Elections and Governance in Nigeria's Fourth Republic

This book is a product of CODESRIA National Working Groups.

Dedication

For those who stood firm,
and sacrificed for democracy that we may have progress

Elections and Governance in Nigeria's Fourth Republic

Edited by

Osita Agbu

CODESRIA

Council for the Development of Social Science Research in Africa
DAKAR

© CODESRIA 2016
Council for the Development of Social Science Research in Africa
Avenue Cheikh Anta Diop, Angle Canal IV
P.O. Box 3304 Dakar, CP 18524, Senegal
Website: www.codesria.org

ISBN: 978-2-86978-639-4

Typesetting: Alpha Ousmane Dia
Cover Design: Ibrahima Fofana

Distributed in Africa by CODESRIA
Distributed elsewhere by African Books Collective, Oxford, UK
Website: www.africanbookscollective.com

The Council for the Development of Social Science Research in Africa (CODESRIA) is
an independent organisation whose principal objectives are to facilitate research, promote
research-based publishing and create multiple forums geared towards the exchange of
views and information among African researchers. All these are aimed at reducing the
fragmentation of research in the continent through the creation of thematic research
networks that cut across linguistic and regional boundaries.

CODESRIA publishes *Africa Development*, the longest standing Africa based social science
journal; *Afrika Zamani*, a journal of history; the *African Sociological Review*; the *African Journal
of International Affairs*; *Africa Review of Books* and the *Journal of Higher Education in Africa*. The
Council also co-publishes the *Africa Media Review*; *Identity, Culture and Politics: An Afro-Asian
Dialogue*; *The African Anthropologist, Journal of African Tranformation, Méthod(e)s: African Review
of Social Sciences Methodology*, and the *Afro-Arab Selections for Social Sciences*. The results of its
research and other activities are also disseminated through its Working Paper Series, Green
Book Series, Monograph Series, Book Series, Policy Briefs and the *CODESRIA Bulletin*.
Select CODESRIA publications are also accessible online at www.codesria.org

CODESRIA would like to express its gratitude to the Swedish International Development
Cooperation Agency (SIDA), the International Development Research Centre (IDRC),
the Ford Foundation, the Carnegie Corporation of New York (CCNY), the Norwegian
Agency for Development Cooperation (NORAD), the Danish Agency for International
Development (DANIDA), the Netherlands Ministry of Foreign Affairs, the Rockefeller
Foundation, the Open Society Foundations (OSFs), TrustAfrica, UNESCO, UN Women,
the African Capacity Building Foundation (ACBF) and the Government of Senegal for
supporting its research, training and publication programmes.

Contents

About the Contributors..vii
Acknowledgements..ix
Abbreviations...xi

Introduction
Osita Agbu 1

1. The Nigerian State and Politics in the Fourth Republic
    Osita Agbu.. 9

2. An Overview of Party Formation in Nigeria, 1960-1999
    Osita Agbu...27

3. Electoral Commissions and the Conduct of Elections in Nigeria:
    The Role of INEC
    Pamela Ogwuazor Momah.. 37

4. Governance and Local Government Elections in Nigeria's Fourth Republic
    Chinwe Nwanna.. 53

5. An Overview of the State Houses of Assembly Elections
    Sharkdam Wapmuk.. 81

6. A Review of the National Assembly Elections
    Sharkdam Wapmuk..99

7. Presidential and Gubernatorial Elections in the Fourth Republic
    Ogaba Oche... 123

8. Consolidation of Democracy and Good Governance in Nigeria:
    The Role of Civil Society
    Ogaba Oche...137

9. Impact of the Elections on Governance: Lessons Learned
    Osita Agbu..149

10. Elections in Nigeria: A Select Annotated Bibliography
    Pamela Ogwuazor Momah 163

11. Postscript 183

About the Contributors

Osita Agbu is a Research Professor at the Nigerian Institute of International Affairs, Lagos, and the editor of this volume. His specializations include Governance and Democratisation, Technology and Development, Post-Conflict Studies and Nigeria's Foreign Policy. He was formerly, editor of the *Nigerian Journal of International Affairs*. His published works include *Ethnic Militias and the Threat to Democracy in Post-Transition Nigeria, 2004; West Africa's Trouble Spots and the Imperative for Peace-Building, 2006; and Ethnicity and Democratisation in Africa: Challenges for Politics and Development,* 2011. He is also published in many reputable journals.

Ogaba Oche is a Research Professor and Head, Research and Studies Department at the Nigerian Institute of International Affairs, Lagos. He had previously lectured at the University of Jos in Plateau State, Nigeria, and has several publications in Political Science and International Relations. His areas of interest include African Politics, International Relations, Strategic Studies, Conflict Studies and Political Economy.

Chinwe Nwanna is a Senior Lecturer in the Department of Sociology, University of Lagos, Nigeria. She has numerous publications in Social Work, Gender and Population Studies, HIV & AIDS, Reproductive Health, Urban Sociology and Labour Migration. Currently, she is the Coordinator of B.Sc. Social Work Programme in the Faculty of Social Sciences, University of Lagos. She is also the Business Manager of *UNILAG Sociological Review,* a journal published by the Department of Sociology. She has received various awards for academic and research excellence including the awards as the Faculty of Social Sciences Distinguished Researcher 2007/2008 Session and the best PhD thesis in the Humanities, 2009.

Sharkdam Wapmuk is a Research Fellow at the Nigerian Institute of International Affairs, Lagos. His research interests include Democratisation, Integration Studies, and Nigeria's relations with the Emerging Powers. He has been published in several journals and has contributed chapters in some books. He is currently a PhD student at the University of Jos, Nigeria.

Pamela Ogwuazor-Momah is the Deputy Director, Readers and Bibliographic Services, Library and Documentation Services at the Nigerian Institute of International Affairs, Lagos. She holds a B.Sc. degree in International Studies from Marymount Manhattan College, New York, USA, and an MLS degree in Library Science from the University of Ibadan, Nigeria.

Acknowledgements

We wish to extend our special gratitude to the Council for the Development of Social Science Research in Africa (CODESRIA) which funded this project under the National Working Groups (NWG) programme. We are also grateful to the following individuals for their support during the project: former Executive Secretary of CODESRIA, Professor Adebayo Olukoshi; the current Executive Secretary, Ebrima Sall, Professor Francis Nyamnjoh, Bruno Sonko, Carlos Cardoso and Oyekunle Oyediran.

Our gratitude also goes to the management of the Nigerian Institute of International Affairs, for granting some of us the time and facilities to conduct this study. In particular, we wish to extend our gratitude to the support staff of the Department of Research and Studies and the ICT Unit of the Institute who provided administrative and technical support to ensure the success of the various workshops on this project.

Finally, the editor wishes to commend all contributors for the zeal, commitment and dedication with which they approached this study. If we have been able to let you in into the intricacies and problems of elections and governance in Nigeria, and ways through which the situation could be improved, then we would have largely achieved the objectives of this study.

Abbreviations

AC	Action Congress
ACN	Action Congress of Nigeria
AD	Alliance for Democracy
AFRC	Armed Forces Ruling Council
AG	Action Group
ANC	All Nigerian Congress
ANPP	All Nigeria Peoples Party
APC	All Progressives Congress
APGA	All Progressives Grand Alliance
APP	All People's Party
CDCC	Constitutional Debate Coordinating Committee
CNC	Congress for National Consensus
CPC	Congress for Progressive Change
DAC	Democratic Advance Movement
DPN	Democratic Party of Nigeria
ECN	Electoral Commission of Nigeria
EFCC	Economic and Financial Crimes Commission
EMU	Eastern Mandate Union
EMBs	Electoral Management Bodies
FEC	Federal Electoral Commission
FEDECO	Federal Electoral Commission
FGD	Focus Group Discussion
FEC	Federal Executive Council
FPTP	First Past the Post
GDM	Grassroots Democratic Movement
GNPP	Great Nigeria Peoples Party
ICPC	Independent Corrupt Practices and other Related Offenses Commission
INEC	Independent National Electoral Commission
ING	Interim National Government
JACON	Joint Action Committee on Nigeria
LCDAs	Local Council Development Areas
LGA	Local Government Areas

LGC	Local Government Council
MDJ	Movement for Democracy and Justice
NACA	National Agency for the Control of HIV/AIDS
NCBWA	National Congress of British West Africa
NADECO	National Democratic Coalition
NCNC	National Council of Nigerian Citizens
NCNC	National Council of Nigeria and the Cameroons
NCPN	National Centre Party of Nigeria
NDDC	Niger Delta Development Commission
NDI	National Democratic Institute for International Affairs
NEC	National Electoral Commission
NECON	National Electoral Commission of Nigeria
NEPU	Northern Elements Progressive Union
NERA	New Era Alliance
NHIS	National Health Insurance Scheme
NLC	Nigerian Labour Congress
NPC	Northern People's Congress
NPN	National Party of Nigeria
NPP	Nigerian Peoples Party
NRC	National Republican Convention
NSM	National Solidarity Movement
OPC	Oodua People's Congress
PCF	People's Consultative Forum
PDP	Peoples Democratic Party
PEF	Police Equipment Fund
PNC	People's National Congress
PRC	Provisional Ruling Council
PRP	Peoples Redemption Party
SIEC	State Independent Electoral Commission
SDP	Social Democratic Party
SMC	Supreme Military Council
TMG	Transition Monitoring Group
UMBC	United Middle Belt Congress
UNIP	United Nigeria Independent Party
UPN	Unity Party of Nigeria
UNCP	United Nigeria Congress Party
UNPP	United Nigeria People's Party
UPP	United People's Party
WASU	West African Students Union

Introduction

Osita Agbu

Nigeria is bedevilled by a myriad of governance problems, often typified by the pre- and post-election crises associated with its democracy. Instances of this abound from the experiences of the 1999, 2003 and 2007 general elections in the country. The conduct of these elections was fraught with such irregularities that many wondered if the country could survive the ensuing crises. Fortunately, it did and has continued to do so amidst a volatile political climate. However, the nagging question remains: for how long will the country continue to bastardise democracy and engage in electoral brinkmanship? The elections of 1999 and 2003 could be considered transitional elections because they marked watersheds in the country's march to civil rule, which had been truncated severally under military rule. We call them"transitional elections' in the sense of movement away from military to civil rule, autocratic to supposedly popular rule, and from the embrace of democracy to its consolidation. While the 2007 elections appeared to have set back the gains made with the democratisation process, the 2011 exercise was a redemption exercise of sorts. The expectation, therefore, is that the 2015 general elections will significantly consolidate democracy after sixteen years of unbroken civil rule, which is a rare achievement in many developing countries, especially in Africa.

In this volume, we argue that the processes leading up to the 1999, 2003 and 2007 elections, the conduct of the elections proper and the post-election controversies have continued to have serious implications for Nigeria's democracy, national stability and development. The poor conduct of elections has directly and indirectly thrown up highly unsuitable people into positions of trust and governance. The quality of governance has therefore suffered as a result of this. It is against this backdrop that we assert that the quality of the electoral process in Nigeria will invariably determine the quality of governance and service delivery in the country.

It, thus, becomes necessary to ask the following questions so as to highlight the key issues connected with the conduct of elections and governance in Nigeria: What has been the character of elections held in Nigeria since 1999? To what extent have successful elections contributed to stability and good governance in the country?

What are the challenges of conducting of credible elections and provision of good governance in Nigeria? What is the link between the character of elections and the character of the Nigerian state? What should we do to ensure that future elections are transparent and contribute to good governance in the country?

These are some of the pertinent questions we intend to examine critically in this volume so as to provide viable answers towards realising Nigeria's development aspirations. In particular, we shall focus on the concepts of elections and good governance as well as issues relating to the Local Government elections (1999, 2003, 2007), gubernatorial and House of Assembly elections (1999, 2003, 2007), National Assembly elections, the presidential elections, and also the role of the Independent National Electoral Commission (INEC) in the electoral process. In addition, the role of the civil society between 1999 and 2007 in the political and electoral processes will be addressed and recommendations proffered towards addressing the problems identified.

Conceptual Issues in Elections and Governance

Several significant studies have been carried out on the various dimensions of elections and governance in Africa generally, and Nigeria, in particular. Some authors, for example, Bratton and Daniel (1999) focused on the matter of second elections and the nexus between the state, conflict and democracy in society. Others focused on human rights abuses and their effect on the conduct of free and fair elections (Human Rights Watch 2007; Ajala and Mbagwu 2007; Ibrahim and Egwu 2005). Sha (2005, 2006) was more concerned with the quality of elections conducted in Nigeria as he assessed Nigeria's democratic transition project. He concluded that there has been too much politics and too little democracy in the elections. Furthermore, Olawale and Adetula (2006), in trying to draw lessons from the 2003 elections in Nigeria, expressed grave concern over the flawed processes that characterise the conduct of future elections and their implications for good governance in the country.

The literature also indicates that elections and post-conflict elections have become important instruments or processes of peace building favoured by the international community in countries emerging from social violence and civil uprising (Shain and Linz 1995; Kumar 1998; Sisk 1998; Ibrahim 2003; IOM 2005; Lopez-Pintor 2005; Wai 2006). While Kumar et.al (2002:6), for example, see elections as primary vehicles for transforming conflict-ridden polities to peaceful ones; Ottaway (2003) considers them a necessary part of building new democratic institutions.

Conceptually, the key question at issue in this study could be appreciated particularly within the scope of the liberal democratic theory. However, the tenets of liberal democracy have variously been criticized by scholars who argue that in reality, democracy is difficult to practice. We know, as postulated by Mafeje (1995), that democracy ordinarily has only one meaning, namely, rule by the 'demos' that is, 'the people' arising from the experience of evolution of democracy in America. That is why we often hear people say that democracy cannot be reduced to the ritual of periodic elections for the purpose of sanctioning elite rule. For yet some others, like the late seminal Nigerian political economist, Claude Ake, the issue of concern is the shift of focus from the people to the elite instead of a shift in the opposite direction. A shift of focus to the people will ideally embrace more of social democracy, rather than liberal democracy (Ake 2000:7).

Democracy, used in its modern sense, could be traced to the 19th century when it was used to describe a representative form of government in which the representatives were chosen by free competitive elections and most male citizens were entitled to vote. In the United States, this state of affairs was reached in the 1820s and 1830s, as the franchise was extended state by state. In France, there was a sudden leap to adult male suffrage in 1848, but parliamentary government was not established securely until 1871. In Britain, parliamentary government had been secure from 1688 onwards, but the franchise was not extended to the majority of male citizens until 1867 (Birch 2007:110).

In addition to Abraham Lincoln's famous definition of democracy as 'government of the people, by the people, for the people; which is obviously rather simplistic though enlightening; Sørensen (2008:27) identifies three main conditions that must be met before democracy can happen. These are competition (among individuals, organisations, groups, political parties for all positions of power on a regular basis that excludes the use of force); participation (that is highly inclusive in selecting leaders and adopting policies through regular and credible elections); and civil and political liberties (sufficient to ensure the integrity of the two previous conditions). For him, therefore, competition, participation, civil and political liberties are the core dimensions of political democracy. However, these are supported by certain pre-conditions relating to the economy, participant political culture, the social structure of the society and international economic, political and ideological factors.

Therefore, what really should be at the heart of the democratic theory is the concern for political inclusiveness and popular participation by the majority of the adult population within the polity. One undeniable political fact, however, is that political participation has always been discriminative in respect of provisions for elections. Even in the context of the Greek City states where democracy had its roots, certain categories of people were excluded from participation in the decision-making process. Demographic imperatives and the increasing complexity of modern industrial societies, it is argued, have made it impossible to practice the Greek form of 'direct democracy'. What has come to replace this historic democratic model is representative democracy. In theory, democracy is a system of government characterised by the participation of the people through their freely elected representatives, by the recognition and promotion of the basic rights of citizens, including the rights of vulnerable groups such as minorities. The central thing about democracy is to ensure that the people have a say over the acquisition and use of power. The defining characteristics of democracy include pluralism and multi-partism; free and competitive politics and elections; popular participation in the political process; respect for the rule of law and respect for human rights and the 'rules of the game', as agreed by all stakeholders. Furthermore, the process of establishing, strengthening or extending principles, mechanisms and institutions which define a democratic regime, is what we generally refer to as democratisation (Omotola 2009:40).

Opinions are, however, divided amongst scholars on the adequacy or otherwise of the status of representative democracy as a desideratum for democratic politics (Odukoya 2006:4). For Ake (2000:7), there is nothing operationally complex and confusing about the concept of democracy '... it means popular power, or in the famous American version, government of the people, for the people, by the people'. The essence, of course, is to devise a system that allows the people to select who should govern them in a popular and transparent manner. Increasingly, it is becoming clear that whereas there are certain irreducible characteristics of democracy, every country or polity will have to eventually evolve the strand of democracy that best suits its history, culture, social values, economy and politics.

The pluralism which democracy values, finds expression in elections as an instrument of popular choice. However, if elections are to be respectable and acceptable and perform its role in political transformation, peace building and conflict resolution, it must be free and fair. In order words, the defining character of good elections is the degree of transparency and popular choices associated with the electoral processes. The people who are qualified to vote must be allowed to freely decide the choice of parties and candidates in an unencumbered manner. This, to a very large extent, is a function of the structure and process of the electoral system and its practice.

The relevant concepts involved in this study include democracy, elections and good governance, political representation and democratization. Elections provide the medium through which the different interest groups within the nation-state can stake and resolve their claims to power through peaceful means. Elections, therefore, determine how political change occurs in a democratic state, and where this fails, the result is usually chaos. In Nigeria, as in many other countries, the conduct of free and fair elections has always been a problem which continues to threaten the very survival of the entity and question the relevance of 'democracy' since the country's political independence on 1 October 1960.

Nigeria is politically plural with about sixty-three political parties and an estimated 70 million voters as at 2010. These features posed a major problem for the organisation of the 2011 general elections. The problem arose both in respect of election management relating to logistics and the activities of some of the politicians who tried to undermine the elections knowing that there was no way they could win in a free and fair contest. The electoral management body – the Independent National Electoral Commission (INEC) – had the herculean task of superintending over the charged elections.

The constitutional provisions on elections and the proper and fair implementation of these are fundamental to the conduct of free and fair elections and the credibility of any democracy. In the Nigerian case, however, there were quite a number of issues relating to the Constitution. It would be recalled that the 1999 Nigerian Constitution was an amended version of the still-born 1995.

Constitution. The Justice Niki Tobi-headed Constitutional Debate Coordinating Committee (CDCC) during the Abdusalami Abubakar regime quickly tinkered with this document (the 1995 Constitution) within a two month period and came out with a new draft Constitution. Because of this, there was little time and inadequate consultation and public hearing to properly receive inputs and debate the provisions of the draft constitution. In short, what the CDCC ended up producing as a draft constitution was far from being the peoples' Constitution (Omotola 2009:45). The Constitution had several conflicting provisions. A troubling feature of this is the over-centralization of powers in one person – the President – thereby constraining the provisions and processes that underlie democracy. This invariably laid the foundation for the several constitutional crises experienced in the Fourth Republic, such as the nature of fiscal relationship between the Local and State Governments, the relationship problem between the Executive and Legislative arms of government and the matter of tenure elongation of Mr President. It was much later, towards the end of the Olusegun Obasanjo Presidency that INEC and the Federal Government sought ways through which electoral reforms and amendment of the 1999 Constitution could be instituted.

On the other hand, the essential principle underlying governance is the exercise of power and authority in both the political and economic spheres (Brautigam 1995:15). There are two approaches to the definition of governance: the neutral and the non-neutral definitions. An example of the neutral definition is that proffered by the World Bank in 1989, which portrayed governance as the exercise of political power to manage a nation's affairs (World Bank 1992). Whilst this definition may be apt in principle, it does not necessarily mean that the institution is a neutral institution. Good governance, on the other hand, is a subset of the wider concept of governance and implies that the government in power upholds the rule of law and is able to provide the basic necessities of life like food, shelter, security and health care to its citizens. Ordinarily, the underlying principle and thrust of good governance is to focus on people as the ultimate object of development. The expectation is that any government truly elected into office by the people will strive to retain the people as its main constituency, and address their needs accordingly. However, these perspectives on governance should not be taken at their face value. There are contextual influences that result in the evolution of 'good governance' as an organising framework for managing resources in different political entities.

It was against the backdrop of the Structural Adjustment Programme (SAP) of the 1980s which produced results far below expectation or which outrightly failed in many countries that the World Bank, in a context of rising capitalism and vanquished socialism/communism, came up with the concept of 'Good Governance'. The good governance agenda entailed countries making changes in their bureaucracies and/or their political systems. In their version of good governance, the World Bank concentrated on managerial and institutional reforms, while bilateral donors were more explicitly political, and, beyond supporting institutional re-arrangements demanded multi-party democracy and respect for human rights as conditions for foreign aid (Leftwich 1993:606). Within this framework of assumed consensus, concepts such as accountability, transparency, participation and empowerment arose, and have since then not necessarily been properly explained, problematized or contextualized especially since SAP was seen by some as part of the governance problem and not the solution (Bangura and Gibbon 1992; Leftwich 1993; Olukoshi and Agbu 1996).

Hyden (1992) interestingly conceived governance as the conscious management of regime structures with a view to enhancing the legitimacy of the public realm, while Bratton and Rothchild (1992:267) noted that it is simultaneously used as an analytical framework for the study and description of legitimate politics and a desirable value. The point however, is that governance provides us with a theoretical and empirical base upon which we can marry formal and informal societal relations, typified by state-society relations. While we discuss democracy and elections, the imperative for good governance cannot be over-emphasized. It is also important to note that while good elections do not necessarily lead to good governance, it is a *sine qua non* for effective governance.

The general elections held in Nigeria in 1999, 2003 and 2007 were expected to enhance good governance with the ultimate goal of ensuring the welfare of Nigerians and improving their lives. However, it is common knowledge that there were very serious shortcomings about the conduct and results of these elections. In addition, the implications of their outcomes still reverberated around the polity many years after. Incidentally, the subsequent 2011 Elections were largely better organised, and the results more credible, mainly because the then acting President, Goodluck Jonathan, did not tamper directly or indirectly with the electoral process or the results. In other words, the implication is that transparent leadership and political will are two very important variables that could propel Nigeria's quest for mature representative politics.

Methodologically, this book proceeds through a mix of institutional level analyses involving group and national level issues as well as the comparative examination of the elections of 1999, 2003 and 2007. The study is not only topical, but fundamentally relevant to the efforts being made to improve the practice of democracy and conduct of elections in Nigeria. The authors who were all participant-observers made use of both the interview schedule instruments and questionnaires instituted at different levels, depending on the issues involved. While the scope of the study was the entire country, there were differences in mode of analyses at the local, state and national levels, and in some cases comparative analysis was used. Whilst each contributing author was given a free hand to determine his/her choice of instrument for data collection, the overall theoretical and conceptual understanding was premised on the basic theoretical tenet of the need for popular democracy.

References

Ake, Claude, 2000, *The Feasibility of Democracy in Africa*, Dakar: CODESRIA.

Brautignam, D., 1991, *Governance and Economy: A Review*, New York: World Bank Working Paper.

Birch, H. Anthony, 2007, *The Concepts and Theories of Modern Democracy*, London: Routledge.

Bratton, Michael and Rothchild, Donald, 1992, 'The Institutional Basis of Governance in Africa', Goran Hyden and Michael Bratton, eds, *Governance and Politics in Africa, Boulder*: Lynne Rienner.

Bangura, Yusuf and Gibbon Peter, 1992, 'Adjustment, Authoritarianism and Democracy in Sub-Saharan Africa: An Introduction to Some Conceptual and Empirical Issues', Gibbon et. al., eds, *Authoritarianism, Democracy and Adjustment: The Politics of Economic Liberalisation in Africa*, Uppsala: Scandinavian Institute of African Studies.

Bratton, Michael and Posner, Daniel, 1999, 'A First Look at Second Elections in Africa, with Illustrations from Zambia', in Richard Joseph, ed., *State, Conflict and Democracy in Africa*, Boulder: Lynne Reinner.

Human Rights Watch, 2007, 'Election or 'Selection'? *Human Rights Abuse and Threats to Free and Fair Elections in Nigeria*, Number 1, 2007, April. (http: //www. hrw.org). 8 May, 2008.

Hyden, Goran, 1992, 'Governance and the Study of Politics', Goran Hyden and Michael Bratton (eds.), *Governance and Politics in Africa*, Boulder: Lynne Rienner. IOM, 2005, 'Training Module for Election Administrators'. (http://www.geneseo. edu/~iompressttaining%module/Intro.htm). 30 January 2006.

Ibrahim, Jibrin, 2003, *Democratic Transition in Anglophone West Africa*, Dakar: CODESRIA. Ibrahim, J. and Egwu S., 2005, *Defending the People's Mandate*, Abuja: Global Rights.

Ibrahim, Jibrin, 2007, *Nigeria's 2007 Elections: The Fitful Path to Democratic Citizenship*, United States Institute of Peace, Special Report 182, January. (http://www. usip.org). 8 May, 2008.

Kumar, Krishna (ed.), 1998, *Post-conflict Elections, Democratisation and International Assistance*, Boulder, Colo.: Lynne Rienner.

Kumar, Chetan, Sara Lodge, Karen Rosmick, 2002, *Sustainable Peace Through Democratisation: The Experiences of Haiti and Guatemala*, New York: International Peace Academy Policy Paper, March.

Labour Election Monitoring Team Nigeria, 2003, *Balloting for Democracy- A Report of the 2003 General Elections*, Abuja: NLC-LEMT.

Leftwich, Adrian, 1993, 'Governance, Democracy and Development in the Third World' *Third World Quarterly*, Vol.14, No.3.

Lopez-Pintor, Rafael, 2005, *Post-Conflict Elections and Democratisation: An Experience Review*, USAID Issue Paper No.8.

Odukoya, A. Adelaja, 2006, 'Election Credibility, Election Monitoring and Peace Building in West Africa', Paper Presented at the *International Conference on Post-Conflict Elections in West Africa: Challenges for Democracy and Reconstruction*, organised by Nordiska Afrikainstitutet, Accra, Ghana, 15 – 17 May.

Ottaway, Marina, 2003, 'The Dangers of Premature Elections'', Statement before the House Armed Forces Committee of the US House of Representatives', 29 October. (*http:// armedservices.house.gov/openingstaementandpresreleases/108thcongress/03-10-29ottaway. html*). 10 May 2006.

Shain, Yoshi and Juan, J. Linz, 1995, *Between States: Interim Governments and Democratic Transitions*, Cambridge: Cambridge University Press.

Sisk, D. Timothy, 1998, 'Elections and Conflict Management in Africa: Conclusions and Recommendations', Timothy D. Sisk and Andrew Reynolds, eds, *Elections and Conflict Management in Africa*, Washington D.C.: United States Institute of Peace Press.

Olawale, A. I., Marco, D. and Adetula, V. O., eds, 2006, *Towards the 2007 Elections: Perspectives on 2003 Elections in Nigeria*, Abuja: Institute of Democracy in South Africa.

Olubunmi, Ajala and Joan, Mbagwu, 2007, *The People's Mandate: Peaceful Elections and How to Make Your Votes Count*, Lagos: Olive Branch Konsult.

Olukoshi, O. Adebayo and Osita, Agbu, 1996, 'The Deepening Crisis of Nigerian Federalism and the Future of the Nation-State', Adebayo O. Olukoshi and Liisa Laakso, eds, *Challenges to the Nation-State in Africa*, Uppsala, Nordiska Afrikainstitutet.

Omotola, Shola J., 2009, 'Democracy and Constitutionalism in Nigeria Under the Fourth Republic 1999 – 2007', *The Constitution*, Vol. 9 No. 1, March.

Sha, D. P., 2005, 'Too Much Politics, Too Little Democracy: Assessing the Quality of Nigerian Democratic Transition Project', *Nigerian Journal of Policy and Strategy*, Kuru: National Institute of Policy and Srategic Studies, Vol. 15, Nos. 1 and 2, December.

Sha, D. P., 2006, 'Vote Buying and the Quality of Democracy', Adetula, V. O. et. al., eds, *Money, Politics and Corruption in Nigeria*, Abuja: International Fund for Electoral Support (IFES).

Sørensen, Georg, 2008, *Democracy and Democratisation: Processes and Prospects in a Changing World*, Colorado: Westview Press.

Wai, Zubairu, 2006, 'Elections as a Strategy for Conflict Transformation and Democratisation in Sierra Leone: A Critique of the Liberal Peace Agenda', Paper Presented at the *International Conference on Post-Conflict Elections in West Africa: Challenges for Democracy and Reconstruction*, organised by Nordiska Afrikainstitutet, Accra, Ghana, 15 – 17 May.

1

The Nigerian State and Politics in the Fourth Republic

Osita Agbu

Introduction

We cannot engage in any far-reaching and grounded discourse of Nigerian politics without first interrogating the character of the Nigerian state in terms of its origin, people, human interactions and economy. Nigeria is made up of some 250 ethnic groups with no common language. However, there are three dominant ethnic groups, namely, Hausa, Yoruba and Igbo, which together constitute a tripod that has serious implications for the socio-economic management and political organisation of the country. Pre-colonial, colonial and post-colonial developments have together combined in shaping the mode of governance in Nigeria. Pre-colonial Nigeria was characterised by the existence of empires, kingdoms and segmented societies like the Habe Kingdom (Hausa) of the fifteenth century, before the ascendancy of the Fulani in 1804 after the Jihad. Other political entities included the Kanem-Borno Empire, Oyo Empire, Benin Kingdom as well as segmentary societies of South Eastern Nigeria. Generally, during the pre-colonial era, four major political systems were identifiable: the emirate system, monarchical system, semi-monarchical system and republican monarchism. In the emirate system, the structure was hierarchical, showcasing a sort of uni-directional flow of authority from the emir to the people. In the monarchical and semi-monarchical systems, authority tended to be pyramidal, for example, in the Yoruba kingdom of Oyo and the Benin Kingdom. Republican monarchism was characterised by decentralist principalities consisting of independent political units or segments with little allegiance to any overarching authority. Whilst the emirate system was synonymous with a subject political culture, the monarchical and semi-monarchical systems embodied a participant political culture, and republican monarchism was characterised by a high level of decentralization and independence.

The point to note is that pre-colonial Nigeria did not have a monolithic political system, and very little commonality existed among the different peoples apart from trading arrangements. Also, at each turning point during the pre-colonial, colonial and post-colonial periods, there were different norms. This does not of course mean that there were no commonalities at all. For example, whilst in many of the societies women could not aspire to political leadership positions, some however created roles for women that were vital for the governance of their societies. Nonetheless, the differences did little to help the emergence of a Nigerian nation. Indeed, the fact that Nigeria is still a corporate entity five decades plus after political independence is nothing short of a miracle considering its colonial legacy.

The nature of the Nigerian state and society is fundamentally anarchical, mainly because of the multiplicity of its ethnic groupings and its mono-product economy superintended by a distorted federal structure. Its political structure and governance have been distorted since political independence in 1960; first, by colonialists; second, by the ethnicised political class; and thirdly; by military politicians. The character of the Nigerian state derives from the various experiences of the past such as the colonial experience, the coercive amalgamation of southern and northern protectorates in 1914, the various attempted and successful *coups d'état* (eleven as at the last count in 1997), ethnic politics, the civil war (1967-1970) as well as deep-rooted distrust among some of the ethnic nationalities, and settler/indigene crises across the country (Moru, 2004). These experiences have continued to shape the structure and dynamics of the Nigerian state system. Unfortunately, this is a structure that also fosters nepotism, undermines creativity and glorifies mediocrity through the misapplication of the federal character provision and quota system in the amended 1999 Constitution. To this extent, access to power and the use of it for primitive accumulation and influence becomes an internecine affair.

The task today is how to understand and eschew the confusion that have arisen from this distortion; which has stultified, stigmatized and puzzled many Nigerian observers. Molding a distinct political form through the deconstruction and trans-formation of the Nigerian state from its inherited form is the most important task before many Nigerians.

In the immediacy, however, and leading up to the present political dispensation, the background could be traced from the demise of the military strongman, General Sani Abacha who died in 1998, and his replacement with General Abdulsalami Abubakar who initiated and superintended the transition to the Fourth Republic that saw a return to civil rule in 1999. The Fourth Republic is sequentially the republican government of Nigeria from 1999, deriving its powers from the 1999 Constitution of the Federal Republic of Nigeria. A widely monitored 1999 election saw the emergence of former military ruler, Olusegun Obasanjo, on the platform of the Peoples Democratic Party (PDP). The election, though widely regarded as hugely flawed, was grudgingly accepted by most of the citizens since the ultimate objective then was to shepherd the military out of the corridors of power. The general election of 2003 was no better, and was roundly condemned as lacking transparency. Again, in the controversial general election of April 2007, Umaru Musa Yar'Adua of the PDP was purportedly elected. The internal processes of the Party which threw him up were obviously flawed as later events were to show. It was generally believed that his candidacy was imposed on the country by the party 'godfathers'. By February 2010, after much political machinations and brinkmanship, a very sick and obviously physically incapable President Musa Yar'Adua, was temporary replaced by Acting President Goodluck Jonathan through the intervention of the National Assembly as an obviously lame Executive Council of the Federation lacked the will and courage to take a decisive action on the health status of Mr. President. This became necessary as the Nigerian ship slowly, but surely headed for the rocks! As at 2010, no one knew how long the Acting Presidency would last. But mercifully, the 2011 general elections proved much better in its organisation and execution by INEC, and delivered to Nigerians better elections and better candidates. Goodluck Jonathan was elected President, and thus the Acting Presidency terminated. This is the background against which we seek to re-visit the concept of the state, impact of colonialism on the state, post-independent politics, the role of the political elite and elections, and the character of the Nigerian state in the Fourth Republic.

The Concept of State

The concept of the state could be traced to two main traditions, the Weberian (Weber 1964) and the Marxist (Marx and Engels 1852/1958). For Max Weber, a state is a human community that successfully claims the monopoly of the legitimate use of physical force in a given territory. The emphasis here is on the claim to the monopoly of the use of force. Indeed, Weber saw the state as an institution, *sui generis*, existing to safeguard and regulate the society. Marxists reject the position of the liberal theory that the state is basically neutral and stands aside to mediate the contradictions inherent in society (Best 1990). Rather, they conceive of the state as a product of the social system that is characterised by class contradictions, struggles and class domination. These classes have different interests. The state is, therefore, an instrument of class domination with class bias to conflicts in society. It is a specific modality of class domination (Ake 1985; Ihonvbere 1989). It is not above class struggle, and can only be an agent of a particular class. In fact, in the *Communist Manifesto*, the state was construed as an agent of the bourgeoisie, thus: 'the executive of the modern state is a committee for managing the common affairs of the bourgeoisie'.

The literature is replete with many more recent descriptions of the state. So, a state could be any of the following depending on its character and manifestation; capitalist, marxist, socialist, communist, colonial, neo-colonial, welfarist, overdeveloped, rentier, prebendal, enduring, juridical, predatory, fictitious, collapsing and collapsed as the case maybe (Leftwitch 2000; Joseph 1987; Zolberg 1995). Nevertheless, these various sub-classifications could also be tied up into two main strands – state-centric and society-centred. There is, therefore, the conceptualization of the state based on the indices of structure, apparatus of power and their functions, and the conceptualization that perceives the state as a consequence of the character of the society, that is, class structure, social norms and the civil society. Whilst the state structure conceptualization is state-centred and professes a realist outlook that perceives the state as a rational unitary actor (Allison 1971), an organisational statism (Niskanen 1974) and an analytical concept (Mitchel 1992); the 'class character' approach is society-centred and encompasses the pluralists who basically see the state as an arena for competition among various interests (Bendix 1967; Dahl 1971; Held 1989). Included among the pluralists are also the structural-functionalists who perceive the state as an instrument of social integration (Parson 1965; Almond and Powell 1966) and the Marxists who see the state as an expression of class struggle and domination (Poulantzas 1978; Jessop 1990). However, common to the pluralists is the notion that the state is a reflection of the society; hence its dynamics encapsulates the norms, intra- and inter-class struggles and politicized ethnic relations. The character of these struggles determines the structure of the institutions and policies of the government. For us, therefore, the society-centred theoretical approach is much relevant to our understanding of the character of the Nigerian state and its politics. And this character cannot be properly understood until we factor in the economic element. Given Nigeria's profile as a largely mono-product oil producing country, the political economy of oil and its contradictions have been a major factor shaping the character of the Nigerian state and its politics.

The Nigerian State

The character of the Nigerian state could be understood in terms of the genealogy of global capital accumulation and the interplay of local and global class relations. The penetration of European merchants into the territory now known as Nigeria eventually led to the emergence of the nation-state whose umbilical cord is strongly tied to capitalism. The state eventually became a tool in the hands of capitalist forces which used it as an instrument to pacify, dominate and keep the pristine forces apart to enable capital accumulation. The dialectics of existing social forces in its struggle with global capital and wealth accumulation led to the continual transformation of the Nigerian state. But in what direction was this transformation headed? It clearly headed towards its continued use as a provider of raw materials (groundnuts, palm oil, cocoa, and oil and gas) for lubricating the engine of capitalist development, largely in the West. In spite of its transformation from being a colonial entity, the Nigerian state retained the fundamental character of not being a popular-national state that represented the interests of the people (Ibeanu 1997:8).

In terms of transformation, though the pristine forces at independence comprising nationalists, traditional leaders and the educated elite, wrested power from the British colonial power, they soon became embroiled in interests struggle. This led to a crisis of nation-building characterised by hegemonic struggles for access to power at the centre. Although, the 1979 Constitution was a watershed experience in Nigeria's constitutional development, the subsequent party politics that emerged was not much different from what existed in post-independent Nigeria. Political parties were largely formed along ethnic lines, while the political class politicized the ethnic divides. Invariably, what ensued from the symptoms of incompetence, ignorance and corruption, was politics of bitterness and winner-takes-all rather than politics of tolerance. The Nigerian state was to witness further crisis relating to revenue allocation, state creation, civil war, power-sharing, and *coups d'états* that almost led to the disintegration of the political entity. Since then, Nigeria has been bedevilled by claims of marginalization, separatist agitations, resource control, inter-communal conflicts and insurgency. Terrorist attacks and rejection of the Nigerian state have become new threats to the corporate existence of the country. It was perhaps the need to arrest some of these crises, promote national unity and command the loyalty of all that led to the much vilified Federal Character Principle and the quota system as affirmative actions to ensure a sense of belonging and loyalty to the federation. The Federal Character Principle demands that government activities and institutions must reflect the diverse ethnic groupings that constitute the geographic expression called Nigeria [Section 14(3-4), 1999 Constitution]. Unfortunately, the reason for enacting this principle was defeated as the dominant and ruling classes distorted its use for selfish ends. The principle enabled them to sponsor candidates to high political positions, increasing their influence and undermining the spirit of the principle. Invariably, policies, programmes, ascendancy to positions of power and influence, wealth and security were determined by a few individuals that re-cycled themselves or their relations and children into positions of power and authority in a patron–client relationship. Government businesses and activities became personalized, laws became personified and dissent and opposition to policies and powers then became suicidal. Invariably, the Nigerian state became privatized (Eze 2009).

- That the character of the Nigerian state is worrisome is not in doubt. Fifty years plus after political independence, the country is still reeling from vociferous and sometimes violent challenges to its power and hegemony in various parts of the country particularly in the East, the Niger Delta, the West, the Middle Belt and the North East, where an insurgency and terrorism is raging led by *Boko Haram*. After over fifty years, the country is today more insecure, less stable and less confident than it was at independence, and this is in spite of the billions of dollars earned from the sale of crude oil and gas. The citizens are, on a daily basis, assaulted, maimed or killed by either the police or armed robbers and assassins, visited with sectarian crisis that the state appears incapable of resolving, decimated by the scourge of poverty and ravaged by bribery and corruption in low and high places. The citizens' agony is compounded by the lack of basic infrastructure such as motorable roads, electricity and potable water as well as other basic amenities which are taken for granted in many other countries. The cries of marginalization and alienation appear therefore to be largely justified. Still, the dominant and hegemonic political elite continue in their profligacy, stealing the people's vote and mandates and abusing the system. This is against the background that at independence, Nigerian nationalists actually believed that a nation had been born. Had they known that in about fifty years the country would have retarded or de-progressed, perhaps the idea and acceptance of the Nigerian geographic space as a political entity would have been re-negotiated to make for more practical association of peoples. The Nigerian state in its *structural and distributive* mode is *highly dysfunctional*, counter-productive and lacking in innovation. Indeed, there is presently palpable anger and alienation in the land.

In other words, the demand for a national dialogue or national conference by some Nigerians was very much justified. A Presidential Advisory Committee was inaugurated 7 October 2013 at Abuja to distil modalities for the National Dialogue, which was chaired by Dr. Femi Okuroumu. The Dialogue eventually held beginning from 17 March to the end of July 2014. The report of the Dialogue is yet to be implemented as there are constitutional issues to resolve.

At present, the existential conditions of the Nigerian people in the face of the scandalous display of unmerited and stolen wealth by a few individuals and public servants create the right condition for the deepening of contradictions and revolutionary pressures. Thus, we experience frequent labour strikes, including the Academic Staff Union of Universities (ASUU) and demonstrations by students of higher institutions either opposing increases in fees or demanding better facilities. Generally, relations between the state, its agents and agencies and the citizenry are characterised by suspicion, demonstrations and communal strife. The state, given its monopoly of power and the use of force, responds with silence, threats, dismissals, imprisonment and intimidation. The dominant moral climate in Nigeria against the backdrop of stolen mandates and corruption in high places is every man to himself and God for us all. There was a time when the attitude was that of 'siddon look', meaning 'let's wait and see', but it seems the masses are now more conscious, and therefore more predisposed to defending their political rights and votes. Still, the 'National Question' continues to resonate even as state elite across all the ethnic groups fight to retain the advantages they currently have in a distorted federation led by a weak and narrow-minded hegemonic political class. However, history has shown that no dispensation lasts for forever. The dissenting voices and opposition currently gathering momentum in the country and awakening political sensibilities will be instrumental in one day upstaging this lethargic political class. It is even now happening with the very destructive Boko Haram Insurgency raging in the North East of the country.

The State in Nigeria is basically a neoliberal state, an appendage of the 1648 Westphalian State in Europe. In fact, as a 'gatekeeper state', it serves as an instrument of capitalist accumulation, which thrives on dispossession of the populace. It can, therefore, not serve as an instrument of good governance for the Nigerian people. Our observation is that the Nigerian political elites have developed a hegemonic project based around three core principles – multiculturalism, economic liberalism and democracy – which incorporate the indigenous peoples into the political system while simultaneously excluding indigenous movement demands that would undermine the political and economic sources of elite power.

In short, the Nigerian state has been shown not to be a neutral institution; rather, it is an instrument of domination, oppression, primitive accumulation and the protection of elite interests. Eze (2009: 449) has observed that the Nigerian state is a product of western imperialism which has continued to be structured and transformed by the dictates of the productive forces it created. Central to this is the fact that state power was established as an instrument of capital formation and wealth development. Consequently, the various pseudo and comprador bourgeoisies prevalent in the socio-economic system compete in a zero-sum game for the acquisition, use and consolidation of state power. The multiple ethnic pluralities of Nigeria, and its politicization provided a fertile ground for the class struggle. The logic of federalism, unity in diversity, equity and justice, led to the introduction of divisive policies such as the federal character principle and the quota system. Before long, this organising principle of inclusion became distorted and found its way into the political arena and political parties. And in a situation in which people who run for electoral positions are selected on quota basis without really winning an election in a free and fair manner, it is no surprise that the country has become saddled with incompetent and visionless individuals whose only goal is to use public office for primitive accumulation of the commonwealth for self-aggrandizement. The country is worse for it today.

The neo-liberal state in Nigeria at this time has a transformed political centre at the core of which people at the highest echelons of government prioritize marketization, corporatization and outsourcing, as well as economic relationships which aid this. The political centre has been captured by entrepreneurs of the state, corporate interests, and the accountancy firms. Thus, political parties are bound to espouse this mantra, not the idea of serving the Nigerian people's interests. Indeed, in this dispensation, political parties promote the neo-liberal culture: a culture which is based on celebrating the cult of the individual, selfishness, greed and the validation of winners. These parties cannot, therefore, be the heralding of a new participatory and popular democracy as proclaimed. Political gangsterism has become the dominant practice in such a framework. In effect, drawing on insights from economic, political, and cultural theories of liberal democratic governance, countries with a history of Western European influence and with British common law origins often have better governance, but this has not been the case in Nigeria. Why? This could be explained by other factors, both exogenous and indigenous to the Nigerian experience. However, we quickly note that multi-party elections alone are not necessarily the only key determinants of good governance.

Colonialism and the Character of the State before Independence

The British colonial authorities kept the different regions of Nigeria apart to further their own interests prior to independence. Through the use of this divide and rule policy, the British did immense harm to any chance of the peoples of these regions seeing themselves as partners in progress for the development of the geographical entity called Nigeria. The use of the indirect rule system worked more successfully in the north than in the south partly because of the emirate traditional political arrangement. This system suited the colonialist who did not have to deal directly with the people. The Muslim religion and the reverence for religious leaders which is very strong in the north of the country were used as organising principles to keep the subjects in check. This approach was partially successful in the west but different in the east. The east, made up mainly of the Igbo nation historically characterised by segmented and acephalous societies, did not have the kind of reverence for authorities that exist in the north. The Igbos are mainly individualistic and entrepreneurial by orientation and believe in their capacity to become successful through personal efforts and not necessarily through collective or institutional means. It is therefore important to note that the pre-colonial arrangement conditioned the colonial. Though the British occupied Lagos in 1861 and indirect rule continued until 1938, the official date of Nigeria's colonization was 1900 when the British succeeded in militarily 'pacifying' the whole country, while the northern and southern parts of the country were amalgamated in 1914 as one country. Thus, history has a lot to contribute to our understanding of the character of the Nigerian state.

Nigeria constitutionally became a quasi-federation in 1951, since then the country has achieved the enviable but problematic status of a full federation with a strong centre, which has increasingly become an albatross difficult to shift. A federal constitution was fully achieved in 1954 with the enactment of the McPherson Constitution. To a large extent, Nigeria is blessed with enormous human and material resources, however, the uneven distribution and irresponsible use of the proceeds from these resources, especially oil revenues have made Nigeria's fiscal federalism problematic, and this has at times led to fundamental differences among the political elite, leading to elite struggles for access to state resources.

Post-Independence Politics, Oil-based Economy and the Political Elite

Although Nigeria achieved political independence on 1 October 1960, it boasted a colonial, political and economic architecture that tended to accentuate the differences amongst the national elite. Post-colonial Nigeria was to become even more antagonistic as life was then 'short and brutish'. At this period, the centre could no longer hold as parochial and voracious elite from the different regions battled for the soul of the country. Nigeria thus witnessed its first military *coup d'état* on 15 January 1966, followed by a reprisal counter coup in July of the same year. With the discovery of crude oil in the Niger Delta in 1958 and with the country being largely run as a mono-product cultural economy, the state witnessed many more *coups d'état,* the last being an attempted coup on 21 December 1998 against Sani Abacha. According to Mimiko (2007:304):

> the very nature of the Nigerian state, oriented towards rent-seeking ends, makes contest for it acute. The state is colonial and clientelist. It lacks hegemony and is oriented basically to promote the rent-seeking proclivities of transient custodians of state power ...The contest for political power in the prevailing context, therefore, becomes a hot context for the main focus of primitive accumulation, and is of necessity conflictual, highly divisive and fundamentally incapable of sustaining a stable pattern of regime change.

The contradictions inherent in an unproductive and oil-based economy was to play itself out in subsequent years as the military, with the help of civilian collaborators, manipulated the ethnic differences, looted the treasury and regrettably succeeded in bastardizing most, if not all of the inherited institutions, norms and values that are germane to good governance and societal cohesion, such as integrity and communal harmony. The country is yet to recover from this.

Therefore, that there are internal contradictions and ongoing class struggles in a rent-seeking Nigerian formation is not in doubt. At independence in 1960, Nigeria emerged as a neo-colonial capitalist state structurally integrated into the world capitalist system. According to Onimode (1981) and Nnoli (1981), the British colonial authority carefully cultivated a local petty-bourgeoisie to whom political power was transferred, while at the same time, retaining with other industrialized capitalist nations their dominance of the economy of the Nigerian state. Nnoli (1981) noted that this emergent petty and comprador bourgeoisie's objective interest largely lay in the consolidation and reproduction of the colonial system of economic life for pecuniary benefits. Since independence, this local ruling class has continued to pursue policies that reproduce the colonially established bourgeois structure. They tend to be externally oriented, have developed tastes similar to those of the western elites, and therefore find it extremely difficult to understand and articulate the need for endogenous development. Hence, the modern Nigerian state invariably acts to preserve the existing social order in which the capitalist mode of production is not only prevalent but consistently reproduced.

The integration of Nigeria into the global capitalist order operates principally for the benefit of the advanced capitalist economies as the role determined for Nigeria is that of an exporter of raw materials and importer of finished or semi-finished goods (Osoba 1978). Indeed, the character of the Nigerian state can be summarized as follows; firstly, Nigeria is a rentier state and proto-capitalist in its aspiration as the Nigerian state promoted capitalist accumulation and the capitalist class formation in a distorted manner. This is evidenced in the fact that the state itself is:

> ... a major owner of the means of production and finance capital. It invested in large scale productive enterprises, on its own or in partnership with foreign and domestic private capital. It took an active part in promoting Nigerian capitalists, through state banks, development corporations and support schemes. Heavy state investments in economic and social infrastructure clearly support further capitalist production (Beckman 1983).

Secondly, the Nigerian state is a neo-colonial state dominated by conservative forces and interests. On many occasions, the state has found it extremely difficult to control the activities of the trans-national companies (TNCs) operating in the country. This is not surprising since more often than not, the ruling and dominant classes either connive with or find it extremely difficult to resist the overtures and offers made by the foreign companies. Also, the instability associated with the country cannot be divorced from the machinations of the multinationals and their activities in the process of production. As a marginalized capitalist formation, the Nigerian state is therefore an organ of international capital, as the real control of its economy is in the hands of external interests or foreign capital. Effectively, then, the Nigerian state can best be described as a comprador state, since state institutions and its officials operate as agents of imperialism. According to Beckman (1982), the Nigerian state is a state of imperialism. Imperialist social relations of production have been domesticated and the state itself is the very linch-pin around which the system of imperialist domination rotates. This is an important phase of imperialist domination from within, with its specific contradiction, and its specific form of resistance. The Nigerian elite have developed capitalist tastes like their counterparts in the West, except that while their counterparts also engage in productive capitalism, the Nigerian elite is quagmired in consumerism.

The Nigerian elite uses its alliance with foreign capital to enhance its class rule and accumulation. Furthermore, the Nigerian state is characterised by the predominance of the public sector in the generation of profits and determination of the production structure in the economy (Ekuerhare 1984). It is also characterised by a primitive accumulation process with the government playing the central role as a breeding ground of indigenous capitalists. This primitive accumulation process is achieved basically through corruption and violence (Iyayi 1986).

We can at this stage ask the question: in whose interest does the Nigerian state act? In fact, while the Nigerian state serves both as an organ for the penetration of global capital and for the emancipation of the domestic bourgeoisie, it cannot be reduced to either. The primary role of the Nigerian state is basically to establish, maintain, protect and expand conditions conducive for capitalist accumulation in general, without which neither foreign nor Nigerian capitalists can prosper. Suffice it to say that the 'Nigerian state' represents the interests of dominant social forces in their relationship with transnational and international interests (Shaw and Fasehun 1980:551). The Nigerian state is, therefore, dependent and its actions are significantly constrained in the global system. A combination of emphasis on the character of the ruling class in the Nigerian formation which is predatory; the class character of the state, which is rentier to the detriment of productive activities; and the role of the transnational corporations and the overriding influence of the global capitalist production system provide a graphic background for understanding the myriad of problems associated with governance and the conduct of elections at all levels in the country.

Hence, it is safe to say that the Nigerian state plays a crucial political role in industrial relations. As a petty-bourgeois state, it supports capital whenever fundamental conflicts arise between labour and capital. It is, therefore, clear that the dominant role played by the petty-bourgeoisie in contemporary Nigerian society has immediate implications for the political and electoral processes. Therefore, power is important, and indeed, is the ultimate prize for the large army of combatants who battle, upon the pain of death, to attain political power. What, however, makes the Nigerian case unique, is the multicultural character of its elite and the tendency to embrace corruption as a means of achieving personal and group interests. Against the background of a skewed political arrangement and an unbalanced federation, in addition to the easy perquisites derivable from occupying positions of authority in an oil-rich country, access to power becomes deadly and electoral integrity is undermined.

Furthermore, the Nigerian state has a structural problem as currently constituted of a 'strong centre' and weak states. This does not allow for the requisite depth of commitment on the part of the citizens. The state is too centralized to deliver quality governance in a highly plural and heterogeneous political context, and is therefore invariably prone to instability. Many have, therefore, repeatedly called for the decentralization of governance with more powers devolved to the states in order to ensure buy-in by the citizenry. The expectation is that with this devolution of powers, the incidence of corruption would reduce tremendously as the penchant for corrupt means of achieving political and/or economic ends will cease.

Generally, the political elite have tended to display a conservative attitude that hardly promotes democracy at the political level. An explanation for this is the dominant place of force and violence in the political life of Nigerians over the years. From colonialism, an authoritarian and exploitative phenomenon, through to military rule, it is surprising that Nigerian governments over the years have not taken the necessary steps to put an end to this ugly phenomenon. The neglect of the debilitating impact of force and violence in the national psyche has contributed to its overriding manifestation in the society and in the democratisation process, including its negative influence on the conduct of elections.

The Nigerian State in the Fourth Republic

Having critically examined the general character of the Nigerian state in pre- and post-colonial Nigeria, what then can we say is the present character of this state? And to what extent has it transformed and in what direction? Cumulatively, the malaise confronting Nigeria increasingly indicates that it is a state in deep crises of nation-building. Nigerian masses are still not sure whether to completely pledge allegiance to the entity, as the central government has not demonstrated serious commitment to protect the lives of the people and provide for their welfare. Hence, it is difficult to obtain the required allegiance from them. The Niger Delta crisis would not have been as intractable as it was if Niger Deltans had some trust in the Nigerian State. It was only when they perceived some sense of seriousness from the Musa Yar'Adua-led PDP government that amnesty was brokered in 2009 and many of the militants laid down their arms. This political mileage is yet to be completely consolidated by government due to unnecessary politicking and the pursuit of selfish interests by some members of the political class. For instance, many observers witnessed in disbelief how some elements of the northern political elite, bent on holding on to power at all cost, insisted on foisting a sick and incapable president on the nation contrary to constitutionally laid down rules. The interest of the hegemonic class is therefore not difficult to understand. Against the voice of the people led by civil society and some notable Nigerians, who clearly called for the Vice-President to take over from the President, the hegemonic political class resorted to lies, trickery and justifications on why a sick president must remain in office. Clearly, their interest negated the public interest and led to uncertainty in governance. Nigeria was being polarized into 'elite-mass' and 'ethnic' cleavages that did not augur well for the country. The country was overheating as conservative and radical forces took different positions.

Therefore, the Fourth Republic, beginning with the election of Chief Olusegun Obasanjo as civilian President in May 1999, has grown out of flawed political processes, intimidation and outright brigandage which combine to undervalue the democratic process. Though government has embarked on several reforms, yet it has continued to lack legitimacy as a result of the flawed elections. Though, the international community was largely benign and chose to accept the results of the 1999 elections for the sake of 'democracy', the 2003 and 2007 Presidential elections also won by the Peoples Democratic Party (PDP) were severely criticized. The reports of both domestic and international observers about the elections pointed out several shortcomings that made the elections unacceptable.

There is a general feeling that the ruling party, the PDP, lack a clear political ideology and direction. Indeed, it could be said that because this party, which claims to have the largest membership of any party in Africa, does not have internal democracy as evident in the conduct of its primaries, a contagion effect has been passed on to some of the other parties, as quite a number of them thrived on the use of 'godfathers' to select candidates for elections. A culture of impunity has characterised Nigerian politics and the conduct of elections in more recent times in Nigeria. Hegemonic and unbridled politics by the major parties have combined to rob the electorate of their constitutional right to elect their leaders. Nigerians often experience what is called 'garrison politics', in which force, intimidation and manipulation of results are used to impose unpopular individuals on the people. It was in the Anambra State Governorship election of February 2010 hotly contested by three political parties, the PDP, All Progressives Grand Alliance (APGA) and the Action Congress (AC) amongst others, that the peoples' votes could be said to have triumphed, despite poor organisation of the elections by the Independent National Electoral Commission (INEC). The voters register was greatly mutilated as many eligible voters could not find their names in the register and therefore could not exercise their franchise. This time, however, the peoples' vote counted because of better voter consciousness and their determination to physically defend their votes by any means necessary. Voters refused to leave the polling stations after casting their votes and made sure that the result from the various polling stations were announced on the spot, approved by all designated party agents and documented. The civil society also played a key role in ensuring that the governorship election was not rigged as they encouraged the people to defend their votes. Anambra State had hitherto been one of the most problematic states where free and fair elections were marred by the nefarious activities of 'godfathers' who used party machinery and coercion to select candidates who would stand for elections, and they would proceed to rig the elections in favour of such candidates. Thus, these corrupt politicians imposed governors on the people in connivance with the security forces. It took several months of legal battle for Peter Obi of APGA to win back his mandate at the electoral tribunal. The point to note here is that without the activities of the civil society groups and the citizens of Anambra State, the cabal that had hitherto intimidated and looted the state would have had their way. In this case, the heightened consciousness on the part of the people on the one hand, and the fear of violent repercussions arising from mass action that could result from rigging the elections made the corrupt politicians to desist from their intransigence.

The flawed elections cannot be divorced from corruption and its implications for the political process. The structure of the Nigerian state is such that corruption remains a major problem and culprits are often let off the hook. Indeed, publicly disgraced government officials and politicians often find their way back into the foray of politics, and end up being given government appointments (Moru 2004).

The character of the Nigerian state has played a dominant role in the formation of a peculiar Nigerian mode of politicking that glorifies selection, rather than merit as a key political variable. This is ironically being replicated in the run-up to the 2015 general elections as the ruling party, the PDP, has its party primaries where it selected and nominated President Goodluck Jonathan as its presidential candidate without subjecting him to any election. For the political class, politics in the Fourth Republic connotes access to power and its uses for personal enrichment. But where is the opposition? The opposition is nowhere to be seen until recently when the Action Congress (AC) became more and more critical of the policies of the ruling PDP . Often, the ruling party is able to get key elected individuals from an opposition party to defect to their side with promises of compensation by the party. This is one of the issues that should be addressed in the political reform measures currently under discussion. For instance, how do you prevent a politician elected on a particular political platform from defecting to another party midstream into his tenure? A new opposition party – the All Progressives Congress (APC) was formed on 6 February 2013 to contest the 2015 general elections against the ruling PDP. It is an alliance of the Action Congress of Nigeria (ACN), the Congress for Progressive Change (CPC), All Nigeria Peoples Party (ANPP), and a faction of the All Progressives Grand Alliance (APGA).

Elections in Nigeria prior to 2011 were not about popular vote but about power relations, patronage and selection. It was about the ability to harass your opponent, threaten his life and those of his family, recruit thugs to cart away electoral materials and intimidate INEC officials, and if possible assassinate your opponent (Moru 2004). It was rare to see an incumbent voted out of office before the 2011 elections. The power of incumbency, stolen taxpayers' money, the police, state and federal electoral officers were invariably bought over or threatened, to prosecute what was taken as a war. The perquisites of office derivable from the successful prosecution of the war was simply too irresistible. The flawed elections, non-transparent party primaries, corruption, intimidation, impunity, violence, assassinations, disenfranchisement and helplessness of the electorate were all possible because the rentier Nigerian state had been hijacked or captured by an unrepentant political class and state elite bent on satisfying their interests and not that of the people. The implication is that any serious attempt at upturning the system will face resistance. But this is to be expected. Nonetheless, a ibrant civil society that refuses to be docile in the face of injustice can remove the stranglehold of the corrupt political class. It is only then that the country can ensure its survival, make progress politically and lay to rest the shadow of disintegration that constantly hangs over the political terrain.

Conclusion

This chapter has tried to interrogate the character of the Nigerian state beginning from the pre-independence period to the present times. However, in doing this, it constantly sought to determine the contemporary nature of the Nigerian state with respect to its politics. This it has done through the various examples discussed. From the initial aspirations of the nationalists who envisaged a strong and a united nation to the current worries about the way democracy is practised in Nigeria, it is obvious that the country has remained non-progressive in its traits and politics. This is primarily because national and transnational forces hold sway, while opposition forces have been too weak to check the excesses of corrupt politicians. It suffices to observe, as Edem (2010) says, that the Nigerian state is a confluence of nationalities made up of 'unreasonable' people (politicians) associating involuntarily in the pursuit of uncommon interests. It is fundamentally held together by its armed forces and controlled by a few influential individuals across the ethnic divide, who time and time again recycle themselves or their relations and children into positions of authority. The country still lacks the essential ingredients of legitimacy as significant numbers of its nationalities have not wholly consented to the political association. The situation is further worsened by poor leadership and institutionalised corruption, which stifle any effort to manage the contradictions and get the country on a progressive path. The state seems set for self-destruct. Attempts to convene an all-embracing national conference were sabotaged for a long time and sections of the country simply refuse to discuss those crucial issues that are germane to the country's progress. Although the country has a myriad of political and social institutions, they are mostly weak and disorganised, and subject to abuse and manipulation by an elite that revel in the weakness of its institutions.

Logic dictates and experience shows that the only way to make progress is through increased pressure on the elite by popular forces (see Graf 1988). This is because in the peripheral capitalist economy called Nigeria, the pattern of elite politics and its domination of popular classes have remained intact. Progress entails organisation, resistance, pressure and, if necessary coercion by counter-hegemonic forces to re-direct the country on the path of peace and stability. So far, Nigeria's contemporary politics has simply been disastrous since there is nothing as criminal and painful as being disenfranchised and having strange elements and corrupt individuals imposed on the people. The end of this is usually violence, chaos and retrogression. The Nigeria of tomorrow must be a Nigeria whose elite are enlightened, rational and people-oriented. An elite that is collectively willing to do the right thing for the country despite their differences. Anything short of this breeds anarchy.

References

Agbu, Osita, 1995, *Crisis of the State and Society in Nigeria: A Case of Leadership Failure*, Conference Proceedings on Nigeria at Crossroads: Which Way Out? Nigerian Anthropological and Sociological Association.

Allison, T. Graham, 1971, *Essence of Decision: Explaining the Cuban Missile Crisis, Ist ed.*, Little: Brown.

Almond, A. Gabriel and G. Bingham Powell Jr., 1966, *Comparative Politics: A Developmental Approach*, Little: Brown.

Beckman, B, 1983, 'Whose State? State and Capitalist Development in Nigeria', *Review of African Political Economy*, No.23.

Bendix, R., 1967, *Nation Building and Citizenship*, Berkeley: University of California Press.

Claude, Ake Claude, 1985, *The Political Economy of Nigeria*, London: Longman. Dahl, R. 1971, *Polyarchy*, New Haven: Yale University Press.

Edem, Orok, 2010, *The Nigerian State and National Security*, (http://nigerdeltacongress. com/narticles/nigerian_state_and_national_secu.htm), 3 Aug. 2010.

Eze, C.M., 2009, 'The Privatized State and Mass Poverty in Nigeria: the Factor of Economic Development Programmes since 1980s', *African Journal of Political Science and International Relations*, Vol.3, No.10, October.

Graf, William, 1988, *The Nigerian State: Political Economy, State Class and Political System in the Post-colonial Era*, London: James Curry and Portsmouth.

Held, D, 1989, *Political Theory and Modern State*, Cambridge: Polity Press.

Ihonvbere, Julius ed., 1981, *The Political Economy of Crisis and Underdevelopment in Africa*, Lagos: JAD Publishers.

Iyayi, Festus, 1986, 'The Primitive Accumulation in a Neo-colony: The Nigerian Case', *Review of African Political Economy*, No.35.

Jessop, B, 1990, *State Theory*, Philadelphia: University of Pennsylvania Press.

Joseph, Richard, 1991, 'Class, State and Prebendal Politics in Nigeria', *Journal of Comparative and Commonwealth Politics*, Vol.21, No.3.

Leftwitch, A, 2000, *States of Development*, Malden: Blackwell Publishers.

Marx, Karl, F Engels, 1852, *Selected Works*, Vol.1, Moscow: Foreign Language Publication House. Best S.G,1990, "State, Capitalist Crisis and Constitutional Reforms in Nigeria", in S.G Tyoden ed., *Constitutionalism and National Development in Nigeria*, Proceedings of the 17th Annual Conference of the Nigerian Political Science Association (NPSA), University of Jos, 21 – 23 November.

Mimiko, O. N. Femi, 2007, 'Political and Constitutional Reforms', in Hassan Saliu et.al. ed., *Nigeria's Reform Programme: Issues and Challenges*, Ibadan: Vantage Publishers.

Moru, John, 2004, 'Rethinking the Nigerian Reform Programme', *Thisday* (Lagos), June 23.

Mustapha, A. R., 1992, "Nigeria: The Challenge of Nationhood", *Nigerian Forum*, NIIA, September – December.

Niskanen, W., 1974, *Bureaucracy and Representative Government*, Chicago: Aldine.

Nnoli, Okwudiba, 1981, A Short History of Nigeria Development', in O. Nnoli ed., *Path to Nigerian Development*, Dakar: CODESRIA.

Okechukwu, Ibeanu Okechukwu, 1997, 'The Nigerian State and Politics of Democratisation', Paper Presented at a *Conference on Comparative Democratisation in Africa*, Cape Town, May 31 – June 1.

Onimode, Bade, 1981, 'Imperialism and Nigerian Development', in O. Nnoli ed., *Path to Nigerian Development*, Dakar: CODESRIA.

Osoba, Segun, 1978, 'The Dependency Crisis of the Nigerian National Bourgeosie', *Review of African Political Economy*, No.23.

Parsons, Talcot, 1965, *Structures and Processes in Modern Societies*, London: Frank Cass.

Poulantzas, N., 1978, *State, Power, Socialism*, London: New LeftBooks.

Shaw, M.T and O. Fasehun, 1980, 'Nigeria in the World System: Alternative Approaches, Explanations and Projections', *Journal of Modern African Studies*, Vol.18, No.4.

Mitchel, T., 1992, 'Going Beyond the State', *American Science Review*, Vol.4, No.86.

Weber, Max ed., 1964, *The Theory of Social Economic Organisation*, New York: Free Press.

Zolberg, A, 1995, 'The Formation of New States as a Refugee-generating Process', E.

Ferris ed., *Refugees and World Politics*, New York: Praeger.

2

An Overview of Party Formation in Nigeria, 1960–1999

Osita Agbu

Introduction

This chapter examines party formation processes in post-independence Nigeria. The chapter serves as a useful background for easy understanding of the character of political parties and party politics in contemporary Nigeria. This is examined against the backdrop of recent transitions to democracy, cognizant of the role that political parties are expected to play as key instruments of democratisation in these transitions. The emphasis on the post-colonial period is to shed fresh light on some of the political features and events of the past that could help critical analysis of the current dynamics of the political environment, including the features, origin, character, organisation and ideological tendencies of the political parties during the transition period.

To begin with, a political party could be defined as a group that is publicly organised with the intention of gaining control of government to realise certain aims or to obtain personal advantages or both (Dunmoye 1990:421). This definition not only captures the essence of what a party should be in terms of its public nature and the fact that it basically seeks to control state power and government. The definition is grounded on the pragmatic understanding of the character of political parties, namely – the quest for personal and group advantages. Indeed, a political party is differentiated from other aggregations of people such as pressure groups because it not only seeks to take over the business of government through constitutionally accepted means, but is also expected to have a relatively longer period of active life.

Over the years, Nigeria has operated a multi-party system of government. This was so during the First Republic (1960-1966), the Second Republic (1979-1983), the aborted Third Republic (1987-1993) and the Fourth Republic (1999 – to date). It was this same system that was recommended during the Abdulsalami Abubakar's transition to democracy between 1998 and 1999. General Abdulsalami Abubakar became Nigeria's tenth Head of State when General Sani Abacha suddenly died in office in June 1998. Surrounded by immense goodwill and encouragement locally and internationally, he initiated a new transition to democracy that ended on 29 May 1999. The point to note is that irrespective of the type of government in place, whether parliamentary or presidential, the party system in Nigeria has remained the same – that is multi-partism – except for the brief period of experimentation with the two-party system which resulted in the 12 June 1983 debacle, when Moshood Abiola, the presumed winner of the largely free and fair election, was prevented from assuming office by a conservative military. Multi-partism in Nigeria is no doubt a recognition of the plural or multi-ethnic nature of the Nigerian society.

Post-Colonial Party Formation (1960-1983)

Though the history of the evolution of political parties in Nigeria dates back to the Clifford Constitution of 1922, the parties that were formed prior to independence in 1960 were all regionally and ethnically based, and were largely the result of the provisions of the parliamentary constitution of 1951. Three major parties and a few minor ones featured predominantly in the politics of the early 1960s. These were the National Council of Nigeria and the Camerouns (NCNC), Northern People's Congress (NPC) and the Action Group (AG); others included the United Middle Belt Congress (UMBC) and the Northern Elements Progressive Union (NEPU). The oldest of the three major parties was the NCNC which was formed in 1944 (Dudley 1982:45). The NCNC was, in fact, the dominant force in Nigerian nationalism until 1951 when the Action Group rose to challenge it. The NCNC later had the problem of how to transform a structure that was principally organised to oppose colonial rule into a vote-winning political party. At this period, it was broad-based, with its influence significantly felt as far as the Cameroons.

The Action Group (AG) on the other hand, was formed in 1951, as an offshoot of a Yoruba cultural organisation known as *Egbe Omo Oduduwa* formed by Chief Obafemi Awolowo and his friends. This party made it clear that it intended to operate principally from the regional level. In a press release issued in 1951, the party announced that it was a "Western Regional Political Organisation, pure and simple". Its aims and objectives were for the advancement of the Yoruba race (Nnabuihe et al 2004:167). This revelation was later to set the tone for other parties to lay claim to hegemony of their regions during subsequent elections (Post

1963:31). This may be regarded as the prelude to the emergence of some regional and ethnically-based political parties in Nigeria.

On the other hand, the Northern People's Congress (NPC) with its base in the North was formed in 1949 on the initiative of some young men, including Abubakar Tafawa Balewa, Yahaya Gusau and Dr. R.A.B Dikko. It was an offshoot of the cultural association known as *Jam'iyyar Mutanen Arewa*. By and large, the North had remained untouched by the nationalist movement that had significant followership in the South of the country. Deliberate British policy, more especially the principle of absolute non-interference with Islamic beliefs, the discouragement of missionary activities for this same reason, and the relative insulation of the North from the effects of modern economic development, had ensured that no significant radical group emerged to challenge the colonial administration. Though, initially perceived with suspicion by the traditional rulers, the party later gained support from them by stating that it intended to work strictly within the limits of the traditional political systems. The NPC subsequently controlled the politics of the North due to its link with the Native Authority.

As earlier mentioned, apart from these three dominant parties, there were many other smaller ones such as the Northern Elements Progressive Union (NEPU), which emerged to challenge the hegemony of the NPC, the United Middle Belt Congress (UMBC) which claimed to represent the Northern minority groups of the Middle Belt, the United Nigeria Independent Party (UNIP) and others (Dudley 1982: 50). These were highly localized parties anchored basically on sectional interests and personalities. Apart from the NCNC, which was initially broad-based in its membership, the NPC and the AG were basically regional parties representing the interests of the ruling class in their respective regions. Of course, these interests were masked as ethnic interests, which contributed gravely to the events which occurred in the 1959 and 1964 Federal Elections. Political unrest and loss of lives and property consequently led to the declaration of a state of emergency in the Western Region and subsequent military intervention of 1966.

The acrimonious politics of the Federal Elections of 1964, the manipulation of ethnicity and lack of political consciousness on the part of the people combined to remotely set the stage for the events of 1966. Pogroms were carried out against easterners in the north of the country resulting in the declaration of the breakaway Republic of Biafra by Colonel Odumegwu Ojukwu on May 30 1966, when it became clear that the Federal Government was not ready to protect the lives and property of easterners. At this juncture, it is important to pause and ask ourselves – what has changed? Are the present parties, in terms of origin, membership, cohesion and ideology any different from the parties of the 1960s? The scenario in the Second Republic (1979-1983) tended to support the view that nothing had changed. On the other hand, the trend of activities in party-formation in the 1998-1999 transition (1998-1999), appears to indicate a fundamental shift. Furthermore, the emergence of the All Progressives Congress (APC), a mega-party of opposition parties and groups with Muhammadu Buhari as presidential candidate for the 2015 general elections could be an improvement of sorts in respect of political party organization. We will come later to this after briefly examining party formation in the Second Republic.

On the Second Republic, by September 1978, the ban prohibiting the formation of political parties was lifted by the military government of General Olusegun Obasanjo, giving rise to a plethora of political associations numbering about one hundred and fifty. By the end of the year, only five of these associations were registered as political parties, namely the National Party of Nigeria (NPN), the Nigerian Peoples' Party (NPP), the Unity Party of Nigeria (UPN), the Great Nigeria Peoples' Party (GNPP), and the Peoples' Redemption Party (PRP). The Nigerian Advance Party (NAP) led by Tunji Braithwaite later joined the fray to contest the aborted 1983 elections.

Of these, the UPN had been in the making long before it emerged in October 1978. In fact, most of the leadership of the UPN were the same set of people that had led the Action Group (AG) in the First Republic (Dudley 1982:186). The UPN claimed to be 'democratic socialist' in orientation, but in practice pragmatic considerations diluted its ideological commitment to democratic socialism. The NPN, on the other hand, initially was nothing more than a collection of rich individuals with enlightened self-interests and a commitment to the maintenance of a free market economy. Though broad-based, it represented the interests of the rich business-managerial class and had a firm base in the North. If the UPN was a reincarnation of the AG, the NPN was a descendant of the NPC and was firmly positioned to the right of the ideological spectrum. The original NPP, led by Ibrahim Waziri was an amalgam of young moderate well-to-do businessmen and representatives of minority groups who felt marginalized in the power equation. Disagreement over leadership led to a split which saw the emergence of the GNPP which professed 'consensualism' ('politics without bitterness'), and the NPP, which espoused a liberal ethic based on 'individualistic'/'collectivist' paradigm. A placing of these parties on an ideological spectrum had the PRP at the extreme left, followed by the UPN, with the NPP at the Centre, followed by the GNPP and then, the NPN at the extreme right of the centre. At least, there was some semblance of ideological predisposition by these parties. This had completely vanished, however, by the beginning of the Fourth Republic.

This positioning notwithstanding, ideological consideration has never been a strong element of Nigeria's party politics. More common has been the politics of personalities based on the ability of local politicians to cajole, buy and ride on the ethnic card as a way of getting to political offices. Indeed, it is clear from the foregoing that the parties of the Second Republic differed little from the major parties of the First Republic. Does this then mean that circumstances have remained the same? Does this mean that ethnic considerations based on the lack of political consciousness still influence the political behaviour of Nigerians? We will next examine the type and nature of parties which subsequently arose during the Ibrahim Babangida and Sani Abacha military-guided transitions, in order to decide whether indeed any changes had occurred or not.

Party-formation under the Babangida-era transition to democracy

The military regime of General Ibrahim Babangida (1985-1993) was characterised by a phased-approach to the political transition project. An important aspect of this programme was the debate over the type of political system Nigeria should adopt. To this end, a *Political Bureau* was set up in 1986 and came up with a report, which recommended among other things a two-party system for Nigeria's Third Republic. Two parties were subsequently decreed into existence by the government – the Social Democratic Party (SDP) and the National Republican Convention (NRC). With the benefit of hindsight, it appeared that this recommendation was apparently an effort to address the cankerworm of ethnicity in Nigeria's troubled political life. However, it could also be said that the 1979 Constitution on party formation enforced a national outlook for all registered parties, which largely attenuated ethnicity. Since then the class interests of the political elite, recruited nationally, have tended to bind them together against the mass of Nigerians. Nothing shows this better than the levity with which worsening corruption has been treated since May 1999.

However, the creation of the two parties was later to be criticized as basically undemocratic, on the grounds that people should ideally be allowed a free choice to associate and galvanize their interests in the way they want and in as many a political grouping as they wish. More significant however, was the result of the annulled June 12 1993 presidential election which saw Moshood Abiola, the billionaire politician poised to win in all sections of the country even in the North, though he was ethnically Yoruba. This was indeed, a novel development which seemed to point to the fact that with consensual agreement on how to organize the political system, it is possible to overcome certain inherently structural and constraining factors that inhibit political development. In this case, it would have been best if the two parties that contested the elections were allowed to *ab initio* evolve independently outside of government interference through the articulation of the interests of groups and individuals. This apart, the former president, Ibrahim Babangida, termed the herding of the various political associations either into the Social Democratic party (SDP) or the National Republican Convention (NRC) as simply a compartmentalization of these interests a little to the left – (SDP), and a little to the right 0 (NRC). (But the constitution of the latter, the military junta's preferred party, was more left-leaning than the former, thus sowing the seeds of confusion in the minds of politicians and the electorate alike). In terms of organisation, the government not only founded these parties, it built their offices all over the country, funded them and had overwhelming influence in their decision-making process.[7] Obviously, both were broad-based, but basically ideologically suspect. It suffices to state that an undemocratic government cannot enthrone democracy, especially one in which it single-handedly dictated the nature and character of the political parties.

The Abacha Transition

Right from the outset, the transition programme master-minded by General Sani Abacha was characterised by insincerity and designs for self-succession. It was a pointer that Nigerian politicians had learned little and forgotten quite a lot when a disproportionate number of them went along with the charade that was then playing itself out in the name of 'self-succession'. Though five parties were eventually registered, namely the United Nigeria Congress Party (UNCP), Democratic Party of Nigeria (DPN), Congress for National Consensus (CNC), National Centre Party of Nigeria (NCPN), and the Grassroots Democratic Movement (GDM), there was very little room for the parties to manoeuvre as the military junta abused all known principles of democratic practice in its bid to achieve Abacha's self-succession design (Agbu 1998). Basically, all the five parties were made up of a mixed-bag of politicians out for what they could get when it was clear that the whole transition was a ruse. Candidates were being disqualified by the government supposedly on security considerations which was really nothing but a way of eliminating anti-Abacha and potentially politically threatening candidates from challenging the hegemony of the favoured party – the UNCP. Basically, all were institutionally and ideologically bankrupt and paraded a significant array of unprincipled characters masquerading as politicians. It, therefore, appeared that not only had things not changed, it had indeed gotten worse. The high point of the charade was when the five political parties mysteriously adopted Abacha as the sole candidate for the planned presidential elections. The sudden death of the dictator on 8 June 1998 put a stop to the travesty and created the opportunity, yet again, for another political transition programme.

Abubakar's Transition

The country, once more, embarked on a new transition under General Abdulsalami Abubakar's military government, which assumed the reins of leadership on 9 June 1998. Abubakar promised to hand over power to a democratically elected president by 29 May 1999. To this end, nine parties were given provisional registration out of the 26 political associations that sought registration. These included the All People's Party (APP), People's Democratic Party (PDP), Democratic Advance Movement (DAM), Movement for Democracy and Justice (MDJ), United People's Party (UPP), Alliance for Democracy (AD), and the National Solidarity Movement (NSM). According to the Independent National

Electoral Commission's (INEC) guidelines for the transition, for any of these parties to qualify for permanent registration, it must score 10 per cent of votes cast in at least 24 states of the Federation and the Federal Capital Territory (FCT) at the Council polls scheduled to be held on December 1998. INEC subsequently issued a code of conduct for parties and warned that 'any political party that fails to abide by the conditions shall have its registration withdrawn' (The Guardian 1998). These conditions included cooperation with INEC, respect for the rights of other parties, freedom to campaign, avoidance of violence and the use of inflammatory languages, rejection of corrupt practices… and assisting in ensuring peaceful and orderly voting on polling day. These conditions notwithstanding, some politicians accused INEC of incompetence and alleged malpractices during voters' registration.

For those political organisations given provisional registration, a comparison with past experiences based on general aggregation of interests, and role of personalities reveal some interesting tendencies. Whereas the parties of the 1960s had very clear objectives, be it national or regional control and/or protection of traditional and minority interests, some of the associations which metamorphosed as parties during this dispensation appeared vague in their party objectives apart from the common goal of seeking political office. However, one thing that was agreed upon by all the parties as a common objective was the fact that they all wanted an end to military rule.

The three registered political parties that satisfied the provisions laid down by Independent National Electoral Commission (INEC) were the Alliance for Democracy (AD), the All Peoples Party (APP) and the Peoples Democratic Party (PDP). Let us briefly examine the origin of these parties.

Alliance for Democracy (AD)

The AD was formed by a number of Southern pressure groups – *Afenifere*, Eastern Mandate Union, People's Consultative Forum, National Democratic Alliance (NADECO), and the Southern Leaders Forum. These groups were basically opposed to the self-succession bid of Sani Abacha (Maja-Pearce 1999).

It is of interest to note that the groundwork for the formation of the AD was very quickly done (Maja-Pearce 1999). Its major component, the People's Consultative Forum (PCF) initially pulled out of the Peoples Democratic Party (PDP), and then also left the All Peoples Party (APP) after raising objections to the presence of pro-Abacha politicians in its fold. They then approached the United Democratic Congress led by Ambassador Tanko Yusuf, and the two formed an alliance known as the Alliance for Democracy (AD). This party dominated the six Yoruba-speaking states of the South-West of Nigeria between 1999 and 2003.

In respect of party philosophy, the AD believed that a restructuring of the Nigerian federation was imperative, including a restructuring of the Police and Armed Forces. It also believed that revenue allocation should be based on derivation and that a Sovereign National Conference (SNC) was a *sine qua non* in deciding how the country should be made to progress. Underlying the restructuring of the Nigerian state is the demand for the devolution of more powers to the states, in the true spirit of federalism. Prominent members of this party were Chief Ayo Adebanjo (Acting National Chairperson), Bassey Etubom Bassey (National Vice-Chairperson), Dr. Chukwuemeka Ezeife, Alhaji Abdul Kadir Daiyabu (National Vice Chairperson), Chief Olu Falae, Chief Bola Ige, Alhaji Yussuf Mamman (National Organising Secretary), Chief Segun Osoba, Dr. Udenta O. Udenta (Secretary) and Senator Bola Tinubu.

All People's Party (APP)

This Party originated out of a meeting held between the Southern Leaders Forum led by Chief Bola Ige and the Conference of Fused Associations led by Umaru Shinkafi in Lagos. Described as a 'rainbow coalition', it initially had Associations like the Peoples National Congress (PNC), United Nigeria Peoples Party (UNPP), the People's Consultative Forum (PCF) also known as *Afenifere,* the All Nigerian Congress (ANC), and the National Unity Party in its fold. The PCF later broke ranks with the APP citing incompatibility with politicians in the party who publicly supported the designs of General Sani Abacha for self-succession.

Prominent members were Alhaji Usman Shinkafi, Dr. Olusola Saraki, Senator Mahmud Waziri (National Chairperson), Chief Emmanuel Iwuanyanwu, Dr. Bode Olajumoke, Chief C. C. Onoh and Gamaliel Onosode.

Peoples Democratic Party (PDP)

Its genesis could be traced to a popular opposition movement called the G34. The G34 had metamorphosed from the Institute of Civil Society which was formed in late 1997 with the aim of enlightening citizens about their rights and obligations under military dispensation. This Institute initially transformed into the Group of 18, mostly northern politicians who were unhappy with the self-succession plan of General Abacha. This group would later be enlarged to 34 members – G34, comprising eminent Nigerians from across the country who privately wrote General Abacha on 24 February 1998 asking him to retrace his his steps (Maja-Pearce 1999). Believed to be fairly well-funded, the organisation had within its fold many retired generals and other senior military officers, which made many sceptical about its objectives and sincerity. The party proper was formed by some of the leading members of the G34 led by Dr. Alex Ekwueme, former Vice-President of Nigeria (1979-1983) in association with other political groups. Some of these groups included the All Nigeria Congress (ANC), New Era Alliance (NERA), and the United Nigerian People's Party (UNPP). With a blend of old and new breed politicians in its fold cutting across all states of the federation, it was considered a broad-based party and stood to gain from the nature of its composition and origin.

Prominent members of the party included Chief Alex Ekwueme (chairperson, Board of Trustees), General Olusegun Obasanjo, Mallam Adamu Ciroma, Chief Solomon Lar (national chairperson), Alhaji Sule Lamido, Chief Jim Nwobodo, Alhaji Abubakar Rimi, Chief Don Etiebet and Dr. Tonye Graham-Douglas. This party was later to win the 1999, 2003, 2007 and 2011 general elections, even though the elections, apart from the 2011 elections, were considered largely flawed, characterised by unreliable voters' registers, poor organisation, intimidation, vote rigging and generally poor election security.

Conclusion

This overview and analysis of the situation during the Abubakar transition with respect to party formation suggests that pluralism is still a major feature of Nigeria's political development. Fundamentally, it appears that nothing has changed in terms of articulating national objectives for the survival of the Nigerian polity. The ideal was the desire for democratic governance, while the reality was the lack of transparency in the political processes. However, what was observed was the reconfiguration of new parties from old ones, with very little changes in terms of core parochial/ethnic and personal interests. However, what should also be noted is the opposition of the new parties to military rule. All wanted an end to military rule. Again, it is fairly evident that the high level of ignorance on the part of the people, which the politicians of the 1960s exploited, was no more readily obtainable on the same scale as before, especially after the destructive manipulations of the Babangida and Abacha transitions which were non-transparent, self-serving and highly destructive of the Nigerian unity project.

A lot still needs to be understood with respect to the myriad of social and political forces in Nigeria with subjective and centrifugal tendencies in the body-politic. Politicized ethnicity and the undue emphasis on the subjective criteria of regional ascendancy have frustrated efforts at national integration and inhibited the healthy growth of a political culture. For Nigerians, at no other time in recent memory were they expected to take more interest in their internal politics than during this very interesting, but volatile Fourth Republic.

References

Agbu, Osita, 1998, 'Political Opposition and Democratic Transitions in Nigeria (1985- 1996)', in Adebayo O. Olukoshi ed., *The Politics of Opposition in Contemporary Africa*, Uppsala: Nordiska Afrikainstitutet.

Dudley, Billy, 1982, *An Introduction to Nigerian Government and Politics*, London: Macmillan.

Dunmoye, T. Ayo, 1990, 'Economic Crisis, Constitutionalism and Poltiical stability in Nigeria', in S. G. Tyoden ed., *Constitutionalism and National development in Nigeria*, Proceedings of the 17th Annual Conference of the Nigerian Political Science Association (NPSA), held at University of Jos, 21-23 November.

Maja-Pearce, Adewale, 1999, *From Khaki to Agbada: A Handbook for the February 1999 Elections in Nigeria*, Lagos: Civil Liberties Organisation.

Nnabuihe, N.S., Aghemale, A., and Okebugwu, N.E., 2004, 'Ethnicity and Electoral Behaviour in Nigeria', *European Scientific Journal*, vol. 2, pp159-178.

Olukoshi, Adebayo and Agbu Osita, 1996, 'The Deepening Crisis of Nigerian Federation and the Future of the Nation-State', in Adebayo Olukoshi and Liisa Laakso eds., *Challenges to the Nation-State in Africa*, Uppsala: Nordiska Afrikainstitutet.

Post, K.W.J, 1963, *The Nigerian Federal Election of 1959*, Oxford: Oxford University Press. R

The Guardian (Lagos), 1998, 'INEC Issues Code of Conduct for Parties', October 23.

Thisday, (Lagos), 1998, 'Government to Punish Hoarders of Voters' Cards', October 22.

3

Electoral Commissions and the Conduct of Elections in Nigeria: The Role of INEC

Pamela Ogwuazor Momah

A Historical Perspective of Electoral Commissions in Nigeria

Other Electoral Management Bodies (EMBs) had existed before the advent of the Independent National Electoral Commission (INEC) in Nigeria. These EMBs with similar powers as INEC were reflections of Nigeria's political life. The number, to a large extent, underscores Nigeria's ability or inability to develop a political culture. What is clear, however, is that each time democracy is truncated by way of military intervention, the yearning for democracy increases and prompts the country to seek recourse in a new EMB.

The first Election Management body was the defunct Electoral Commission of Nigeria (ECN), which conducted the pre-independence elections of 1959. With the advent of independence, the government of Abubakar Tafawa Balewa set up the Federal Electoral Commission (FEC), which conducted the 1964 and 1965 elections. Following the first military *coup d'état* of 15 January 1966, the FEC was dissolved. It was not until 1978 that the Obasanjo military administration set up another electoral body; the Federal Electoral Commission (FEDECO). FEDECO conducted the transitional elections that ushered in Nigeria's Second Republic with Alhaji Shehu Shagari of the National Party of Nigeria (NPN) emerging as the President. Hardly had democratic rule taken off than it was extirpated in 1983 and FEDECO was promptly dissolved in 1987, when the administration of General Ibrahim Babangida began one of Nigeria's longest transitions to civil rule programmes. He set up the National Electoral Commission (NEC). NEC worked assiduously until the annulment of the presidential election in June 1993. General Sani Abacha, who took over power as Head of State from Chief Ernest Shonekan, Head of the Interim National Government (ING), then replaced NEC with the National Electoral Commission of Nigeria (NECON) which conducted another set of elections to the local government councils to the National Assembly. The elected officers had not, however, been sworn into office before Abacha suddenly died in June 1998, aborting the process. General Abdulsalami Abubakar dissolved NECON in 1998 and established The Independent National Electoral Commission (INEC). (INEC'S Retreat, Kaduna, 16-20 August 2009).

Since independence, Nigeria has had eleven Chief Electoral Officers, the first being Chief Eyo Esau, who midwifed the 1964/1965 elections, while Dr. Abel Guobadia was in charge in 1999, and Professor Maurice Iwu superintended the body from 2005 to 2010. Professor Attahiru Jega, a political scientist has been in charge as INEC Chairman since 2010 (see Appendix).

Electoral Commissions and Elections in Nigeria

Most Nigerians believe that electoral commissions are central to the problems associated with the conduct of elections in Nigeria. The Electoral Commission of Nigeria (ECN) conducted the 1959 elections that led to the first neo-colonial civilian government in Nigeria. The outcome of the election was controversial and it led to the controversial 1964 regional elections in the Western Region. The controversies surrounding the 1964 elections were the basis for which the military decided to overthrow the civilian government in 1966 (Iyayi 2006:11). In 1979, FEDECO conducted elections that gave rise to the famous two-thirds of nineteen states' crisis. This controversy escalated because the military were alleged to be in favour of a particular group of people that they wanted to hand over power to (Iyayi 2006:11). In 1983, FEDECO was seen as instrumental to the return of NPN, the ruling party, into power by announcing that the number of registered voters had increased from 48, 499,07 in 1971 to 65, 304,818, in spite of the fact that the 1979 figure was considered to be highly inflated (Iyayi 2006:11). Similarly, the results of the 1999 elections were seen to have been pre-arranged with INEC so as to make the electoral process and results legitimate (Iyayi 2006:11). Again INEC was seen as part and parcel of the enormous fraud that characterised the 2003 and 2004 elections. According to the Transition Monitoring Group (TMG), INEC contributed its own fair share of electoral problems in the 2003 elections. The lack of clearly designated compartments for thumb-printing undermined the secrecy of the vote and exposed the voters to machinations of those that would have preferred 'community voting'. INEC also did not make adequate arrangements for the transportation of sensitive election materials to the polling stations and collation centres. Result sheets disappeared and re-appeared in different forms at collation centres whilst corrupt party agents simply sold unused ballot papers to the highest bidder. Following the reversal of the process for the order of the elections by INEC, voters deserted the state House of Assembly elections. Thus no voting took place in these elections, although winners emerged from the process.

The 2007 elections fell short of national, regional and international standards for democratic elections. They were marred by very poor organisation, lack of essential transparency, widespread procedural irregularities and substantial evidence of fraud. According to the European Union Observer Mission:

> The voter registration exercise conducted by INEC was marred by delays due to lack of available Direct Data Capturing Machines, technical breakdowns and establishment of illegal voter registration centres. The quality of the final voter register was poor and included under age voters, double entries, missing and blurred pictures of voters. The voter register was not displayed at the local level as required by law and was partly posted prior to Election Day for orientation purposes only. Permanent voter registration cards were not issued due to late publication of the final register.

The above observation suggests that electoral commissions in Nigeria have so far tended to serve the interests of the ruling party in power and have thus contributed to election problems in Nigeria. But these observations do not necessarily explain why these commissions do so (Iyayi 2006:12).

There have been instances when the election tribunals set up to adjudicate on the conduct of some elections had established that INEC was partisan, but the full weight of the law was never brought on those INEC officials. Lack of punishment, of course, results in impunity. Elections are conducted with billions of naira, and with frequent nullifications and high turnover of results, billions of naira go down the drain as yet another huge amount of money is budgeted for yet another re-run. Nobody has been prosecuted for such huge waste of the country's resources.

Purpose of the Study

- To provide a critical analysis of the role INEC played at the state and federal levels in the 1999, 2003 and 2007 elections; determine its strengths and shortcomings, so as to proffer an appropriate solution to the country's electoral problems.
- To examine INEC as an institution in the context of its independence, impartiality, transparency, and accountability.
- To examine the institutional weakness of Nigeria's electoral processes and the legal framework for the conduct of elections as they relate to INEC.
- To establish the fact that the institution that is charged with managing the conduct of elections has a vital role to play in the growth and development of the nation's democracy.
- To proffer recommendations as to how INEC can conduct transparent and credible elections, so as to improve political stability and good governance in Nigeria.
- To provide a guide for INEC or any other future electoral body.

Methodology

The study is both historical and analytical. The historical approach provides the genesis of INEC, while the analytical approach assesses the effectiveness of INEC in the performance of its functions. The analysis is approached from an institutional perspective and closely examines INEC's ability to function as a neutral, fair and transparent umpire during elections. The study used secondary sources of data collected from INEC offices in Abuja, Enugu, and Lagos, and materials from other libraries.

Key Concepts

Democracy – According to the Webster dictionary, this is government by the people; rule of the majority; a government in which the supreme power is vested in the people and exercised by them directly or indirectly. Democracy is a human right,as such, it is included in a number of the most important international human rights standards, such as the Universal Declaration of Human Rights Art.1, which states that

> Everyone has the right to take part in the governance of his country, directly or indirectly, or through freely chosen representatives…

Art.3 states that

> The will of the people shall be the basis of the authority of the government; this will be expressed in periodic and genuine elections that shall be held by secret vote or by equivalent free voting procedures.

Thus democracy respects human rights and therefore also respects the rule of law, because the rule of law is part of human rights.

Elections – According to Okoye (2003: vii), elections are – A complex set of activities with different variables that act and feed on one another. It can be defined as a 'formal' act of collective decision that occurs in a stream of connected antecedent and subsequent behaviour. It involves the participation of the people in the act of electing their leaders and their participation in governance. Elections are not necessarily about Election Day activities, although it forms an important component. It encompasses activities before, during and after elections. It includes the legal and constitutional framework of elections; the registration of political parties, party campaigns, the activities of the security agencies and the government in power. It includes the authenticity and genuineness of the voter's register. It includes the independence or lack of it, of the electoral agencies and organs. It includes the liberalism or otherwise of political processes in the country and the independence of the adjudicating bodies in elections.

In a democratic nation, periodic elections of the executive and legislators constitute the principal institutional device for making sure that the government shall derive its just power from the consent of the governed. Elections are central to the functioning of modern democracy (Singh and Mishra 1991).

Voting – This is the simplest form of democratic participation and it is the most formal act of political participation, but not the exclusive form of citizens' involvement in the political system. It is one procedure generally accepted as binding within the political society, through which citizens make an explicit choice between alternatives in elections (Singh and Mishra 1991). The goal of any voting system is to establish the intent of the voter, and through it transfer the intent to the vote counter. The efficiency of the voting method and the accuracy of the vote counter are the crucial determinants of the ability and capacity of the system to correctly determine the wish of the voter (Iwu 2008:1).

Elections/Electoral Commissions – According to Wikipedia online dictionary, it is in theory a non-partisan body that determines election procedures and district boundaries and oversees the conduct of elections. It is also an impartial administrator, with an independent body, being available to adjudicate in electoral disputes, re-engineer the political process, conduct elections and implement the various regulations devised to prevent every imaginable form of election misconduct (Derbyshire and Debyshire 1993:130). A neutral electoral commission is thus one of the fundamental pre-requisites for a truly free and fair election and the establishment of true democracy in any nation.

INEC and its Institutional Framework

The commission is made up of a chairman and 12 national commissioners. The commission was established in accordance with section 153 (f) of the Constitution of the Federal Republic of Nigeria. The functions of the Commission, as stipulated in part 1 of the Third Schedule to the 1999 Constitution, are as follows:

- Organize, conduct, and supervise all elections and matters pertaining to elections into all elective offices provided in the Constitution of the Federal Republic of Nigeria 1999, as amended or any other enactment or law.
- Register political parties in accordance with the provision of the relevant enactment or law.
- Monitor the organisation and operation of the political parties, including their finances.
- Arrange for the annual examination and auditing of the funds and accounts of political parties and publish a report of such examination and audit for public information.
- Conduct registration of persons qualified to vote and the preparation, maintenance and revision of the register of voters for the purpose of any election.
- Monitor political campaigns and provide rules and regulations, which shall govern the political parties.
- Ensure that all Electoral Commissioners and Electoral Returning Officers take and subscribe to the oath of office prescribed by law.

- Delegate any power to any Resident Electoral Commissioner.
- Carry out such other functions as may be conferred upon it by a Decree or any other enactment of law.
- Divide the area of the Federation or as the case may be, the area of a state, local government or area council into such number of constituencies as may be presented by law, for the purpose of elections to be conducted by the Commission.

Guiding Principles

The principles that guide INEC in the fulfilment of its mission and vision are:
- Transparency: INEC will be open and transparent in all its activities and in its relations with political stakeholders, media organisations, INEC service providers and the people of Nigeria.
- INEC will strive to be truthful and honest in all its dealings with people, its political stakeholders and each other.
- Credibility: INEC will strive to ensure that the people of Nigeria and in particular the political stakeholders will readily accept all its actions.
- Impartiality: INEC will endeavour to create a level playing field for all political actors.
- Dedication: INEC will be committed to providing the highest quality election services to the people of Nigeria and will also work to ensure that merit will continue to be the basis for compensation, promotion and recruitment of staff.

The Commission consists of a Chairman who is the Chief National Electoral Commissioner, and twelve other members, known as National Electoral Commissioners. The Chairman and members of the Commission are appointed by the Head of State, Commander-in-Chief of the Armed Forces. In each state of the Federation and the Federal Capital Territory Abuja, there is an office of the Commission and a Residential Electoral Commissioner, who is appointed by the Head of State. The Commission also has a Secretary who is the Administrative Officer of the Commission.

Nigeria has a Federal system of government, with different tiers of jurisdiction, involving several levels of elections.
- Presidential Elections.
- Elections at the Federal Level, for the Senate and the House of Representatives.
- Elections at the State level, the elections of Governors and State legislators
- Elections at the local government level.

Result of Findings

Going through various copies of the Electoral Magazine, an INEC publication, collected from the INEC offices, Professor Iwu is described as a man who introduced a lot of innovations into the electoral process, the Electoral Institute, now Electoral Institute of Nigeria, being one of them. Although the man has been castigated, vilified and abused, INEC strongly believes that the myriad of negative comments by people after elections is due to not having correct information. However, the facts remain that Iwu should bear responsibility for the bastardization of Nigeria's electoral process between 2005 and 2010. His intransigence in defending the indefensible – rigging of elections, ballot box stuffing, imposition of candidates, doctoring of election results and outrightly imposing those who never won primaries within their parties as elected cannot be forgotten. He was indeed, the face of Nigeria's democracy in its most decadent state.

However, for INEC, the panacea for election rigging is the electronic voting system, which has four major components: electronic voter register, voter accreditation and authentication, electronic balloting and electronic transmission of results. These would eliminate violence, money laundering, ballot box stuffing, fraudulent counting of votes and resultant manipulation in elections.

Going through the official report of the 2007 general election by INEC, some issues are highlighted as having hindered the elections and INEC's performance in particular. These include:

- Lack of financial autonomy was a major problem, which resulted in undue delays with ultimately detrimental consequences.
- Electoral constituency delimitation. This did not allow for a proper level playing field for political participation in elections.
- The deployment of appropriate technology i.e. electronic voting machines were proposed and not approved by the National Assembly.
- The majority of the political parties were not represented at the polling centres so as to minimize complaints and irregularities.
- The Constitution does not specifically provide the power for the commission to disqualify candidates whose submitted claims are found to be false.
- The Commission's resort to receiving electoral logistic support from the state and local government. Although, this is good in itself, it needs to be investigated to ensure that INEC staff are not blackmailed or compromised at the grassroots level by politicians.
- Producing sensitive election materials abroad result in delivery delays, thus crippling logistic plans.
- The inability of the various commands and security organisations to deploy their personnel to all the 120,000 polling units nationwide during

elections is a serious challenge. This is the reason why cases of ballot snatching and other forms of electoral offences happen during voting.

- Nigeria's vast terrain and geographical complexity poses logistical problems in distributing materials to all nooks and crannies of Nigeria. Staggering elections could solve this problem even though it will probably create other problems, e.g. a bandwagon effect in voting pattern.

- The principle of first-past-the-post, whereby the candidate with the majority of votes is declared the winner, even with the slimmest number, allows nomination/ substitution of candidates, which has been the bane of Nigerian electoral system. INEC advocates for the proportional representative system, where the emphasis is on the political party that is allocated a seat, based on the percentage of votes scored in elections.

Despite what INEC might think of its performance during elections, the majority of national and international observers and the generality of the Nigerian public, think otherwise. Monitoring of elections in Nigeria and other developing countries is done in order to put a stamp of credibility on the outcome of such elections. The Carter Centre in collaboration with the National Democratic Institute for International Affairs (NDI), based in Washington D.C., that had President Carter and General Colin Powell in its large delegation, was amongst those who monitored the 1999 general elections. Their observations are well-documented in the literature, including the following:

- The monitors in the 1999 were unanimous in their verdict that there were massive irregularities in all the elections. The international monitors put the voter turn out to be 20 per cent while the election results indicated 30 – 40 per cent (Aluko, 1999:2).

- President Carter, though a personal friend of Obasanjo, refused to put his stamp of approval on the presidential vote – 'There was a wide disparity between the number of voters observed at the polling station and the final results that was reported from several States' (Aluko 1999: 2)

- The Transition Monitoring Group (TMG), a coalition of 70 human rights and civil liberty NGOs, said that both sides committed fraud. Yet the 1999 elections was upheld and given legitimacy by INEC.

After the 1999 elections, political observers were not comfortable with the fact that the president was vested with the power to appoint the Chairman and members of INEC. Section (1) of the 1999 Constitution of the Federal Republic of Nigeria, gives him these powers and the arrangement allows the Commission to draw its funds from the Presidency. Analysts believe that with this arrangement, the incumbent could always use his position to influence INEC. They doubted very much that a chairman appointed by the president and who depends on him for funds can, in practical terms, be an impartial umpire (Okusabor 2001:5). Indeed, since these funds are not personal, the real explanation for dancing to the whims and caprices of Mr. President could lie elsewhere, and my suspicions are lack of integrity and corruption.

In the 2003 elections the EU Observation Mission, noted that:

- The electoral preparation by INEC, particularly the registration of voters, started late; and thus led to recurrent delays during the course of elections.
- INEC did not disseminate adequate guidelines and instructions on matters regarding political party campaigning and candidate nominations.
- The number of total registered voters by INEC shortly before Election Day varied greatly and fuelled suspicion, particularly as the process of detecting and deleting millions of applications in a short period was herculean.
- The established parties were identified as being involved in malpractices. INEC was unable to counter such tendencies, as a result of insufficient level of logistical and inadequate implementation of its own procedures.
- The 2002 Electoral laws that guided the 2003 elections stipulated that INEC should issue guidelines on campaigns, but it failed to do so.
- INEC's training capacity was small, in regards to the number of people who had to be educated on electoral matters.
- INEC's organisational, technical and structural shortcomings opened up new doors for fraudulent activities conducted by the parties and their candidates.

Ogunsanwo (2003:14-15) commenting on the 2003 elections said that INEC was certainly and genuinely not in absolute control of activities on election day. He also pointed out that INEC could not vouch for the integrity of the election officials who were engaged all over the country (Ogunsanwo 2003:15). He further pointed out that a major flaw in INECs management of the 2003 General Elections was the declaration of individuals who did not contest elections as winners i.e. those who neither won party primary elections within their party caucus, nor were known candidates (Ogunsanwo 2003:16).

The report of the EU Observation Mission on the 2007 elections pointed out that the 'elections at both state and federal levels were marred by very poor organisation, lack of essential transparency, widespread procedural irregularities, substantial evidence of fraud, widespread voter disenfranchisement at different stages of the process, lack of equal conditions for political parties and candidates and numerous incidence of violence'.

The 2007 elections were regulated by the 1999 Constitution and a new Electoral Act was adopted for this – The 2006 Electoral Act. Atiku Abubakar's disqualification by INEC resulted in significant logistical problems for the presidential elections, following the 16th April decision of the Supreme Court, to allow Atiku to run for the 2007 Presidential elections. Generally, several logistical problems were experienced:

a) INEC failed to provide information on the final number of candidates and the final number of voters per constituency and the number of ballot papers that were printed and distributed, and it made no provision for results to be posted at the polling stations.

b) There was a lot of delay in completing the voter registration exercise, which in turn affected the distribution of permanent voter registration cards.

c) Ballot papers were produced with pictures missing and names misspelt in some cases.

d) INEC failed to distribute the ballot papers on time to states, and from there to the LGAs, wards, and polling stations. This led to serious delays and disruptions and, in a number of cases, cancellation of election. In Lagos State, some candidates' names were missing from the Senate and House of Representatives ballot papers, causing a cancellation of elections in two senatorial elections in the state. In Enugu, polling did not start before 1500hours. Although INEC was aware of the serious delay in opening the polling station, no regulation was issued to extend the official polling hours. In Enugu North, it was found that completely different results in favour of the ruling parties were recorded on the result sheet, when compared to those of six polling stations.

e) The voter registration exercise conducted by INEC was marred by delays, due to lack of Direct Data Capturing Machines, technical breakdown, and battery and light problems.

Observations

Going through the litany of irregularities that marred elections in Nigeria in the 1999, 2003 and 2007 elections in particular, it is obvious that a big problem exists with election management in Nigeria, even if INEC feels that most of the ills plaguing elections had nothing to do with it. The then President, Musa Yar' Adua in reaction to the irregularities that characterised the 2007 general elections, said that he was going to carry out a radical restructuring of the Nigerian electoral system, when he was sworn in on the 27 May 2007. Consequently, on 28 August 2008, a 22-member Electoral Reform Committee, headed by retired Honourable Justice Mohammed Lawal Uwais, former Chief Justice of Nigeria, was set up. His mandate was to examine the entire electoral process with a view to ensuring that the quality and standard of our general elections are raised, thereby ensuring transparent democracy (Ayonrinde 2009:1).

The Electoral Act 2006 is a great improvement on the Electoral Act 2002, which regulated the 2003 elections. It contained some measures to make INEC more efficient, such as the appointment of the Secretary by INEC, instead of the

President. It also provided for the financial independence of INEC by setting up a fund for it. This fund was, however, not established for the 2007 elections. It provided clear procedures and timetable for the voter registration exercise. It did not, however, address the issue of INEC's independence. The Chairman and the 37 Resident Electoral Commissioners are still appointed by the President after consultation with the Federal Executive Council and the Senate. There is no requirement for results to be displayed at polling stations and for a breakdown of polling station results to be displayed. There is also no clear procedure for handling of complaints and appeals before election day. Also, no specific time limit is provided for the publication of results and for the determination of election petitions (Report of the EU Observation Mission 2007).

The pertinent question here is: can an electoral management body be impartial, taking into account that it is the President that appoints its Chairman and Commissioners and also finances it? Could Iwu have been able to go against the wishes of the President who said categorically to the hearing of all Nigerians that the *forthcoming election is a 'do-or-die affair? Winning in the forthcoming election is a matter of life and death for PDP. I will not hand over power to anybody who will not continue the reform agenda'* (Akogun 2007:17). It therefore follows that the independence of INEC is a fundamental pre-requisite for the success of elections and democracy in Nigeria.

Nigeria has had very poor antecedents in conducting free and fair elections, elections having consistently been mired by poor organisation by the Electoral Management Body, leading to questionable voters' registration, the disenfranchisement of credible voters, intimidation, bribery, violence and outright manipulation of results. Decades of these bad experiences have made most Nigerians lose faith in the electoral process (Olutola 2007:16).

President Yar'Adua thus started off on the right footing, by setting up the Uwais Electoral Reform Committee, which had on 12 December, 2008, submitted the following recommendations:

a) Creation of three commissions, viz (1) Electoral Offences Commission (2) A Constituency Delimitation Commission; and (3) A Political Parties Registration and Regulatory Commission. These were all in the bid to unbundle INEC.

b) Putting the power of appointing the Chairman of INEC in the hands of the Judiciary and Legislature.

c) making constitutional allowance for Independent candidacy.

d) Disposing of electoral litigation before elected officials are sworn in.

e) Applying stiff punishment on of electoral offences at special tribunals.

f) Banning cross carpeting by office holders.

g) Including civil society organisations in INEC board.

h) Providing of security of term for INEC members to insulate them from external forces.

i) Shifting the burden of proof from petitioners to INEC, where widespread malpractices are alleged.

j) Abolishing the Residential Electoral Commissioners.

The Uwais Committee prepared three draft bills along with the report: Bill amending the 1999 Constitution, Bill Amending the 2006 Electoral Act and a Bill to Establish the Electoral Offences Tribunal.

A nine-member Committee of the Federal Executive Council, led by Dr. Shettima Mustapha, was set up to draft a white paper from the report. The draft White Paper agreed basically to the Uwais report, and adopted the recommendation that the National Judicial Council should appoint the INEC Chairman, after the position has been duly advertised.

This recommendation led to the setting up of another three-man Committee led by the Attorney General of the Federation, Michael Aondoakaa. The Committee rejected the recommendation of the Uwais Committee, on the appointment of INEC Chairman and said that the President should appoint the Chairman, subject to the approval of the National Assembly. It also disagreed that all petitions should be exhausted before an elected officer is sworn in. It said election petition could last up to six months. It agreed on the unbundling of INEC, but rejected the inclusion of the Nigerian Labour Congress in the INEC board. It called for an independent candidate to make a financial deposit that would be determined by INEC. The burden of proof it says should still remain with the petitioner and not INEC.

For a government which says that it is keen on electoral reforms, it would seem that the government turned down all the recommendations that would make the executive unable to control INEC and make the rigging of elections easier to unravel in court and less rewarding for the perpetrators (Ayorinde 2009:4).

While looking at INEC, one cannot fail to mention the positive initiatives and programmes it had for the 2007 general elections:

(1) Awareness campaigns in the media through jingles about Nigerians' civic duties and obligations.

(2) Training of INEC staff as well as ad-hoc staff.

(3) Partnership with the Nigerian and international civil society organisations, setting up of stakeholders forums.

(4) Establishment of an Electoral Institute in each of the six geo-political zones (Kwaja 2007).

2010 Electoral Act

At the 15th African Union Summit held in Uganda in 2010, President Goodluck Ebele Jonathan said 'I would not also want to conduct an election in which people would raise issues. I want a situation where at the end of elections nobody will go to court because there would be no reason for people to go to court'. The National Assembly in 2010 approved the 2010 Electoral Act in preparation for the 2011 general elections in Nigeria. Here some degree of independence has been granted INEC, which will now get its funds from the consolidated fund. In general, it appears that significant progress has been made in respect of the Electoral Act, to allow for a freer and fairer election under the administration of Goodluck Jonathan.

The changes in the 2010 Electoral Act mostly reflect the suggestions of the Uwais-led Electoral Reform Committee (ERC), and that of the new INEC chairman, Alhaji Attahiru Jega. Some of the following changes were made:

(1) Elections will be divided into Federal and State government elections. The National Assembly and the Presidential elections will take place before the State Governor and State Assembly elections.

(2) Under section 78 of the amended law, parties that fail to win a seat in either the National Assembly or State Legislative bodies can be unregistered. This means that at least 50 political parties can be removed from the official list of political parties.

(3) Section 91 places a cap on how much money can be spent on an individual campaign. Presidential aspirants are limited to spending a N1 billion while gubernatorial candidates can only spend N200 million. National Assembly aspirants can spend N40 million and State Assembly aspirants can spend only N20 million. Under section 92(3), all political parties have to submit their expenses to the commission six months after elections, duly signed by political party auditors and the chairmen. Failure to do this leads to a conviction and/or a N1 million fine.

Conclusion and Recommendations

When all is said and done, restructuring and re-organising the electoral framework is only a small part of the bigger challenge that Nigeria faces. The democratic environment in Nigeria needs to be reformed because, generally, Nigerians do not have much confidence in the elections, umpired by an Electoral Management Body that is in the pocket of the ruling political party. There has to be an attitudinal change amongst political stakeholders. A new electoral mindset has to emerge. Take the elections that took place in Ghana in 2008, John Atta Mills, a Professor of Law and an opposition candidate emerged as the President, defeating the incumbent in office. This was not the first time it would be happening in Ghana; the immediate former President John Kuffor attained this feat when he defeated and took over from the Jerry Rawlings' ruling party in 2000. Nigerians must stop seeing elections as something that must be won at all costs. It is not a do-or-die affair, contrary to Obasanjo's claim in 2007. Nigeria's political elite must not put their selfish and greedy desires above national interest. Nigerians should be allowed the right to choose their leaders. Election campaigns must be based on solid and concrete issues. Issues-based campaigns and the candidates' strategies are the keys to gaining the support of voters. The political campaigns should not be an avenue for thuggery and assassination of political opponents. If politicians say that they have come to serve the people and not their own interests, then the people's right to choose their own leaders and ask questions about how they are governed must be allowed.

Another question to be asked is the readiness of the political elite to ensure proper implementation of the Electoral Act and to respect the peoples' will? If they are really determined to serve the people, then the will of the people would be of paramount importance to them, and they would only be able to rule because the people want them to rule them, and not because they managed to rig their way into office by using the electoral umpire to legalize their nefarious acts. To crown it all, they expect that the people would give their full support to their programmes when they know that they never gave them the mandate to rule. It only follows that if you have voted a certain political party into office, you would be committed to its programmes and would want it to succeed. Most of the unpatriotic acts of Nigerians are due to the fact that they believe they had nothing to do with the installation of the government of the day, so they do not really care if it succeeds or fails.

In Nigeria, the political class needs to seriously alter their mindset, before any legal framework can work. This turn-by-turn Nigerian mentality, for a piece of the national cake is killing democracy in Nigeria. The best legal framework amounts to nothing without value change at the appropriate levels of society. We need to get our priorities right. If integrity, honour and truth mean nothing to our political elite and leadership, then democracy, which is a human right, will continue to elude us. There is a need for those who are examining the electoral reforms instituted by the late President Yar'Adua to be sincere to themselves and Nigerians as a whole. They should put Nigeria first and do what is right for the country. Fortunately, the foot dragging on the electoral reforms was addressed to a large extent when President Goodluck Jonathan signed the 2010 Electoral Reform Act into law. Having good legislation is one thing, but making it work so that free and fair elections are conducted in Nigeria, is another thing, because, as was said earlier, even the best legal framework will amount to nothing if Nigerians do not change the way they think and what they value.

As regards INEC, going through its mandate, vision statement and guiding principles, it is clear that Nigerians would be pleased if these laudable goals could be achieved by the Commission. But it is obvious that this is not being done satisfactorily yet. This chapter recommends the following for INEC:

(1) INEC should start planning early, in order to forestall a repeat of the previous lapses.

(2) INEC should learn to listen to the complaints of the masses if it wants to be respected. After all, there are only a handful of politicians who are going to rule the majority. If the majority is complaining, then INEC owes the masses the duty to listen and see what they can do to address the issues raised.

(3) The way INEC officials are maligned by the generality of Nigerians is enough for the officials to stand up and say no to being used for the selfish gains of anybody. Its leaders should have the nerve to resign if need be. Their integrity should be of paramount importance to them.

(4) INEC will still be held responsible for the activities of its ad-hoc staff. So to say that they committed the atrocities is no excuse. It is INEC's duty to see that it trains these categories of staff well, as they would be held responsible for what they do or do not do.

(5) INEC has to be more committed to voter education. This has to be done at the grassroots level where there are many uneducated people. The local language should be used, so that the people can understand what their rights are and how valuable their votes are.

(6) Amendment of the 2010 Electoral Act has been completed, so that INEC has some level of financial autonomy. However, the funds have to be released in time so that it can be adequately utilized for proper preparation for the elections.

(7) INEC Chairman should not be appointed by the President, so that he does not have to keep on looking over his shoulders.

(8) INEC has to sort out all outstanding issues on electoral constituency delimitation, for fairer political participation in future elections.

(9) INEC has to know how to properly handle electronic voting. Officers have to be adequately trained on how to use the machines. There must be enough machines and stand-by generators in case of electricity failure, and for areas where there is no electricity. A technology-based balloting system, if properly and wholesomely implemented, would solve a lot of problems, like ballot box stuffing, use of fake voters and general manipulation of results etc.

(10) Nigeria has a vast terrain, which is complex in nature. INEC should be allowed to stagger the elections. There are places like the creeks of the Niger-Delta, which might not be so easy to get to. Logistics has always been

one of the main problems INEC has encountered. Staggering elections over a period of one month could help INEC's logistics problems.

(11) The Nigerian Security and Printing Mint should be able to print ballot papers for elections. If we are serious there will be no fraud. Getting these materials printed abroad causes immense logistic problems as well as depletion of foreign exchange.

INEC should realise that it is the institution charged with supervising Nigeria's elections. The politicians seeking office are only a handful of representatives of the people. The masses to be ruled are in the majority. It is its duty of INEC to ensure that the majority get their wish; nobody but they can do this for them. Thus if the people's choice of who to govern them is going to be attained it is only INEC that can make sure that their wishes are fulfilled. Doing the bidding of a handful of people in power would result in a disgruntled populace who are far removed from those that have stolen their votes and make a mockery of democracy. In this case, governance would suffer as the level of service delivery will be low.

References

Akogun, Kunle, 2007, 'April Polls: Voting for Another Impasse', *Thisday,* June 3.

Aluko, Mobolaji, 1999, *Monitoring Nigeria's Elections-The Carter Formula,* Buttosville, MD.USA,

Ayorinde, Olujun, 2009, 'Thinkering With A Report', *Views,* 10:56.368

Derbyshire, J.N., and Derbyshire I., 1993, *World Political Systems,* Chambers.

Iwu, Maurice, 2008, 'Electronic Voting and the Future of the Electoral System in Nigeria', *The Nigerian Electoral Journal,* Vol.2., No.1., May.

Iyayi, Festus, 2006, *Elections, INEC and the Problems of Elections in Nigeria,* Abuja: INEC. Kwaja, Chris.2007, 'INEC and Management of Elections: Lessons from Nigeria', retrieved from (http://www./afrimap.org/english/image/paper/kwaja-inec-nigeria-EN-0pdf)   05   May 2009.

Ogunsanwo, Alaba, 2003, 'Keynote Address', in Remi Anifowose and Tunde Babawale, eds, *2003 General Elections and Democratic Consolidation in Nigeria.* Lagos: Friedrich Stif- tung.

Okaisabor, Thompson, 2001, 'INEC and 2003', *Daily Times,* 9 Sept.

Okoye, Festus, 2003, 'Do the Votes Count?' Final Report of the 2003 General Elections of Nigeria.

Olutola, Bello, 2007, 'Elections and the Challenges of Nation-building', *The Punch,* April 13, INEC, 2009,

'Report of the INEC's Retreat on the Operational Plans for 2011 General Elections', held from the 18-20 August 2009, in Kaduna. retrieved from (http:www.Nigerdeltacongresss. com/marticles/monitoring_Nigeria_elec- tions-t.htm). May 2009.

Singh S., and Mishra, Suresh, 1991, 'Powers of Elections Commission: A Legal Perspective', *The Indian Journal of Public Administration,* Vol. xxxvii, No.3:361.

4

Governance and Local Government Elections in Nigeria's Fourth Republic

Chinwe Nwanna

Introduction and Statement of Problem

Local governments and elections are two essential features of modern democracies. They help to establish, nurture and sustain democracy and democratic political culture. Elections provide the electorate with the power to freely participate in choosing their leaders and in providing the much-needed support and legitimacy to the state. Leaders are made accountable, and the institutions that create the stability of the political system are strengthened (Fage 2007). Local governments, on the other hand, are viable instruments of grassroots political participation and socialization. In theory, they are generally viable instruments in the democratisation of modern governments, while elections are means of ensuring regular changes of governments. Despite this, the Nigerian experience has been very disappointing. After several attempts at democratisation, the country is yet to evolve a viable, virile and stable democracy that will elicit popular support or even have direct bearing on the lives of the ordinary people. This is so because the so-called elected governments often lack legitimacy. Fundamentally, the primary role of local governments is to promote the spirit of local self-help and self-reliance, community sense of unity and achievement, through a network of grassroots and civil society organisations.

The most fundamental weaknesses of local governance in Nigeria are non-delivery, lack of accountability and corruption. The institution of local government in Nigeria has failed to enhance its capacity, to engage and mobilise the people and respond to their needs, and to administer effectively and responsibly the various local services. Ojofeitimi (2000) has observed that local governments have failed woefully in providing good governance. They have failed in their areas of primary responsibility – provision of such basic services as primary education, primary health care, refuse collection and refuse disposal, street drainage and lighting, provision of potable water, care of the destitute, provision of comfortable stations, clean and hygienic markets, security, etc.

Local government elections in the country had been on non-party basis from 1987 to 1998. They were first held in 1987 during the Babangida Administration. This was the first time local government chairmen were elected through universal adult suffrage. There were local government elections in 1996, 1997 and 1998 but all proved problematic. In 2003, local government elections were postponed against the provisions of the Constitution. Some states conducted local government elections in 2007 which were marred by violence, fraud and rigging; while some, like Lagos and Jos, conducted theirs in 2008. Others, like Anambra State, did not have local government elections until January 2014. This particular State had been ruled for many years by four successive governors – Chris Ngige, Peter Obi, Andy Uba and Virginia Etiaba and again Peter Obi without local council chairmen. They appointed Caretaker Committees to run the affairs of the local governments in the state. It has also been observed that local government elections were generally marred by violence, fraud and rigging. Thus, the purpose of this study was to examine the role of local government elections in the governance of the people from 1999 to date in three states of the federation.

Specifically, the objectives of the study were to:

a) Explore the level of citizens' participation in the local government elections in 1999, 2004 and 2007/2008.

b) Assess the challenges of local government elections in Nigeria in 1999, 2004 and 2007/2008.

c) evaluate the successes or failures of the local governments in the provision of basic social services to their citizens.

d) highlight the level of involvement of citizens in the provision of basic social services in their various LGAs

e) suggest ways of achieving good governance at the local government level.

The following research questions formed the basis of this study:

a) What was the level of citizens' participation in the local government elections in 1999, 2004 and 2007/2008?

b) What were the challenges that affected local government elections in 1999, 2004 and 2007/2008?

c) Which of the basic social services were provided by the local governments from 1999 to date?

d) Were the citizens involved in the provision of basic social services in their LGAs?

e) What can be done to correct any observed anomalies?

Local Government – Conceptual Discourse

In modern usage, local government is equated with grassroots participatory democracy. It refers to self-government of the local community for local community by its elected local inhabitants (Fage 2007)). In fact, it is within the framework of grassroots democracy that the 1976 Nigerian Local Government Reform Guidelines defined local government as: government at the local level exercised through representative councils established by law to exercise specific powers within areas defined. These powers should give the council substantial control over its local affairs as well as staffing and institutional and financial powers to initiate and direct the provision of services and to determine and implement projects that complement the activities of the state and federal government in their areas. They are also to ensure, through devolution of functions to these councils and through the active participation of the people and their traditional institutions, that local initiative and response to local needs and conditions are maximized (Reform Guidelines 1976:1).

From this, it is clear that the concept of (modern) local government involves a philosophical commitment to the idea of democratic participation in the governing process of a country at the grassroots level. The implication of this is that, the higher-level government voluntarily grants a certain degree of legal and administrative autonomy to a local community so as to enable the community perform specific functions within the broad national policy framework. By so doing, the operation of local government is confined to a specific geographic area within which the local community enjoys local 'self-government'. Self-government here does not mean that the local government becomes a local sovereign political entity. Rather, the term connotes that the local government council is at liberty to make bye-laws to enable it perform specific functions, have control over its finances, recruit and discipline its staff and formulate policies to usher in development programmes within the broad national objective(s).

Local governments could also be understood as administrative offices that are smaller than a state or province. The institutions of local government vary greatly between countries, and even where similar arrangements exist, the terminology often varies. Common names for local government entities include state, province, region, department, county, prefecture, district, city, township, town, borough, parish, municipality, shire and village (Ojo 2007). However all these terminologies are often used informally in countries where they do not describe a legal local government entity. Local governments are set up to bring government closer to the grassroots people – i.e. people in the communities, be it urban or rural. The Local Government in Nigeria forms the third tier of government, coming after the Federal and State Governments.

According to Green 'Local government is an essential instrument of national or state government for performance of certain basic functions which can best be administered locally on the intimate knowledge of the needs, conditions and peculiarities of the areas concerned' (see Akinboye 2007). The constitutional guarantee of an autonomous local government system in Nigeria is a clear indication that grassroots administration in the country's political system is a fact of life (Akinboye, 2007).

The most authoritative and generally acceptable definition is that provided by the United Nations Office for Public Administration. This defines local government as a political sub-division of a nation or (in a federal system) state, which is constituted by law and has substantial control of local affairs, including the power to impose or exact labour for prescribed purposes (UN Report, 1960:3; cited in Akinboye 2007). A clearer picture of this definition reveals quite poignantly that local government is 'local', in the sense that it has to do essentially with a group of people having something of a common outlook and living in a close vicinity in a particular locality; and is 'government' in the sense that it is not just a mere delegation of powers from state or central government but has effective autonomous legal status (Akinboye 2007).

In the light of the above definitions, the definition provided by the 1976 Nigerian Local Government Reform Guidelines was adopted in this study.

Governance

The concept of governance is a contested one. Adejumobi (2004) maintains that it is a concept that is notoriously slippery, frequently used by social scientists and practitioners without a concise definition. It has been variously conceptualized to suit legal, political and economic systems or ideologies. However, one strand that runs through all the definitions is that governance has to do with the relationship between the government and the governed. The Universal Declaration on Human Rights defines governance as the process whereby public institutions conduct public affairs, manage public resources and guarantee the realisation of human rights (UNHCR 2002). In this regard, governance is perceived as the process through which the leaders have as their basic guide and target, the guarantee of basic rights of the governed. This approach has its foundation basically in the Universal Declaration on Human Rights which proclaimed human rights 'as a common standard of achievement for all peoples and all nations'. This definition is basically saying that public resources should be managed in such a way and manner as to guarantee the basic civil, political, economic, social and cultural rights of the people.

Another school of thought views governance in a technical sense. In this case, the concept borrows directly from its usage in the corporate world. It implies the efficient management of state institutions. Issues of public accountability, transparency in government procedure, rule of law, and public sector management are emphasised. This is the restricted view of governance adopted by the World Bank (Adejumobi 2004). The essence of this governance approach is to discipline the state and its institutions for economic purposes. Adejumobi (2004) further states that governance is the acceptable face of spending cuts. Governance is the political construct of a minimalist state.

A third perspective to governance is a holistic one that transcends the state and its institutions. Governance is seen as the process of steering state and society towards the realisation of collective goals. It points to the dynamic, but problematic and often times contradictory relationship between the state and society (Adejumobi 2004). In this direction, a meeting of experts convened by the United Nations Economic Commission for Africa (UNECA) defines governance as a process of social engagement between the rulers and the ruled in a political community. Its component parts are rule-making and standard-setting, management of regime structures and outcome and results of the social pact (Adejumobi 2004)). The United Nations Development Programme (UNDP) describes governance as 'the totality of the exercise of authority in the management of a country's affairs, comprising of the complex mechanisms, processes and institutions through which citizens and groups articulate their interests, exercise their legal rights, and mediate their differences. It encompasses the political, economic, legal, judicial, social and administrative authority and therefore includes; government, the private sector and the civil society' (World Bank 1999). In every legal or political system, there are rules guiding resource allocation and exploitation. This is to ensure even distribution of resources. Taxes and other revenues are imposed and collected for or by the government. In this same system also, there are natural and human resources which are to be harnessed by the government. The manner in which the government does the above for the overall benefit of the people and to enhance development is regarded as governance.

While there are variations in this holistic conception of governance, there is a consensus on the major actors or agencies of the governance project. These are the state, the civil society and the private sector. The state, though under enormous attack in the regime of market economy, remains a major actor in the governance agenda.

The latter conception of governance, though broader, is not unproblematic. It also has an economic undertone, in which the private sector is deliberately emphasised. The essence is to promote and reinforce a market economy. The rural population that constitutes the bulk of Africa's population do not feature overtly in this conception of governance, whereas the civil society that is basically urban-based, and the private sector that is small and limited in Africa are prioritized.

The UNDP further stresses that governance is the exercise of economic, political and administrative authority to manage a country's affairs at all levels. It comprises the mechanisms, processes and institutions, through which citizens and groups articulate their interests, exercise their legal rights, meet their obligations and mediate their differences. The main drivers in this approach to governance are government institutions and the civil service. This definition is predicated upon the fact that the Constitution confers legislative, executive and judicial powers upon certain persons and institutions, the exercise of which will either constitute good or bad governance. Governance, in this respect, being the ability of the concerned institutions of government to play creditably, their rightful roles of legislating for the order, peace and good governance of their area of operation, executing government policies for the public good and creating a forum for the adequate redress of wrongs. Another important area is that of creating opportunities for interest articulation and aggregation. Individual members of any given society should be able to form groups or elect to join any of their choice. Governance entails government being able to make good use of these diverse interests for the benefit of the society at large.

Good governance flows logically from the concept of governance. According to Ahmed Mohideen, governance becomes 'good', when it operates in accordance with legal and ethical principles as conceived by society and seeks to provide a guide and direction to itself through standards and norms embedded in the governance idea (see Adejumobi 2004). The urge to steer state and society according to defined rules and procedures, and ensuring that governance in all its ramifications serves the interests of the greatest number of people in society through a collective, participatory endeavour.

Theoretically, understanding the role of government in any society relates directly to the fact of state-citizen relations in respect of the *Social Contract*, in which the state provides security and welfare for the citizens, and the citizens in turn reciprocate by recognizing the authority of the state and paying taxes to it. This relationship is further strengthened in a democratic environment where the citizens are allowed to freely elect their representatives through a transparent process. It is when this process is undermined that we see individuals selected rather than elected, and this could have serious long-term consequences for the health of the polity even at the local level.

Historical Perspective on the Nigerian local government system

Local government has been variously conceptualized. In its generic sense, the term refers to self-government by the local community. From this broad and all-encompassing sense, therefore, one can argue that both the idea and practice of a 'local self-government" predated British colonialism. Fage (2007) contends that long before the British colonialists' conquest, the various communities that were later to form modern Nigeria had one form of local administration or the other. For instance, centralized states such as Borno, the Hausa states, Oyo and Benin kingdoms had a hierarchical system comprising of a central administration, a local government administration and a field administration. At the helm of affairs was a supreme leader (king, emir, etsu and oba, etc.) who ruled the entire kingdom or emirate with the help of traditional council at the local government level, where title holders (appointed by and responsible to the supreme leader) administered their respective local areas. Beneath the title– holders were indigenous rulers (field administrators) through whom the entire local government administration was carried out. In fact, even in the decentralized states like the Igbo, Tiv, etc, there was a system of local government administration based on lineage. Here the lowest level of the administration was the village, while its upper level were groups of villages that had common ancestry.

Local governments in Nigeria have undergone so many transitions since the colonial period. Between 1950 and 1975, the country's systems of local governance moved from the colonial inheritance of indirect rule through Native Authorities to elected councils (Adedeji 2000). In his contribution, Ojofeitimi (2000) asserts that local government in Nigeria has had a chequered history. He discerns six phases, during which local government's fortune rose and ebbed. The first phase, commencing in the early 1950s, witnessed early efforts at democratisation. It marked the end of 'Indirect Rule' system with the attendant dominance of traditional rulers in grassroots governance and the experimentation by two of the regional governments (East and West) with English-Style Divisional, District and County Local Governments. The local government councils in the East were wholly elected. In the North, the Chief-in-Council replaced the Sole Native Authority while traditional districts and village group/villages remained as subordinate administrative organs of the Native Authority. Thus, by the end of the 1950s, there were high expectations that the 1960s would witness the emergence of a virile, effective and democratic local government.

He noted that during the second phase, which began in the early 1960s and which terminated with the end of the Civil War in 1970, the hope for a democratic system of local government was dashed. Various developments, both political and economic, took their toll on the structure, staffing, services and finances of local government. The multi-tier system introduced in the 1950s in the Eastern and Western regions was abandoned in favour of the one-tier system of local government. State government developed the field administration of their various ministries instead of strengthening local governments by making more funds available to them. Local governments, to all intents and purposes, became mere extensions of the state bureaucracy. The replacement of elected councils in the Western Region by nominated ones in 1963 completed the dismantling of the representative/democratic edifice.

The third phase inspired and epitomized by the Local Government Reforms of 1976 witnessed a determined effort by the Federal Government to revamp, rationalize and rehabilitate the system of local government. By October 1979, it could be safely stated that the rehabilitation of local government had been satisfactorily executed. Many years later, the country was still bedevilled by the dichotomy between the state and local government in respect of fiscal control and autonomy of local government. Unfortunately, the fourth phase of local government administration (1979 to 1983) which held out high hopes for the consolidation of local government as a democratic and results-oriented system collapsed, due to its dependent nature on the state as a constituent unit in the Nigerian federation. Indeed, local government was virtually brought back to the unenviable position that it was in before the Local Government Reforms of 1976.

The fifth phase (1984 to 1993) witnessed efforts of the Buhari and Babangida administrations, especially the latter, to salvage local government from the mess that it was plunged into between 1979 and 1983. The first set of local government chairmen was then elected. The dominance of state governments was greatly reduced with the abolition of the state ministry for local governments. Their share of federally-allocated revenue was increased from 10 per cent to 15 per cent and subsequently 20 per cent. This reform also made it possible through the provision of the clause of 'Recall' for the people of the locality to recall councillors found wanting in the discharge of their duties.

The last phase (1994 to date) has been characterised by efforts to modify and resuscitate the system of local government following the political crises caused by the annulment of the 1993 Presidential Elections which virtually paralyzed the operations of government at federal, state and local government levels for several months. Local government council elections were held in March 1996 on a non-party basis. The way and manner the election was managed by the Abacha regime caused some concern in some sections of civil society that the government sought to control the transition process. By the second quarter of 1996, the General Abacha regime had created six additional states to calm frayed nerves so that he could drum up support for the transition programme (Ojo and Azeez 2002). The country witnessed another round of local government elections in April 1997 which were considered to be free and fair. Later, all the councils that emerged from the elections were dissolved by the Abubakar government and sole administrators were appointed to manage their affairs. In 1998, another local government election was held before the general election. Meanwhile, the Abacha regime had created more local government areas by adding 179 to the list – thus bringing the total number of local government areas to 768.

Legal Framework for Local Governments in Nigeria

Section 3(6) of the Constitution of the Federal Republic of Nigeria (CFRN) 1999 emphatically guarantees democratically elected local government administration in the country while 7(6) talks about statutory allocation provisions to local governments by both the National and State Assemblies. In Section 7(4) the government of a state is enjoined to ensure that every person who is eligible to vote and be voted for in a House of Assembly election is also given the right to vote and be voted for at a local government council election.

Furthermore, Section II of the concurrent legislative list says that 'the National Assembly may make laws for the Federation with respect to the registration of voters and the procedure regulating elections to a local government council' while Section 12 of the concurrent list says 'Nothing in paragraph 11 hereof shall preclude a House of Assembly from making laws with respect to election to a local government council in addition to but not inconsistent with any law made by the National Assembly' In consonance with the provisions of Section 7(5), functions of local governments are set out in the Fourth Schedule of the 1999 Constitution. Part VII of the Electoral Act 2006 comprising Sections 120 to 123 sets up the procedure for Local Government Council Elections.

Research Design and Methods

Research design

The study adopted a non-experimental research design. Three states were selected on purpose because of their peculiarities. Two of them were problem states – Anambra and Plateau, representing South-East and North-Central geo-political zones, respectively. The third state was Lagos which had been consistent in the conduct of local government elections. Anambra had not had any local government elections since 1999 while Plateau experienced crisis after 2008 local government elections.

Anambra State

The original Anambra State was created in 1976 when East Central State was broken into Anambra and Imo States. Then, it comprised the present Anambra State and Enugu State including the Abakaliki part of Ebonyi State, with Enugu as its capital. During further state creation in August 1991, Enugu State with Abakaliki was excised, leaving Anambra State as currently constituted, with Awka as its capital. The state derived its name from the Anambra River, the largest, most southerly, left bank tributary of the River Niger. With a total land area of 4,416 sq. km, Anambra State is situated on a generally low elevation on the eastern side of the River Niger. It is located in South-East Nigeria, and bounded by Delta State to the west, Imo State to the south, Enugu State to the east and Kogi State to the north. It has one of the highest population densities in Nigeria. The state comprises numerous thickly populated villages, a number of small towns and a few major towns; some areas are so thickly populated that the estimated density is 1500-2000 persons living within every square kilometre.

Anambra State had a population of 4,182,032 as at March 2006 (Federal Government Printer [FGP] 2007). The indigenous ethnic group in Anambra State is the Igbo (98 per cent per cent of population) and Igala (2 per cent of the population). Most of the population is rural, although over the last two decades rural-urban migration has stretched the meagre urban services to a breaking point. This pattern of human migration has posed serious problems for the state's resources, fragile infrastructure, environmental sanitation, erosion control and social services. This pressure is especially evident in its huge commercial city of Onitsha. Consequently, potable water, electricity and decent housing for the residents of Onitsha have become a luxury. Anambra is rich in natural gas, crude oil, bauxite, ceramics and almost 100 per cent arable soil. Most of its natural resources remain largely untapped.

Administratively, the state consists of twenty one local government areas. There are three senatorial districts in the state, namely: (a) Anambra North, (b) Anambra Central, and (c) Anambra South. Most of the population of Anambra State consists of members of the enterprising Igbo ethnic group who are renowned for their resourcefulness and entrepreneurship. The Anambra Igbo can be found in all nooks and crannies of Nigeria, as well as in virtually every part of the world. Wherever they find themselves, the entrepreneurial skills of the Igbo stand them out in all their fields of endeavour.

Anambra State citizens, who refer to themselves as 'Anambrarians' are also educationally advanced. Literacy rate in the state is comparatively high, and there is an abundance of well educated and skilled personnel in virtually all fields of endeavour. Anambra State is the home state of many prominent Nigerians such as Nnamdi Azikiwe, former Governor-General and President of Nigeria; renowned writer Chinua Achebe and Chukwuemeka Odumegwu Ojukwu, the civil war Biafran Leader.

Lagos State

Lagos State was created on 27 May 1967 by virtue of the State Creation and Transitional Provisions of Decree No. 14 of 1967, which reconstructed Nigeria's federation into 12 states. The State is located in the south western part of Nigeria. Administratively, Lagos State is divided into 20 local government areas (LGAs) and 37 development areas. By the results of 1991 census, Lagos State had the highest population of 5,725,116 which was over 5 per cent of the national estimate of 88,992,220 (National Population Commission [NPC], 1998) with a landmass of 3,577 square kilometres representing 0.4 per cent of the total landmass of the federation. However, in the 2006 census figures, Lagos had over 9.0 million inhabitants (FGP 2007). The Lagos State Government has however declared that the figure was unacceptable because a parallel census conducted by the state produced a much higher figure of 17.6 million people (Obia 2007). The fact is that it is believed that Lagos State has a population figure far higher than the official census figure.

Lagos State is inhabited predominantly by the Aworis and Eguns who are Yorubas in Ikeja and Badagry divisions, respectively. Generally her ethnic configuration is diverse, with Yorubas constituting 65 per cent, Hausa 15 per cent, Igbo 15 per cent and others 5 per cent (Lagos State website 2004). Until

12 December 1991, Lagos served as the federal capital of the country. It also serves as the industrial and commercial hub of the nation with a Gross National Product (GNP) that triples that of any other West African country (Lagos State Government 2006). The five LGAs investigated in Lagos State were: Lagos Mainland, Kosofe and Ajeromi-Ifelodun as urban LGAs while Ikorodu and Epe were studied as rural LGAs.

Plateau State

Plateau State, which derives its name from the Jos Plateau State is located in Nigeria's middle belt and shares common boundaries with Benue, Nassarawa, Kaduna, Taraba, Bauchi and Gombe States. With an area of 26,899 square kilometres, the state has an estimated population of 3,178,712 people (FGP 2007). The state is named after the picturesque Jos Plateau, a mountainous area in the north of the state with captivating rock formations. Bare rocks are scattered across the grasslands, which cover the plateau. The altitude ranges from around 1,200 meters (about 4000 feet) to a peak of 1,829 metres above sea level in the Shere Hills range near Jos. Years of tin mining have also left the area strewn with deep gorges and lakes.

Plateau State is a product of half a century of boundary adjustments arising, on the one hand, from the ambition of the colonial masters to create a province which consisted largely of non-Muslims under one Resident, in order to protect the railway line being constructed at that time and guarantee the sustenance of tin mining activities which began in 1902, and the strong desire of the peoples in the area for political self-determination, on the other hand.

In the formative years of British colonialism in Nigeria, much of Plateau State was part of Bauchi Province. In 1926, Plateau Province, comprising Jos and Pankshin Divisions, was carved out of Bauchi Province. At various times between 1926 and 1976, the boundary of Plateau Province oscillated, paralleling the general trend of political development in the country, as the government of the day acquiesced to the agitation of different ethnic groups to be merged with their kith and kin that were of larger concentrations in other provinces. During this period, therefore, some administrative units or divisions, as they were then called, from neighbouring provinces were added to or subtracted from Plateau Province. In May 1967, Benue and Plateau Provinces were merged to form Benue-Plateau State, one of the twelve states into which the military administration of General Yakubu Gowon divided Nigeria in place of the four existing regions then.

The division of the country into smaller semi-autonomous states was strategic and an attempt to introduce a sense of balance between the north and the south, and to save the federation from total disintegration, which was imminent from the polarization of the country along ethnic lines after the bloody military takeover of 1966 and the subsequent crisis which led to an attempted secession by the

Eastern Region. Benue-Plateau State emerged as one of those large states of the Federation where pressure was mounted on the Federal Government immediately after the civil war for the creation of more states.

When the country was however further divided into nineteen states in 1976, Plateau Province was severed from Benue-Plateau State to become Plateau State. In 1996, the present Nassarawa State was carved out of the western half of Plateau State by the Abacha military regime. In 1976, Plateau State had fourteen local government areas (LGAs). New LGAs were carved out of the large ones in 1989, 1991 and 1996, so that today, the new Plateau State is subdivided into seventeen LGAs. The state has over forty ethno-linguistic groups. Each ethnic group has its own distinct language, but as with the rest of the country, English is the official language in Plateau State; Hausa is also a medium of communication and commerce as is the case in most parts of the North and Middle Belt of Nigeria.

Research Method

A cross-sectional survey was employed to elicit qualitative and quantitative data from the population. Data were collected at one point in time through the use of interviews and Focus Group Discussions (FGDs).

Study populations

The units of analysis for the survey were household individuals and Local Government employees in the studied population. This constituted the quantitative aspect of the study.

Sample and Sampling Techniques

Sample size for the study was computed based on the proportion of females to males in 2006 census data. Women were 48.78 per cent while men were 51.22 per cent of the total population of Nigeria as at March 2006. The computed sample size was 1,650. Due to limited fund, 25 per cent of the number i.e. 412 was finally accepted.

However, 455 respondents were studied because populations of Anambra and Plateau states were raised in order to allow for comparative analysis. The states were allocated sample sizes based on the proportional distribution of their populations to the total 2006 census figures e.g. Anambra State has a total population of 4,182,032, which is 2.99 per cent of the total population of Nigeria. The population of Plateau State is 3,178,712, representing 2.27 per cent of the total and Lagos State – 9,013,534 representing 6.44 per cent of the total. This implies that 225 respondents in Lagos State; 112 in Anambra State and 75 in Plateau State should be studied. However, in order to get the least number that was adequate for comparative analysis between rural and urban populations, the populations of Anambra and Plateau states were increased. Consequently, 120 and

110 were studied in Anambra and Plateau states, respectively i.e., for Anambra State 70 urban dwellers and 50 rural people were studied. In Plateau State, 60 urban and 50 rural dwellers were interviewed. In each selected local government area, five employees of local governments were also investigated except in Plateau State where only 11 Local Government employees were interviewed. Their total number was not included in the sample size.

Multi-stage random sampling method was used to select the 455 respondents. The first stage involved identifying and selecting the states from the zones. In the second stage, considering that each of the states has three Senatorial Districts, there was allocation of sample slots to the states based on the proportion of each state to the total population size of Nigeria using the 2006 census figures as provided by the National Population Census. The third stage was the selection of 25 per cent of LGAs (which in Lagos was five LGAs) from the Senatorial Districts in the states. Consideration was given to the urban-rural spatial distribution such that in a peculiarly urban state like Lagos, 60 per cent of the respondents were drawn from urban LGAs while 40 per cent were drawn from the rural LGAs. It thus follows that three urban LGAs (Lagos Mainland, Kosofe and Ajeromi-Ifelodun) and two rural LGAs (Ikorodu and Epe) were selected for the study in Lagos.

In Plateau and Anambra States, one rural LGA and two urban LGAs were investigated in each since their sample sizes were less than that of Lagos State. In Anambra, Awka South and Onitsha North were the urban LGAs selected, while Awka North was the rural LGA. In Plateau State, Jos North and Jos South formed the urban LGAs while Barkin-Ladi was the rural LGA studied. From the selected LGAs, a minimum of 25 per cent of the wards were selected in the fourth stage. From the selected wards, 25 per cent of the streets were selected randomly. From the selected streets, households were selected systematically and then the final sampling unit was the consenting individuals in the fifth stage. This constituted the eligible respondents. Efforts were made to have a gender balance of 50 per cent males and 50 per cent females in the final sampling unit but in some instances women declined to respond to questions. With respect to ethical considerations, respondents' oral consent was obtained. They were not coerced.

Research Instruments

Since the study was carried out in both rural and urban areas, interview schedule was employed as most of the population might be semi-literate or non-literate and if there was need to probe further in order to get clear answers this was made possible. The interview schedule was structured with closed-ended and a few open-ended questions based on the objectives of the study. The interview method was complemented by Focus Group Discussions (FGDs). The content of the instrument was highly specific to the elections and governance of the LGAs. Two sets of interview schedules were developed, one for the individuals and the other for the LG officials.

Focus Group Discussions (FGDs)

The FGDs were helpful in the collection of qualitative data. There were four FGDs in each state, one for each of the following categories of participants: (a) Male youths (18-29 years); (b) Adult males (30 years and above); (c) Female youths (18-29 years); (d) Adult females (30 years and above). There were six people in a session, a moderator and a note-taker.

A pre-testing of the research instruments was conducted outside the LGAs under study.

Data Collection

The survey was conducted from June to July 2009. Research team consisted of sociologists and political scientists: the principal investigator, three state supervisors and eleven research assistants (RAs) (5 in Lagos State; 3 in Anambra State and 3 in Plateau State). The state supervisors and RAs were recruited among the residents in the states under study. All the RAs were trained for one day. The training focused on the objectives of the study, the techniques of interview and how to approach and develop rapport with the respondents. The aim of the training was to ensure that the interviews were conducted in similar ways in order to enhance comparability of information and to minimize interview bias. The individuals were selected on the basis of possession of demonstrated and adequate social research skills and experience.

Data Analysis

Data were analysed using version 15 of the Statistical Package for Social Sciences (SPSS). Quantitative data were presented in frequencies and percentages while qualitative data were used to buttress the findings of the quantitative data.

Challenges of the Fieldwork

One major problem was that of recall on the part of the respondents since the study was in retrospect. It was also not uncommon for the respondents to demand financial rewards for their time and cooperation. Rains constituted another major challenge. These problems were addressed as they arose. The training equipped the RAs with the necessary skills to overcome the challenges. During the training, emphasis was on communication skills and interpersonal relations which should enhance rapport with diverse respondents in the communities of interest. The recruitment and training ensured that RAs were people who understood the local terrain as well as the language of the communities under study. These ensured that the survey gained acceptance of the local population and also took care of the uneducated.

Findings

Social Demographic Profile of the Respondents

The total number of respondents investigated was 455, comprising 120 from Anambra State, 225 from Lagos State and 110 from Plateau State. Disaggregating into rural and urban locations, 60 per cent of the respondents were from the urban centres in both Anambra and Lagos States while in Plateau we investigated 54.5 per cent of urban dwellers (see Table 4.1). In other words, 58.7 per cent of the total respondents were urban dwellers. Out of the total respondents, 55.8 per cent were males while 44.2 per cent represented females. In spite of our efforts to investigate equal number of males and females, many women declined to participate. About three fifths of the total respondents were married (60.7 per cent) while one-third of them were never married. Educational levels of the respondents indicated that 30.1 per cent had acquired tertiary education and 17.4 per cent, professional education. About one-quarter of the total respondents had obtained other forms of education such as Modern 3, Pitman etc. With respect to occupational status, 25.7 per cent of the total respondents were self-employed and artisans accounted for 14.7 per cent, while others were distributed as follows: students (14.3 per cent), private sector employees (10.5 per cent) and civil servants (9.9 per cent). The respondents were predominantly Christians as they accounted for three quarters of the sample. The next dominant religion was Islam (22.0 per cent).

Table 4.1: Social Demographic Profile of the Respondents

Characteristics	Anambra N = 120		Lagos N = 225		Plateau N = 110		Total	
	N	%	N	%	N	%	N	%
Urban	72	60.0	60	54.5	60	54.5	267	58.7
Rural	48	40.0	90	40.0	50	45.5	188	41.3
Gender								
Male	61	50.8	126	56.0	67	60.9	254	55.8
Female	59	49.2	99	44.0	43	39.1	201	44.2
Marital status								
Single	48	40.0	50	22.2	51	46.4	149	32.7
Currently married	59	49.2	167	74.2	47	42.7	273	60.0
Divorced/ separated/ widowed	7	5.8	8	3.5	9	8.1	24	5.3
No response	6	5.0	–	–	3	2.7	9	2.0
Education								
None	5	4.2	4	1.8	3	2.7	12	2.6
Primary	15	12.5	11	4.9	8	7.3	34	7.5

Secondary	7	5.8	12	5.3	3	2.7	22	4.8
Tertiary	43	35.8	82	36.4	16	14.5	141	31.0
Professional	17	14.2	30	13.3	32	29.1	79	17.4
Others	32	26.7	86	38.1	44	38.9	162	35.6
No response	1	0.8	–	–	4	3.6	5	1.1
Occupation								
Unemployed	4	3.3	7	3.1	14	12.7	25	5.5
Housewife	6	5.0	7	3.1	10	9.1	23	5.1
Pension/Retired	6	5.0	2	0.9	3	2.7	11	2.4
Student	29	24.2	18	8.0	18	16.4	65	14.3
Farmer	6	5.0	3	1.3	8	7.3	17	3.7
Self/Own	25	20.8	75	33.3	17	15.5	117	25.7
Self/Informal	6	5.0	14	6.2	1	0.9	21	4.6
Art	6	5.0	60	26.7	1	0.9	67	14.7
Unskilled	4	3.3	–	–	–	–	4	0.9
Private sector	10	8.3	23	10.2	15	13.6	48	10.5
Civil Servant	16	13.3	10	4.4	9	17.3	45	9.9
Others	–	–	1	0.4	3	2.7	4	0.9
No response	2	1.7	5	2.2	1	0.9	8	1.7
Religion								
Traditional	5	4.2	2	0.9	3	2.7	10	2.2
Christianity	114	95.0	133	59.1	95	86.4	342	75.2
Islam	–	–	90	40.0	10	9.1	100	22.0
Others	1	0.8	–	–	1	0.9	2	0.4
5.00	–	–	–	–	1	0.9	1	0.2

Political Behaviour

Participation in Local Government Elections

In this section, the political behaviour of the respondents was assessed. In Table 4.2 all the studied states conducted LG elections in 1999 but at the time of the study, Anambra State had not yet held another one. Lagos and Plateau States were supposed to hold LG council election in 2003 and 2007 but they were delayed to 2004 and 2008 respectively because of some political reasons. The level of awareness of local government elections in the three periods under review showed a similar pattern. 84.8 per cent, 81.1 per cent and 80.9 per cent of the respondents were aware of the local government council elections of 1999, 2004, and 2008 respectively. These varied from one state to another. For instance, in 1999, 70.8 per cent of Anambra State respondents compared to 92.4 per cent of Lagos State and

84.5 per cent of Plateau State respondents knew about the LG council elections. The level of awareness in Lagos and Plateau States increased to 97.3 per cent and 88.2 per cent respectively in 2004. By 2008, almost all the respondents in Lagos State and 99.1 per cent respondents from Plateau State knew that local government elections were held.

Table 4.2: Respondents' Participation in Local Government Elections

	Anambra N=120			Lagos N= 225			Plateau N =110		
Aware of LGA elections	1999	2004	2008	1999	2004	2008	1999	2004	2008
Yes	70.8	-	-	92.4	97.3	99.1	84.5	88.2	89.1
No	29.2	-	-	7.6	2.7	0.9	15.5	11.8	10.9
Take part in elections	1999	2004	2008	1999	2004	2008	1999	2004	2008
Yes	55.0			62.7	76.0	68.4	60.0	60.0	64.5
No	43.3			37.3	24.0	31.1	40.0	40.0	34.5
No response	1.7			–	–	0.4	–	0	0.9
If no, why	1999	2004	2008	1999	2004	2008	1999	2004	2008
Didn't know	9.2			2.7	0.4	0.4	0.9	0.9	--
Didn't know anybody	1.7			4.0	1.8	1.3	6.4	6.4	6.4
Not interested	7.5			15.6	14.7	24.0	15.5	16.4	18.2
Not my business	4.2			1.8	0.9	0.4	6.4	3.6	3.6
Others	24.2			12.9	6.2	4.0	10.9	8.2	6.4
No response	53.3			63.1	76.0	69.8	60.0	64.5	65.5
If yes, in what capacity	1999	2004	2008	1999	2004	2008	1999	2004	2008
Vice chairman	0.8			0.4	–	–	0.9	-	-
Councillor	0.8			–	–	–	1.8	-	-
Voted	55.8			59.1	72.4	65.3	52.7	53.6	53.6
Campaigned	2.5			3.1	2.7	3.1	4.5	9.1	12.7
No response	40.0			37.3	24.9	31.1	40.0	37.3	33.6
Whether the respondents belonged to any party	1999	2004	2008	1999	2004	2008	1999	2004	2008
Yes	35.8			25.8	26.7	28.4	45.5	54.5	38.2
No	57.5			73.3	72.4	70.7	52.7	43.6	57.6
No response	6.7			0.9	0.9	0.9	1.8	1.8	4.2

About 43.3 per cent of respondents from Anambra State, 37.3 per cent from Lagos State and 40 per cent from Plateau State did not take part in 1999 local government council elections (see Table 4.2). The situation improved in Lagos State but remained the same in Plateau State until 2008 when fewer people declined to participate (34.5 per cent). Reasons provided for non-involvement in the elections were apathy, not familiar with the contestants, not their business and therefore unconcerned or that they travelled outside the states. However, the study showed that 55.0 per cent of respondents from Anambra State, 60.0 per cent from Plateau State and 62.7 per cent from Lagos State actually participated in the LG elections of 1999. The findings revealed in Table 4.2 that the respondents participated in various capacities. Major mode of participation was voting, although some respondents contested as Vice Chairmen, councillors while others campaigned for others. Political party membership was not common among the respondents because majority of the total respondents did not belong to political parties. For instance, in Table 4.2, 73.3 per cent of Lagos State respondents, and more than one half of both Anambra and Plateau State respondents affirmed that they did not belong to any political party in 1999. Lagos and Plateau States ran almost similar patterns in 2004 and 2008 elections as in 1999. This indicates the level of apathy among the electorate.

Challenges of Local Government Council Elections

In 1999 LG council elections, 50.8 per cent, 48.2 per cent and 35.6 per cent of the respondents from Anambra, Plateau, and Lagos States, respectively, did not know whether all the contesting parties were represented (see Table 4.3). This could be attributed to low level of campaigns and too many political parties which usually confuse the electorate. However, 35.8 per cent of Anambra State respondents, 62.2 per cent of those of Lagos State and 38.2 per cent of Plateau State respondents ascertained that all political parties were represented during the voting exercise.

In 2004 and 2008, Anambra State did not hold any LG elections but for Lagos State, the findings revealed that a higher proportion of the respondents (70.7 per cent) than that of 1999 (62.2 per cent) testified that all the parties involved were represented. On the contrary, in Plateau State a lower percentage (21.8 per cent) than that of 1999 (38.2 per cent) reported so. By 2008, the proportions of respondents who affirmed that all parties were represented dropped to 52.9 per cent in Lagos State and 18.2 per cent in Plateau State. By this time, LG council elections were characterised by rancour, accusations and counter-accusations by various parties. A greater proportion of those who said that some political parties were not represented were found among the Plateau respondents throughout the three periods under review. They revealed that some parties declined to participate. For instance, in Lagos, the Peoples Democratic Party (PDP) declined to participate in 2008 because of the issue of 20 Local Government Councils and 37 Local Council Development Areas (LCDAs). Thirty-one political parties indicated their interest in participating in the local council poll in the state.

Voters' turnout in 1999 was encouraging in all the states investigated. About 62.5 per cent of Anambra State, 69.8per cent of Lagos State and 75.5 per cent of Plateau State respondents said that the turnout of voters was impressive. In Lagos State, people's turnout was more impressive in 2003 than in 1999 as 80.4 per cent compared to 69.8 per cent of the respondents said that the citizens came out en mass to vote, but this percentage dropped to 67.1 per cent in 2008 (see Table 4.3). On the contrary, in Plateau State, the percentage of respondents who said that there was a mass turnout of voters dropped from 75.5 per cent in 1999 to 70.9 per cent in 2004 but increased to 80.0 per cent in 2008.

However, in 1999, one in four of Anambra State respondents, one in ten of Lagos State and a little above one in five of Plateau State respondents reported that the voters were bribed by the political parties while 15.8 per cent, 7.1 per cent and 13.6 per cent of Anambra, Lagos and Plateau respondents respectively claimed that the voters were compelled to vote for parties which were not their choices in the same year. Furthermore, 15 per cent of Anambra State, 4.9 per cent of Lagos State and 15.5 per cent of Plateau State respondents reported that LG Chairmen and councillors declared as having won the elections did not actually win. This is probably because these politicians exercise their political powers by putting their friends and clients on the state payroll as council employees, thus ensuring them a secured livelihood.

Table 4.3: Challenges of Local Government Council Elections

	Anambra N=120			Lagos N= 225			Plateau N =110		
All parties were represented	1999	2004	2008	1999	2004	2008	1999	2004	2008
Yes	35.8			62.2	70.7	52.9	38.2	21.8	18.2
No	4.2			1.8	3.6	18.2	10.9	21.8	30.9
Don't know	50.8			35.6	23.6	27.6	48.2	52.7	47.3
No response	9.2			0.4	2.2	1.3	2.7	3.6	3.6
People came out to vote	1999	2004	2008	1999	2004	2008	1999	2004	2008
Yes	62.5			69.8	80.4	67.1	75.5	70.9	80.0
No	1.7			0.9	2.2	14.2	1.8	9.1	3.6
Don't know	21.7			27.1	16.9	18.2	20.0	18.2	13.6
No response	14.2			2.2	0.4	0.4	2.7	1.8	2.7
Whether the electorate were bribed	1999	2004	2008	1999	2004	2008	1999	2004	2008
Yes	25.8			10.7	15.6	10.7	22.7	30.0	42.7

No	25.8			52.4	58.7	55.6	19.1	20.0	12.7
Don't know	36.7			34.2	24.9	33.3	57.3	50.0	42.7
No response	11.7			2.6	0.9	0.4	0.9	–	1.8
Whether the electorate were permitted to vote for the contestants of their choices	1999	2004	2008	1999	2004	2008	1999	2004	2008
Yes	39.2			61.3	65.8	62.7	42.7	37.3	39.1
No	15.8			7.1	8.4	7.6	13.6	23.6	33.6
Don't know	30.0			29.8	24.4	29.3	40.9	37.3	26.4
No response	15.0			1.8	1.3	0.4	2.7	1.8	0.9
Whether the declared winners actually won	1999	2004	2008	1999	2004	2008	1999	2004	2008
Yes	31.7			63.6	68.4	67.1	37.3	28.2	13.6
No	15.0			4.9	7.1	5.3	15.5	30.0	40.9
Don't know	39.2			29.8	23.6	27.1	45.5	40.0	42.7
No response	14.2			1.8	0.9	0.4	1.8	1.8	2.7
Whether problems were encountered during the elections	1999	2004	2008	1999	2004	2008	1999	2004	2008
Yes	20.8			2.7	4.0	2.2	9.1	17.3	29.1
No	40.8			68.4	73.3	77.3	44.5	29.1	20.9
Don't know	23.3			28.4	20.9	18.7	44.5	42.7	29.1
No response	15.0			0.4	1.8	1.7	1.8	10.9	20.9

With regards to whether the electorate was bribed in 2003, 30 per cent of Plateau State and 15.6 per cent of Lagos State respondents said yes. Furthermore, 23.6 per cent of Plateau State and 8.4 per cent Lagos State respondents said that voters were not allowed to cast votes for the parties of their choice. About 30.0 per cent of Plateau State and 7.1 per cent of Lagos State respondents reported that the declared winners did not actually win the elections.

The next LG elections did not hold in 2007 as planned. Lagos and Plateau States cast their votes in 2008 while in Anambra State, no LG council elections was held since that of 1999. Around 67.1 per cent of Lagos State and 80.0 per cent of Plateau State respondents declared that the turn out for voting was satisfactory. More than two-fifths of the Plateau State sample and one in ten respondents from Lagos State claimed that voters were offered bribes. There is no difference between 2003 and 2007/2008 proportions of the respondents who said that the chairmen and councillors did not win in Lagos State but in Plateau State, the proportion increased from 30.0 per cent to 40.9 per cent between the same periods under review.

The respondents were asked if they witnessed any problems during the polls. About 20.8 per cent of Anambra State respondents compared to 9.1 per cent of respondents of Plateau and 2.7 per cent of those of Lagos State reported that there were problems. By 2003 and 2008 the percentages of Plateau State respondents who said there were problems had increased from 9.1 per cent in 1999 to 17.3 per cent in 2003 and 29.1 per cent in 2008. There were reported cases of delay in the provision of electoral materials, snatching and stuffing of ballot boxes, rigging and violence.

The literature indicates that the local government elections of 2003/2004 were marred by violence and intimidation (Human Rights Watch 2004). Local government elections had originally been scheduled to take place in 2002, but were repeatedly postponed. The official reasons given for these postponements related mostly to logistical and administrative preparations. But many Nigerians speculated that the delays were more likely to have been motivated by political considerations. After the terms of local government councils expired in May 2002, state governors appointed local transition or 'caretaker' committees to take the place of elected local government councils. A federal government announcement in June 2003 that the system of local government administration would be subjected to a wide-ranging review meant that local government elections were, for a while, indefinitely suspended; in the meantime, local governments continued to be controlled by unelected individuals, picked by state governors. When the elections were eventually announced for March 2004, many of these individuals were reluctant to give up these lucrative positions. Human Rights Watch also documented several cases in which members of these transition committees were implicated in acts of violence against their perceived opponents during the 2003 elections (Transition Monitoring Group (TMG), (2004).

The 2003 elections had already demonstrated that the fiercest battles for political control were played out at the local level, and local disputes were the motivation behind many of the most serious incidents of violence. The 2004 local government elections confirmed this pattern. Violence broke out in many locations before, during and after polling day on March 27, leading to dozens of deaths. In addition to battles between supporters of different political parties, the period of the local government elections saw an intensification of internal fighting, in particular within the PDP, with different factions vying for control of local government positions. From February 2004 onwards, there were several incidents of apparently politically-motivated killings and attacks in different parts of the country. For example, on 6 February, Aminasoari Dikibo, National Vice-Chairman of the PDP for the South South Zone, was shot dead in Delta State. In Kogi State, the chairman of the State Independent Electoral Commission, Philip Olorunnipa, was killed on 7 March, and the PDP candidate for the chairmanship of Bassa local government, Luke Shigaba, was killed on 3 March. Also on 3 March, a vehicle carrying the Benue State Governor, George Akume, was attacked; the Governor escaped unhurt, but a friend travelling with him, Andrew Agom (who, like the governor, was a PDP member), and a police officer were both killed. There has been speculation that some of these incidents may have been caused by infighting within the PDP.

Between January and April 2004, there was also an intensification of inter-communal violence in areas such as the Niger Delta and the central Plateau State. Not all these incidents were directly related to the elections, but some analysts argued that the climate of heightened political tension created by the prospect of elections contributed to the increase in violence, especially in Delta State.

On the actual election day of 27 March, numerous incidents of violence and intimidation and clashes between supporters of different parties and candidates were reported across the country. The geographical spread of locations from which electoral violence was reported during the local government elections might have been even greater than during the 2003 general elections. Whereas the worst violence in 2003 was concentrated in the south-south and southeast, violence around the 2004 local government elections erupted in multiple locations across the country. In an initial non-exhaustive count of incidents reported by the end of March 2004, Human Rights Watch noted at least 22 states (out of Nigeria's 36 states) in which killings and other types of violent clashes were recorded by election observers, journalists and other sources (Transition Monitoring Group (TMG), (2004). Between late March and early April, there were reports of further incidents, including killings, some of which might have been linked to the aftermath of the elections (*Daily Champion* 2004; Associated Press 2004)

In addition to the violence, election observers reported widespread rigging of election results. Elections did not take place at all in several locations, in some cases because state or local authorities had chosen alternative dates, and in other cases, such as in Warri in Delta State, because state governments feared that elections would aggravate ongoing violence. The cancellation or postponement of elections was in itself a source of further frustration and anger among some communities. Where elections did take place, there was a very low voter turn-out; observers speculated that people had been discouraged from voting by a mixture of apathy, fear, and disillusion with the 2003 elections (The Transition Monitoring Group (TMG 2004).

In other parts of the country that conducted their local government elections in 2007, violence, fraud and rigging were also experienced. In Plateau State, clashes between the Hausa-Fulani settlers and the indigenes of Jos and between the Muslims and Christians erupted in Jos after the local government elections in 2008, with at least 312 people killed and also the military and the police were alleged to be involved in extra-judicial killings (International Crisis Group, 2012). The Plateau State Independent Electoral Commission (PLASIEC), announced the results of the 17 local government elections, which were won by the ruling People's Democratic Party (PDP). The Plateau State Independent Electoral Commission said the election was free, fair, credible and peaceful but the riots started when some Hausa-Fulani thought that the Plateau State Independent Electoral Commission (PLASIEC) attempted to alter the votes in favour of the ruling People's Democratic Party (PDP) against their candidate of All-Nigerian People's Party (ANPP). They set a church on fire. It was reported that the trouble started when an agent of one of the political parties was killed at Kabong, where results for Jos North were being collated. The ANPP candidate was said to be leading by about 26,000 votes. The International Crisis Group (2012:12) reported that the central collation centre was changed at least three times and the final counting took place in a primary school situated in a different LGA. Yet, the Hause-Fulani's attacks happened before the results were announced.

Assessment of Provisions of Social Services

Local government is a grassroots government and one of the indices of governance is provision of social services. It became imperative to assess how the LGAs had affected the lives of their respective citizens. Between 1999 and 2004, construction of roads (42.5 per cent) was a prominent programme in Anambra State while in Lagos State – potable water (46.2 per cent), refuse disposal (25.3 per cent), street drainage (28.4 per cent), security (20.4 per cent), cleaning of markets (20.4 per cent), environmental sanitation – were provided by the local governments studied (Table 4.4). In Plateau State, the results showed that the LGAs were unpopular as very few respondents testified that social services were provided during the periods under review. With respect to citizens' participation in the provision of social services, 45.8 per cent of Anambra State respondents confirmed that the community members contributed to the provision of social services. In Lagos state, 30.2 per cent of the respondents were in the negative while 39.6 per cent were not sure whether people participated or not.

Between 2004 and 2008, 26.7 per cent and 26.2 per cent of Anambra and Lagos State respondents said that roads were constructed. Similarly, in Lagos State, street drainages were constructed and provision of potable water (36.4 per cent). About 22.7 per cent of respondents from Lagos State affirmed that security was provided (23.6 per cent), cleaning of markets and environmental sanitation (31.1 per cent) between 2004 and 2008. Around 28.3 per cent of Anambra State respondents claimed that people participated in the construction of roads in the state. Although Plateau State respondents could not testify to the provision of social services, they were able to report that their people participated in the provision of social services. For instance, 23.6 per cent, 22.7 per cent and 26.4 per cent of the respondents were certain that their community members took part in the provision of services during the periods under study.

Despite the fact that no LG elections were held in 2004 and 2008 in Anambra state, from 2008 till date of the study showed that social services were provided. For instance, between 2004 and 2008, 26.7 per cent of the respondents said that roads were constructed, 15.8 per cent said health centres were built, 9.7 per cent said classrooms were constructed, refuse disposal was certified by 5.8 per cent, provision of security (5.0 per cent), construction of markets (4.2 per cent), and environmental sanitation (3.3 per cent). There were caretaker committees appointed in each LGA. In Lagos, 26.2 per cent of the respondents mentioned road construction, 38.7 per cent refuse disposal, street drainages (39.6 per cent), potable water (36.4 per cent), 22.7 per cent security, 23.6 per cent cleaning of markets and environmental sanitation (31.1 per cent). For Plateau State, the proportions of the respondents who testified that social services were provided were lower than those found in Anambra and Lagos States e.g while 26.7 per cent and 26.2 per cent of Anambra and Lagos State respondents claimed that their LGAs provided roads for them only 10 per cent of the Plateau State respondents could account for that in their LGAs. Others were health centres (16.4 per cent), building of classrooms (10.9 per cent), refuse disposal (10.0 per cent), street drainages (19.1 per cent), potable water (6.4 per cent), security (5.5 per cent), cleaning of markets (3.6 per cent), and electricity (4.5 per cent).

People's participation in the provision of social services empowers them to be effectively involved in creating the structures and designing policies and programmes that serve the interests of all and effectively contribute to the development process and share equitably in its benefits. In this wise the respondents' level of participation was assessed. With regards to people's participation in the provision of social services between 2004 and 2008, 8.3 per cent, 34.7 per cent and 19.1 per cent of the respondents from Anambra, Lagos and Plateau States respectively reported that their communities did not participate in the provisions of the services mentioned above.

Table 4.4: Assessment of Provisions of Social Services

	Anambra (Yes)			Lagos (Yes)			Plateau (Yes)		
	1999-2004	2003-2008	2008 to date	1999-2004	2003-2008	2008 to date	1999-2004	2003-2008	2008 to date
Construction of roads	42.5	26.7	25.0	19.6	26.2	8.9	14.5	–	11.8
Health centres	15.0	15.8	12.5	5.8	2.7	1.3	11.8	16.4	9.1
Classrooms	11.7	9.2	5.0	2.7	3.6	3.6	12.7	10.9	3.6
Refuse disposal	8.3	5.8	5.0	25.3	38.7	51.6	10.9	10.0	9.1
Street drainages	4.2	0.8	0.8	28.4	39.6	50.2	12.7	19.1	7.3
Potable water	15.0	1.7	2.5	46.2	36.4	26.2	7.3	5.4	8.2

Security	11.7	5.0	3.3	20.4	22.7	22.2	3.6	5.5	6.4
Cleaning markets	9.2	1.7	4.2	20.4	23.6	26.2	3.6	3.6	5.5
Cleaning environment	10.0	3.3	5.0	27.1	31.1	40.0	4.5	5.5	12.7
Your community took part	1999-2004	2003-2008	2008 to date	1999-2004	2003-2008	2008 to date	1999-2004	2003-2008	2008 to date
Yes	45.8	28.3	26.7	12.4	6.9	5.8	23.6	22.7	26.4
No	14.2	8.3	8.3	30.2	34.7	38.2	19.1	19.1	23.6
Don't know	34.2	30.8	31.7	39.6	38.7	44.0	45.5	42.7	33.6
No response	5.8	32.5	33.3	17.7	17.7	12.0	11.8	15.5	16.4

From 2008 till date of the study, the following were identified by respondents to have been provided in Anambra: road construction (25 per cent), health centres (12.5 per cent), classroom (5.0 per cent), refuse disposal (5.0 per cent), building of markets (5.8 per cent), cleaning of markets and environmental sanitation (5.0 per cent) each. In Lagos state, respondents testified that the following services were rendered: classroom construction (3.6 per cent), security (22.2 per cent), cleaning of markets (26.2 per cent) and environmental sanitation (40.0 per cent). Plateau State respondents indicated that they had these services provided for them: road construction (11.8 per cent), health centres (9.1 per cent), classrooms (3.6 per cent), refuse disposal (1.1 per cent), street drainage (7.3 per cent), potable water (8.2 per cent), security (6.4 per cent), building of markets (5.5 per cent), cleaning of markets (4.2 per cent) and environmental sanitation (12.7 per cent). About 26.7 per cent of Anambra State and 26.4 per cent of Plateau State respondents admitted that their communities participated in the provision of social services.

Chairmen's Performance Evaluation

The councillors do not involve the people in the provision of social services. This is demonstrated in Table 4.5. Between 1999 and 2004, half of the respondents in Anambra State, more than three-fifths in Lagos State and over two-fifths of Plateau State respondents declared that the councillors never invited them to discuss issues that concerned them. Similar patterns were observed between 2004 and 2008 and from 2008 to date.

Evaluation of the councillors by the respondents was not favourable in all the periods under review. The respondents said the LG Chairmen did not fulfil their campaign promises after getting into offices. For example, between 1999 and 2004, 49.2 per cent of Anambra State respondents, 57.3 per cent of Lagos State and 54.5 per cent of Plateau State respondents testified that the LG Chairmen did not do all they promised during the campaign periods. This pattern was almost similar in the other two eras under review.

Despite all the aforementioned, the Chairmen were rated fairly well by the respondents in all the periods under review except in Anambra State where there were no chairmen but caretaker committees. Be that as it may, the Sole Administrators were not favourably rated.

Table 4.5: Evaluation of Performance of the Chairmen

Your councillor invited you	1999 2004	2003- 2008	2008 to date	1999- 2004	2003- 2008	2008 to date	1999- 2004	2003- 2008	2008 to date
Yes	8.3	4.2	5.0	5.8	4.4	3.1	7.3	13.6	13.6
No	57.5	41.7	38.3	65.8	72.4	74.7	48.2	42.7	47.3
Don't know	28.3	21.7	21.7	28.4	21.8	21.8	42.7	40.9	36.4
No response	5.8	32.5	35.0	–	1.3	0.4	1.8	2.7	2.7
Fulfilled his campaign promises	1999 2004	2003- 2008	2008 to date	1999- 2004	2003- 2008	2008 to date	1999- 2004	2003- 2008	2008 to date
Yes	6.7	2.5	1.7	5.3	6.2	4.9	4.5	9.1	7.3
No	49.2	48.3	45.8	57.3	62.2	61.3	54.5	55.5	49.1
Don't know	11.7	13.3	8.3	24.9	17.8	18.7	37.3	26.4	20.0
No response	32.5	35.8	44.1	12.4	13.8	15.1	3.6	9.1	23.6
Appraisal of the LG Chairmen's performance	1999 2004	2003- 2008	2008 to date	1999- 2004	2003- 2008	2008 to date	1999- 2004	2003- 2008	2008 to date
Excellent	1.7	0.8	0.8	0.4	0.4	0.9	–	0.9	–
Very good	5.8	3.3	4.2	0.9	3.1	3.1	0.9	–	3.6
Good	25.8	10.0	10.8	36.4	38.7	42.7	17.3	17.3	19.1
Fair	25.8	19.2	14.2	34.2	32.9	35.6	38.2	51.8	37.3
Poor	10.0	10.0	10.0	12.4	14.2	12.4	25.5	19.1	24.5
Very poor	11.7	10.8	10.0	4.9	4.9	3.1	9.1	5.5	5.5
Unbearable	5.8	5.8	7.5	0.9	0.9	0.4	6.4	5.5	8.2
Others	4.2	6.7	6.7	4.9	1.8	0.9	0.9	–	0.9
No response	9.2	33.3	35.8	4.9	3.1	0.8	1.8	–	–

Recommendations

Based on the findings from the study, the following are recommended:

- The study revealed gross apathy among the respondents. A significant proportion of the respondents was unaware of the elections and did not participate in the LG council elections. Concerted voter education should be conducted to improve voters' awareness about elections. Contestants should endeavour to have robust campaigns to sell their programmes to the electorate prior to every election. Secondly, Nigerian democracy is still evolving, therefore, to improve the electoral process and address the apathy among the citizens, citizens' votes must count and enlightenment exercise should be organised for the electorate. It is basically the legitimacy deficit of the government at different levels that gives rise to apathy. In addition, contestants should be clearly identified in the electoral process. And campaign debates to clarify parties' manifestos should be encouraged.

- Major challenges observed from the study were delay in the provision of electoral materials, snatching and stuffing of ballot boxes, rigging, use of financial incentives to sway voters, intimidation of voters and violence. Political parties and INEC should agree on a Code of Conduct and ethics for the elections. Agreement on a Code of Conduct and campaign ethics would send a major signal to the population that the political leadership of the country is committed to the evolution of modern democratic practices.

- In as much as the respondents mentioned construction of roads, refuse disposal, street drainages, potable water, security, cleaning of markets, environmental sanitation as services that were provided by the Chairmen, a lot still has to be done. In fact, in Anambra State, the only visible service is road construction. The Chairmen need to be educated on their duties as soon as they assume office. There is no doubt that the social contract has not been consummated in states like Anambra from the study carried out. Raising the political consciousness of the people, as well as check-mating the elite through civil society action are important ways of ensuring that the people have capacity to demand for and get the type of governance they want.

- It was revealed in this study that the citizens were not involved in the provision of social services, however, it was confirmed that community members contributed to the provision of the social services. The councillors did not consult the people before providing any social services. Here again, education of the elected chairmen and councillors is necessary.

References

Adedeji, A., 2000, 'Renewal of Search for Systems of Local Government that Can Serve the Common Good', in Adedeji, A and Ayo, B. eds. *People-Centred Democracy in Nigeria? The Search for Alternative Systems of Governance at the Grass-roots*, Ijebu Ode: African Centre for Development and Strategic Studies.

Adejumobi, S., 2004, 'Democracy, Good Governance and Constitutionalism in Africa', in Odion-Akhaine, S. ed., *Governance: Nigeria and the World*, Ikeja-Lagos: Centre for Constitutionalism and Demilitarisation (CENCOD).

Akinboye, S., 2007, 'Reflections on Local Government Reforms in Post-independence Nigeria: The Imperative of a New Agenda for Grass-roots Development', in Ani- fowose, R. and Babawale, T. eds, *An Agenda for a New Nigeria: The Imperative of Transformation*, Lagos, Concept Publications LTD.

Associated Press, 2004, 'Nigeria Youths, Security Forces Battle Over Disputed Election Results; 30 Feared Dead', *Associated Press*, April 5.

Daily Champion, 2004, 'Edo Still Boils Two Days After Local Government Poll', *Daily Champion*, March 30.

Fage, K. S., 2007, 'Local Government Elections and Democratisation in Nigeria', *Sunday Triumph*, April 29.

Federal Government Printer (FGP), 2007, 'Legal Notice on Publication of the Details of the Breakdown of the National and State Provisional Totals 2006 Census, *Federal Republic of Nigeria Official Gazette*, No. 24, Vol. 94, Lagos: 15 May 2007: B175 – 198.

Guidelines for Local Government Reform, 1976, http//:www.guardiannewsngr.com/ news/ article 01, accessed 14 April 2011.

International Crisis Group, 2012. 'Curbing Violence in Nigeria (I): The Jos Crisis' *Crisis Group Africa Report* N°196, 17 December.

Lagos State Government, 2004, *History of Lagos*, Lagos: Lagos State Government.

National Population Commission, 1998, *1991 Population Census of the Federal Republic of Nigeria*, Abuja: NPC.

NHCR., 2002, Human Rights in Development (1996 – 2002), Geneva: Switzerland.

Obia, V., 2007, "Census: An unusual survey", *Sunday Independent*, February 11, 2007: B8

Ojo, E. O. and Azeez, A., 2000, 'The Military and Democratic Transition in Nigeria 1976-1999)', *Nigerian Journal of International Affairs*, Vol. 28, Nos. 1 and 2.

Ojo, M. J., 2007, 'Money Politics and Local Government Elections: the Need for Control', Paper Presented during the FOSIECON Conference in Asaba, Delta State, 11-12 July.

Ojofeitimi, T., 2000, 'Yesterday's Hope and Today's Disillusionment: Whither Local Government in Nigeria?', in Adedeji, A and Ayo, B. eds. '*People-centred Democracy in Nigeria? The Search for Alternative Systems of Governance at the Grass-roots*', Ijebu Ode: African Centre for Development and Strategic Studies.

Simon, D., 2004. 'Recent Trends in Development Theory and Policy Implications for Democratisation and Governance', in Odion-Akhaine, S. eds., *Governance: Nigeria and the World*, Ikeja-Lagos: Centre for Constitutionalism and Demilitarisation (CENCOD).

Transition Monitoring Group (TMG), 2004, 'Preliminary Report Issued on the Local Government Council Elections held on Saturday, March 27, 2004', Abuja.

UNDP, 1997, *Reconceptualising Governance*, New York.

World Bank, 1999, *Managing Development: The Governance Dimension*, World Bank, June.

5

An Overview of the State Houses of Assembly Elections

Sharkdam Wapmuk

Introduction

In this chapter we critically examine the nature and character of elections conducted in the State Houses of Assembly in 1999, 2003 and 2007. Not only is the State House of Assembly a replica of the National Assembly, it has also suffered the same fate under past military regimes. The state assemblies in Nigeria were also suffocated out of existence and were only restored with the return to democracy in 1999 (Alabi 2008). Though certain areas of jurisdiction may differ, its importance in the operation of democratic government at the state level can be seen in the functions it carries out. As the law making body at the state level, the state legislature is the source of laws that define the parameters of governance in the state. Second, through the scrutiny of state budgets, the state legislature plays an important role in determining government policies and programmes. Third, being an elected assembly that is closer to the people, the state legislature serves as a barometer for assessing public opinion on the operation of government. The closeness of the state legislature to the people helps it to articulate the peoples' needs and aspirations in theory (Hamalai 1996). In practice, however, what we have is a case of illegitimacy of government marginalizing some segments of the constituency from governance, and benefitting from democracy dividends. Apart from carrying out the important function of legislation at the state level, the state legislatures hear petitions, exercise powers of oversight over the executive, confirm appointments and check other agencies of government. This quality control function is essential for providing effective governance.

Given the important role of the legislative arm of government at the state level, the nature and character of elections that produce members of the state legislature are fundamental. Important as elections are in the democratic process, as the means through which people choose between different political parties and candidates offering different programmes, they have also proved to be problematic in some cases, particularly where the people are denied the actual rights of choosing their representatives through free and fair contests (Obi 2008:20). Ndadozie (2008:45) observed that of the two types of democracies, namely direct and representative democracies, it is only through the electoral process that the representative democracy can be practised. This is so because direct democracy is no longer feasible in a modern society. It is against this background that some have argued that without elections, democracy cannot be practised or institutionalised (Bratton, 2008). It has also been observed that political succession, especially when viewed in terms of elections, has been a problem of democratisation not only in Nigeria, but Africa as a whole (Okoosi-Simbine 2008:3). Attempts by civilian governments to organize elections in the past in Nigeria have been fraught with various problems, which in most cases were cited by previous military regimes as reasons for their incursion into politics. The inability of civilian governments to conduct free and fair elections acceptable to all in the 1964/65 and 1983 general elections and the violence that followed contributed to the collapse of the First and Second Republics (Mohammed 2008:188; Dudley 1982; Osaghae 2002:152).

The recent democratic experiment in Nigeria has raised serious questions about democratic consolidation in the country. Ibrahim (2007) argues that the manner in which the elections of 1999, 2003 and 2007 were conducted in the country shows that it is more or less mimicking democracy. As noted by Kurfi (2005:101), rigging is almost synonymous with Nigerian elections. The rigging of elections has not only frustrated the aspirations of Nigerians, it has also paved way for persons of questionable character to occupy various positions of public trust, including the posts of legislators. This process of political disempowerment runs counter to the tenets of democracy. Elections are supposed to give people the power to decide how they are ruled and who rules or represents them. The elections conducted for the State Houses of Assembly and other elective positions in Nigeria, therefore, falls short of the expectation of Nigerians This chapter critically examines the conduct of the State Houses of Assembly elections in Nigeria up to 2007. Given the fact that Nigeria has 36 states and a Federal Capital Territory in Abuja, the desire to undertake a critical examination of the State Houses of Assembly elections conducted in 1999, 2003 and 2007 and to also closely engage the stakeholders necessitated our selecting three states for study. These are Borno State (North East), Plateau State (North Central) and Lagos State (South West).

Methodological and Theoretical Perspectives

Sources of data and information: Data for this work were obtained from both primary and secondary sources. The field research involved the conduct of face-to-face interviews with law makers and officials of INEC. Focus Group Discussion (FGD) involved citizens of voting age (18 and above). This was conducted in Jos-South (Urban), Jos-North (Urban) and Barkin Ladi (Rural) in Plateau State; Maiduguri (urban), Bama (Urban) and Konduga (Rural), in Borno State and Somolu, Lagos Mainland and Eti-Osa Local Government areas of Lagos State. Discussions were also held with individuals, journalists, activists and community groups. The researcher also obtained information from relevant texts, journals, magazines, newspapers, official publications and historical documents and this was analysed through content analysis.

In respect of theory, the chapter followed the general thrust of the tenets of representative democracy, on the understanding that elections serve as vehicles for effecting changes of government through the citizenry electing selected members of the society presented by the political parties. From this perspective, the political process is expected to be transparent, and the elections free and fair, whilst political and human rights of the populace and contestants are respected and upheld.

Political Parties and the Selection of Candidates

The 1999 elections were supervised by the military government of General Abdulsalami Abubakar. Three political parties which eventually emerged after the nine that participated in the local government elections, fielded candidates for the State Houses of Assembly elections in the country. These parties were People's Democratic Party (PDP), All Peoples Party (APP), now the All Nigerian People's Party (ANPP) and the Alliance for Democracy (AD). Although people were sceptical of the political transition, political activities gathered momentum following the release of a political transition programme by General Abdulsalami Abubakar. This was not surprising considering the many unfulfilled promises and political manoeuvring by the past military regimes to hand over to democratically elected government. The selection of candidates for the State Houses of Assembly elections by the three registered political parties for the 1999 elections was not without challenges; however, the characteristic nature of the candidate selection process was connected to the fact that politicians did not want to do anything that would further prolong military stay in power (Yaqub 2004). Prior to the elections of 2003, some political associations in December 2002 obtained a court judgment allowing them to form political parties contrary to the stand of the electoral commission, which had insisted on using stringent measures to register and control the political parties. As an outcome of the judgment, by the February 2003 general elections, about 30 political parties had been registered to contest the elections (Sha 2006b). Despite the increase in the number of political parties, the nature of campaign and electoral process were hardly different from those of the 1999 elections. Particularly in the area of funding of political parties and candidates contesting for seats in the State Houses of Assembly, the incumbent candidates and political parties in power had the upper hand.

Campaigns for the State House of Assembly Elections

The State Houses of Assembly campaigns ahead of the 1999 elections, which were initially characterised by an atmosphere of uncertainty later attracted the participation of the masses. In Barkin Ladi LGA of Plateau state, majority of those seeking to be elected to the State House of Assembly staged their campaign rallies at party offices. In some parts of Borno State, the campaigns involved, among other activities, the use of drummers who sang the praises of the candidates they supported. The candidates of the three political parties that fielded candidates for elections, namely the PDP, APP and AD staged almost similar campaigns. In the case of the 2003 elections, the late release of the dates of the elections by INEC affected the campaigns by the political parties. This created an atmosphere of haste and confusion in the electoral process, including the campaigns. In Plateau State the campaigns featured the use of mostly posters which were pasted indiscriminately on residences and public places, and writings on rocks and bridges. Compared to the presidential and gubernatorial election campaigns, those seeking elections into the State Houses of Assembly made less use of the print and electronic media. Even those who made use of the print and electronic media hardly focused on, and addressed specific issues beyond the general promise to improve the lives of the people; they also engaged predominantly in sloganeering. As a result of poor usage of the print and electronic media, most of the voters did not know the candidates seeking election for the State Houses of Assembly elections even within their constituencies. In some cases, the campaigns deviated to digging up unpleasant stories about their opponents and calling for their disqualification. Some even resorted to removal of opponents' posters.

To a large extent, most of the campaign strategies were sustained during the 2007 campaigns. Most of the candidates also sought to identify with political financiers and godfathers, whom they held in awe as the guarantors for successful election into the State Houses of Assembly.

The State Houses of Assembly Elections

The 1999 State Houses of Assembly elections took place on 9 January. It has been observed that the transition to civil rule elections held in 1999 contained serious electoral flaws; however, these were overlooked because of the desire to ensure the exit of military dictatorship. The State Houses of Assembly elections for 2003 took place on 3 May. It was noted that voters' turnout was low in many areas arguably due to fatigue as a result of the staggered nature of the general elections, the disenchantment with the conduct and outcome of the National Assembly and the Presidential/Gubernatorial elections, and the apparent cynicism of voters that winners for the State Houses of Assembly elections were already predetermined and that voting would not really change anything. In some cases in Plateau State, it was the aggrieved political parties and/or candidates that instructed their members and supporters to boycott the elections. Some Nigerians did not attach much importance to the elections into the State Legislatures as that of the National Assembly and the positions of the president and governors. Apart from the poor voter enlightenment by the political parties and politicians, some political parties dismantled their campaign structures immediately after the Presidential and Gubernatorial elections. As such, most people did not know the candidates seeking for elections to the State Houses of Assembly.

The conduct of the State Houses of Assembly elections also witnessed several challenges as some of the polling units not only opened late, but also lacked relevant election materials. Because of the late commencement of voting some voters left and never came back to vote. People who needed assistance to vote were assisted by party agents who pressurized them to vote for particular candidates. In addition, election monitors such as the Transition Monitoring Group (TMG) reported that numerous cases of electoral fraud and malpractices, including 'under-age voting, multiple voting, stuffing of ballot papers into ballot boxes, snatching of ballot boxes, falsification of results, and so on, were observed in many states in different parts of the country' during the 2003 elections (TMG 2003:73). The State Houses of Assembly elections for 2007 were held at the same time with the gubernatorial elections on 14 April. Some argued that the 2007 elections were programmed to fail (Ibrahim 2007). This is arguably connected to the pre-election problems, the poor preparation and management of the elections by the Independent Electoral Commission (INEC) such as the voter's registration exercises, voter's education, distribution of voting materials and many others. The presence of the police and other security agencies did not deter party agents from influencing voters and in some areas clashes occurred among party supporters as revealed by one of the local observer groups – the Justice, Development and Peace Commission (JDPC).

Assessment of the Conduct of the State Houses of Assembly Elections and Performance of the State Legislators in Plateau State

Jos-North LGA: Participation in the State House of Assembly Elections

The FGD in Jos-North LGA showed that most people participated in the 1999, 2003 and 2007 elections as voters and only a few as active members of various political parties in the state. The choice of participation in most cases stemmed from the level of interest of the electorate in the process and their support for particular political parties and candidates. Though both men and women of voting age were free to participate in the elections, some pointed out that they did not participate because of either a lack of interest or because they did not know the candidates seeking elections. The FGD in Jos North LGA agreed that most people switched between different political parties between 1999 and 2007. While all the political parties participated in the 1999 elections, not all participated in the 2003 and 2007 elections. Some of the political parties did not have candidates seeking elective positions on their platforms. It was the consensus of the FGD that not all candidates that emerged as winners in the past elections actually won. The negative role played by the State Independent Electoral Commission (SIEC) officials in support of some candidates and also the role played by political god- fathers and political financiers were said to be the deciding factor in who emerged victorious at the elections. It also observed that most people became desperate to become state law makers due to the sudden wealth accumulated by those that became legislators from 1999. As a result, the 2003 and 2007 elections were characterised by more desperate competition by the candidates to attain political offices at all cost. The 1999 elections were said to be more peaceful compared to the 2003 and 2007 elections where the supporters of various political parties such as the PDP and ANPP clashed. The elections were also characterised by several problems such as thuggery by party supporters, late arrival of voting materials and early closure in some centres and missing names from voters list. In some centres where supporters of political parties clashed, the presence of security agencies made little or no difference. In some cases party agents and supporters continued to campaign at the election centres and sought to influence voters, especially those that needed help during elections right under the watch of the security personnel.

Assessment of the Performance of the Legislators at the State Level

The FGD in Jos-North was of the general opinion that the performance of the state legislators in terms of representation, law making and constituency development was very low. The performance level, in some cases, was gauged on the promises made during campaigns which were rarely, if ever fulfilled. Most people could not make input into the law making process because they did not have access to the state legislators. Some electorate noted that the state legislators who had almost become permanent residents in the state capital mostly seek to re-connect strongly with the people at the grassroots only when they are seeking for re-election to the State House of Assembly or other positions. The electorate lacked awareness of legislation that could improve their lives which were sponsored and/or supported by their representatives at the state levels.

Jos-South LGA: Participation in the State House of Assembly Elections

Generally, people had different reasons for participating or not participating in the State House of Assembly elections of 1999, 2003 and 2007. While some argued that they participated in the elections because they wanted to elect the persons who would represent their interest at the state level, others supported particular candidates to win elections because of close or personal relationships. Some of the voters also pointed out that they did not participate in the elections because they were completely unaware of the dates for the state assembly elections and who the candidates were. Some faulted the candidate selection process of the major political parties, particularly the PDP and ANPP as biased in favour of richer, more influential candidates and those with links to political god-fathers, who also sponsored such candidates. Most people participated more as voters than as card carrying members of any political party. The PDP emerged as the dominant political party in the 1999 State House of Assembly elections. By 2003 elections, it was felt that the PDP was dominated by state government officials. This made some of the members of the PDP, who also desired to contest the state assembly elections, to decamp to either ANPP or AD. It was the consensus of the FGD in Jos South that politicians seeking elective positions as state legislators displayed desperation for the office right from the campaigns. Consequently most of them devised different strategies to win at all costs, including the use of monetary inducement. Some candidates, especially women, complained of being denied party tickets after spending on campaigns and mobilisation of the electorate. Some decided to team up with the candidate selected by the party, while others switched to a different political party. The FGD disagreed that the legislators declared as winners in the 1999, 2003 and 2009 State House of Assembly elections actually won. Some members of the FGD argued that the elections held in 2007 was a case of competitive rigging by politicians, including those seeking elections to the State House of Assembly. As was the case with the National Assembly elections, the State Houses of Assembly elections of 1999, 2003 and 2007, in varying degrees, were characterised by problems of poor management, interference by state officials and clashes among political groups supporting different candidates.

Assessment of the Performance of the Legislators at State Level

It was the consensus of the FGD in Jos South LGA that the performance of the legislators at the state level fell far short of the expectations of the voters. People expected that state legislators, in addition to performing the functions of representation and law making, would regularly visit their constituencies and assist the people with various development projects such as roads, water supply, schools, health clinics, markets and others. The FGD conducted in Jos South LGA revealed that the legislators from 1999-2003, interacted better with the people in Jos South than those who represent them from 2003-2007 and after the 2007 elections. While some who were close to the legislators had access to them, some argued that the lawmakers did not impact on their lives in any meaningful way, since they could not gain access to them, and did not know how to contribute to governance. Even where state legislators had attempted to make impact on their constituencies by offering scholarships, distribution of school books, and, in some cases, provision of free medical services, these activities mostly go unnoticed because only a few people are able to access and derive benefits from such services. What could not be ascertained at the time of this study was whether these came from the pockets of the legislators or from their constituency allowances. There was also poor communication between the state legislators and their constituencies. As a result of poor communication between the law makers and their constituencies, many were uninformed of the constituency projects executed by the law makers. The people were also unaware of various roles played by the state legislators in the area of law making in support of their constituencies.

Barkin Ladi LGA: Participation in the State Houses of Assembly Elections

The elections for the State Houses of Assembly in Plateau State in 1999 witnessed low participation in many parts of Barkin Ladi Local Government Area. In many respects, most people were not optimistic that the military would actually hand over to the democratically elected government. The previous transition programmes mid-wived by the past military regimes before that of General Abdulsalami Abubakar's in 1998, were carefully designed to enable self-succession of the incumbent military leader(s). While some people participated more actively in the 2003 State House of Assembly elections, others who did not argued that their votes would make no difference since the candidates had already been chosen by the PDP. More candidates indicated interest in contesting the State House of Assembly elections in 2007. This included female candidates who also took active part in the election campaigns. The youth also participated actively in the elections. However, a youth leader in Barkin Ladi LGA argued that the candidates in the dominant party in the state (PDP) used the youth during elections and dumped them thereafter. Most people participated more as voters than as card-carrying members of political parties in Barkin Ladi LGA. While some remained in the same political party from 1999, others changed political parties in the 1999, 2003 and 2007 elections. Some candidates who failed to secure party ticket for elections to the State House of Assembly moved to other political parties with their supporters with the hope of succeeding in the other political parties. It was the consensus of the FGD in Barkin Ladi that all the registered political parties were represented in the 1999 elections. However, not all political parties were represented in the 2003 and 2007 elections because some of the political parties had no candidates seeking elections for legislative positions in the State House of Assembly. During the 1999 elections, voter turnout was reported as low when compared with the governorship and presidential elections. The voter turnout was said to be higher for the 2003 elections than the 2007 elections for the state legislature. The FGD conducted in this LGA revealed that monetary inducement was used to lure voters by politicians seeking elections to the State Houses of Assembly. However, this was reported to be lower compared to the governorship and presidential elections. It was the consensus of the FGD that not all state legislators declared as winners in elections of 1999, 2003 and 2007 actually won the elections. The FGD also observed that the 2007 elections was the worst election in Nigeria's political history going by the various problems that characterised its organisation, conduct and attitude of the election management body which denied that the election was flawed. Among other things, the elections were widely condemned due to many irregularities, fraud, and violence.

Assessment of the Performance of the Legislators at the State Level

Though most state legislators are supposed to be closer to the people, the electorate reported that they lacked access to them. The very few state lawmakers who established constituency offices at their home bases hardly visited. The constituency offices actually came alive only during election campaigns or when other party activities were to be held. Because of the poor communication between the state lawmakers and their constituencies, most people were not informed about the legislations sponsored or supported by them that could improve their lives. It was also the consensus of participants at the FGD that most lawmakers diverted money meant for constituency projects for personal use. They also noted that most of them were unaware of such projects executed by the legislators at the state level. On the whole, individual state legislators were said to have performed below the expectations of voters in Barkin Ladi LGA from 1999-2007.

State House of Assembly Elections in Lagos State

Somolu LGA: Participation in the State House of Assembly Elections

In terms of participation in the elections of 1999, the FGD in Somolu noted that people took active part in the elections because they were tired of military rule. Their participation in the State House of Assembly elections in 1999 was further bolstered by the release of the transition programme and subsequent conduct of the local government elections in 1998 by the Abubakar regime. The 2003 and 2007 state assembly elections had lower participation of voters due to '*disenchantment with democracy*'. The people's expectations that their standard of living would improve with the return of democracy did not materialize. Most people who participated in the elections of 1999, 2003 and 2007 did so as voters. Some who participated as candidates for elective positions and lost the elections argued that they were rigged out by their opponents with the collaboration of INEC.

To understand why some people prefer to participate as voters, campaigners, members of political parties and/or election observers, we need to understand how they perceive the political terrain. One candidate who contested for the state assembly elections pointed out that 'to be a politician you need to be strong and ready to put your life on the line'. Apart from the fear of political opponents, the electorate argued that politics is highly monetized and expensive. It has thus become a lucrative business for political financiers and godfathers, who demand 'dividends' from those they instal in political office. The FGD in Somolu observed that because of the poor nature of campaign by some candidates seeking election into the State House of Assembly, most voters did not know them even on the elections days. The voters noted that in most cases, politicians would still achieve their aim of rigging the election irrespective of whether they voted or not. As far as the state assembly elections were concerned, the politicians demonstrated their desperation for political office during the 2007 elections than in any other election since Nigeria returned to democracy in 1999. Various forms of inducements were used to seek support, ranging from promising scholarships to indigenes, giving free medical care and using monetary inducements. Some became so desperate that they employed political thugs to intimidate their opponents. These thugs played very negative roles during elections with some deliberately fomenting trouble in order to facilitate the rigging of elections in favour of their preferred candidates. The FGD in Somolu observed that it is questionable that those declared as winners in the 1999, 2003 and 2007 elections for the state assembly elections actually won the elections. Many problems were encountered during the campaigns and on election days. These included political violence and the collusion of state officials and the police in the rigging of elections.

Assessment of the Performance of the Legislators at the State Level

The FGD in Somolu was of the consensus that the performance of the state legislators from 2003-2007 and, to a lesser extent, 2007 to date could be said to be better than those legislators from 1999-2003. They argued that though the people sometimes had access to the state legislators, not much was done to improve their welfare. Most of the politicians made promises without the intention of fulfilling them. That notwithstanding, while some of the lawmakers made efforts to fulfil campaign promises, others had not. The FGD also noted that some of the electorate and groups frequently made demands on the state lawmakers that were rather self-serving and not necessarily in the interest of the generality of the people

Eti-osa LGA: Participation in the State Houses of Assembly Elections

The voter turnout in the elections to a large extent indicated the level of participation by citizens in elections. The FGD in Eti-Osa LGA argued that the experience of people under military rule impacted on their participation in the 1999 elections. The FGD also observed that more people contested the state assembly elections in 2003 and 2007 than in 1999. While majority participated in the elections as voters in 1999, 2003 and 2007, some noted that they did not participate because they did not know whom to vote for. Some reported switching political parties in the 1999, 2003 and 2007 elections. Most of the people, however, did not partake in the campaign, but rather participated as voters in these elections. The FGD in Eti-Osa was of the view that though the politicians seeking election into the State House of Assembly used various forms of inducement to elicit votes, these could not be compared to those of the governorship elections in the state. The State Houses of Assembly elections of 1999, 2003 and 2007 were characterised by many lapses and malpractices. Some of the problems actually started with the disenfranchisement of the people during the registration of voters. While some of those registered were under-aged, others who were of the voting age had their names omitted in the final list that was released. The FGD noted that some of the problems encountered during elections involved INEC officials who did not or could not prevent under age voting, partisanship of its officials, and ensuring secrecy in balloting. The security officials also failed to provide adequate protection at the voting centres.

Assessment of the Performance of the Legislators at the State Level

The FGD in Eti-osa LGA was of the consensus that members of the State House of Assembly did not perform well from 1999-2007. While majority reported not knowing the state legislators, others noted that though they knew them, they had no access to the lawmakers. People argued that they had no way of knowing whether the legislators sponsored or supported any legislation that could have improved their lives between 1999 and 2007. They also claimed to be ignorant of the number of constituency projects executed by the state lawmakers from Eti-Osa LGA. Most respondents rated the performance of the lawmakers from 1999-2003 as poor;those from 2003-2007 as fair; and those from 2007 as poor.

Lagos Mainland LGA: Participation in the State House of Assembly Elections

The FGD of Lagos Mainland LGA noted that the State House of Assembly elections attracted less participation when compared to the presidential and gubernatorial elections of 1999. Some argued that they did not have confidence in the military transition programme after several failed transition programmes in the country. The FGD also observed that even in the 2003 and 2007 elections, people participated more actively in the presidential and gubernatorial elections than in the state assembly elections. While majority participated as voters, others were ordinary party members. Those who were members of political parties were mainly in the Alliance for Democracy (AD) or Peoples Democratic Party (PDP) from 1999-2003 and some decamped and joined the Action Congress (AC) when it replaced the AD in September 2006, while others stayed in the PDP or joined other numerous political parties that were formed as from 2002. The AD, PDP and ANPP fielded candidates for the 1999 elections. However, in the 2003 and 2007 elections, not all the political parties had candidates seeking elections for the State House of Assembly. While the PDP and AD candidates were the main contenders in the 2003, the PDP and AC struggled for the state legislative seats in the 2007 elections in Lagos. The FGD noted that the candidates seeking elections used monetary and other forms of material inducement to influence the electorate. It was the consensus of the FGD that not all those declared winners in the state assembly elections actually won in the 1999, 2003 and 2007 elections. According to them, not only was the 2007 state assembly election brazenly rigged, it also was also violent, as a result of the clashes of AC and PDP supporters in some areas. Voting in some centres in the Lagos Mainland LGA was so undermined by open display of rigging, intimidation and violence by armed thugs that the elections cast serious doubts on the possibility of achieving the consolidation of democracy in Nigeria.

Assessment of the Performance of the Legislators at the State Level

The FGD also observed that because of the cosmopolitan nature of Lagos State, most people were likely not to know the state lawmakers. Some reported knowing the state legislators but having no access to them. The FGD also agreed that there was poor communication between the state legislators and the voters in their constituencies. Most members of the state assemblies became distant after they got into office. Most people noted that they did not know the number of legislations sponsored/supported by the legislators that could be said to have improved their lives. It was the consensus of the FGD that the state lawmakers performed below the expectation of the electorate, particularly in the areas of constituency service and representation.

State Houses of Assembly Elections in Borno State

Maiduguri LGA: Participation in the State House of Assembly Elections

Two major political parties, the PDP and ANPP emerged as the major contenders in the 1999 state assembly elections in Borno State. In Maiduguri, the state capital, where the Kanuri are in the majority, those contesting for the state assembly seats adopted different campaign strategies, including marching from street to street and organising rallies using the local languages of Kanuri and Hausa. While the men and women in Maiduguri participated actively as voters during the elections of 1999, 2003 and 2007, the youth wing of political parties participated actively in the campaigns. The smaller groups that were formed by the youth and, in some cases women, had the financial backing of politicians and political parties in the state. Some of the youth groups such as the 'ECOMOG', named after the Economic Community of West African States (ECOWAS) Monitoring Group, were rather used by the politicians for their 'personal security'. Some of the politicians seeking election into the State House of Assembly moved around with the 'ECOMOG' boys to protect themselves from political opponents. The ANPP, PDP and AD presented candidates for the 1999 State Assembly elections in Maiduguri. In the case of the 2003 and 2007 elections, majority of the political parties did not have candidates seeking election. In the 2003 elections, the contest for State Assembly seats was more or less between the supporters of the former governor, Mallam Mala Kachalla, and the ANPP governorship candidate, Senator Ali Modu Sheriff. Those contesting the State House of Assembly maintained close alliance with the governorship candidates as a way of attracting more support from the people. This was the consensus of FGD in Maiduguri. The elections of 1999, 2003 and 2007 were characterised by various problems, such as the partisanship of election officials and security agencies, invasion by political thugs, under age voting and some cases of meddling by traditional rulers. Some voting centres were stationed either near or in front of the residence of traditional heads. The ballot box of a centre in Borno was taken to the house of a traditional head, while people stood outside waiting. The presence of the INEC officials and security personnel at such centres did not make any difference.

Assessment of the Performance of the Legislators at the State Level

The FGD observed that most people in Maiduguri did not know the state legislators. As a result, most people whose inputs into the lawmaking process were not sought by the lawmakers made no contribution in this regard. The state lawmakers, after the elections, became distant from the people. Most people also lacked knowledge of the legislations that had been sponsored by their representatives at the state that could improve their lives. It was also the consensus of the FGD in Maiduguri that the state lawmakers performed below the expectation of the people between 1999 and 2007.

Konduga LGA: Participation in the State House of Assembly Elections

The FGD noted that the people of Konduga LGA participated more actively in the 1999 and 2003 elections than in 2007. The majority of the participants in the elections who were card-carrying members of political parties were men. With the exception of a few, most women who participated as voters were not members of any political party in Konduga LGA. The women interviewed observed that the dominance of men in politics could be seen in the composition of Borno State House of Assembly. Some were of the opinion that politicians were not to be trusted because they never keep the promises made to the electorate; hence the lack of interest in politics by the electorate. The FGD in Konduga pointed out that elections conducted in the local government were characterised by challenges. Some of those encountered on the Election Day actually stemmed from the nature of political campaigns such as the unhealthy competition between and within the various political parties, and name calling among politicians and party supporters. The partisanship of some electoral officials at the local government level further compounded the problems. It was the consensus of the FGD that those seeking election as state legislators used various forms of inducement, including money, to solicit for votes. The youth who had participated actively in the political rallies and campaigns, some of whom were under-aged, took part as voters in the elections. Some electoral officials were suspected to be members of the ruling party posted to do the bidding of the government in the local government. There were also clashes in some areas between the supporters of the PDP and ANPP. The FGD agreed that some of the state legislators declared winners in the 1999, 2003 and 2007 did not win the elections. The 2007 elections were described as the worst in the local government since the return to democracy in 1999. Politicians desperate for political offices employed every possible means, including the use of political thugs and influencing security officials, to intimidate voters unwilling to vote for them.

Assessment of the Performance of the Legislators at the State Level

The FGD in Konduga LGA was of the opinion that the performance of members of the state house of assembly was not different from members of the national assembly in terms of consultation and involvement of the people in the governance of their own affairs. The state legislators were rated poorly in the area of rendering constituency services such as assisting the people with community development, immunization, roads, schools and farming implements. Most people saw the state lawmakers as controlling very large finances. Generally, there was poor communication between the state legislators and their constituencies. However, the state legislators visit their constituencies more frequently during campaigns and when seeking re-election. Most people also lack knowledge of any legislation sponsored/ supported by their legislators since coming into office. Some legislators are said to have scholarship programmes and other support programmes such as free medical tests and drugs, for the less privileged, however, only a few were able to access the services. The state legislators were said to have performed poorly between 1999 and 2007.

Bama LGA: Participation in the State House of Assembly Elections

The youth in Bama LGA were generally attracted to political activities, especially campaign and elections activities. Sometimes, the people abandoned their farming or trading activities, which majority of them are engaged in, during campaigns and elections. Participation was said to be lower in the 1999 elections than in 2003. In the 1999, 2003 and 2007 elections, with the exception of those seeking political offices and party members, others participated as voters. Unlike the 1999 State Houses of Assembly elections where all the political parties were represented, in the 2003 and 2007 elections, some political parties did not have candidates seeking to be elected to the State House of Assembly. The 1999 elections were contested by three political parties, while the 2003 elections had about thirty political parties and by 2007 the number had increased. Some reported that their names were omitted in the voters register in spite of the fact that they had registered as voters. Some politicians took advantage of the high participation of the youth, some of whom were under aged and used them as political thugs. INEC officials did not prevent the under aged voters majority of whom had registered during the registration exercise from voting. It was the consensus of the FGD that candidates declared winners in the past elections of 1999, 2003 and 2007 could hardly be said to have won. The consensus was that politicians made efforts to outsmart each other by way of rigging the elections. The use of financial/material resources to influence the voters in Bama appeared a normal process and fits a pattern where the candidates with more financial resources and who rigged most are usually declared winners. The FGD observed that in the 2007 elections, the conduct of the elections was compromised as a result of the partisanship of INEC officials and some security agencies who supported particular candidates and political parties.

Assessment of the Performance of the Legislators at the State Level

The FGD observed that most people in Bama did know the names of their legislators, even those who were popular during campaigns, and have very low opinion of most of them in terms of performance especially in the area of constituency service. This is apart from the other problems of effective representation, application of people-friendly laws, oversight functions and corruption. Even though these questions were not posed in these exact words, the FGD did allude to problems of governance, representation and corruption. But given that these were grassroots people, this could not be substantiated. What we documented here are true reflections of the information obtained from the FGD. Most members of the FGD also point out that they did not have access to the legislators. As such they lacked opportunity to make input into the laws made by their representatives. Most people in the local government were not aware of the number of constituency projects executed by legislators at the state level since the return to democracy in 1999. Against this background, the state legislators were said to have performed below the expectation of the electorate.

Conclusion

From the foregoing, it could be said that the struggle to institutionalise representative democracy in Nigeria as a whole, and at the state level in particular, through the conduct of elections has been fraught with shortcomings. This was particularly revealed in the examination of elections of 1999, 2003 and 2007 conducted for the State Houses of Assembly. The state legislature, as we noted, is a replica of the national assembly that operates within the jurisdiction of the powers assigned to it by the 1999 Constitution. Since the local governments and state assemblies are potentially closer to the people at the grassroots level, their participation in governance is key to the consolidation of democracy in the country. However, our examination of the State Houses of Assembly elections conducted in 1999, 2003 and 2007 showed that elections have proved to be unhelpful as a reliable way for citizens to choose individuals to represent them, and also as a platform to choose among laws to be made by their representatives and implemented at the state level for the development of the states.

Our findings show that although the electorate generally have different reasons for participating in elections, the failure to conduct free and fair elections for the State Houses of Assembly, and other elective positions, could lead to loss of faith in the system and create dissatisfaction with democracy (Alemika 2007:11). In some states such as Borno, where the youth took active part in the state assembly elections campaigns, the politicians took advantage of their involvement to recruit underaged voters and political thugs to intimidate opponents during the elections. Our findings also show that electoral officials as well as security personnel tended to be partisan in the conduct of the state assembly elections. The desperation by the politicians to secure elective seats in the state assemblies in the country has tended to increase the struggles for these positions in form of 'competitive rigging', thus reducing the elections to a situation where the candidates and parties that rig most are declared winners (Ibrahim 2007; Kurfi 2005).

In terms of performance of the state legislators, the study noted from the FGD, interviews and discussions that most of the state legislators do not maintain close contact, communication and interaction with the people after elections. Constituency offices tended to become active only during electoral campaigns and elections proper. In some cases, the representatives do not maintain functional constituency offices. The study reveals that a wide representational gap exists between the state legislators and their constituencies. It also reveals that there is a general mistrust of state legislators as rather self serving. The wide consensus of the FGDs in Borno, Plateau and Lagos states are that most of the people are not aware of legislations initiated/ supported by their state representatives. The electorate even rate most of their legislators lower in the area of constituency services and involvement in community developments. Even in the few instances where the legislators were said to have made efforts to fulfil their campaign promises, the services provided are accessible to only a few. Generally, as pointed out by respondents from the FGD, interviews and discussions, the State Assembly elections are not given adequate attention in terms of preparation by the elections management bodies as well as political parties and the active participation of the electorate. Some of the candidates seeking election to the state house of assembly, lacking adequate party support rely on political financiers and god-fathers to attain their goals. Indeed, this appears to be the case at all levels of political contest from the Presidency to the local government elections.

The elections that produce members of the state legislature are fundamental since they also determine the quality of governance and development at the state level. State elections therefore ought to be not only competitive, free and fair, and inclusive of all stakeholders at the state level, but should also, in the true sense, provide an avenue for the concrete expression of peoples' choices and their representatives, as well as their participation in governance.

References

Akinbobola, A., 2003, 'The Nigerian Political Party System and the 2003 General Elections', in Anifowoshe R. and Babawole T, eds, *2003 General Elections and Democratic Consolidation in Nigeria*, Lagos: Fredrich Ebert Stiftung (FES).

Akinboye, S., 2004, 'Nigeria's 1999 Multiparty Elections: An Overview of Electoral Con- duct and Results', in Olurode L. and Anifowoshe R. eds, *Issues in Nigeria's 1999 General Elections* Lagos: Rebonik Publications

Alabi, M.O., 2008, 'The Electoral Act 2006 and the Conduct of 2007 Elections in Ni- geria', in Saliu, H.A. et al., *Nigeria Beyond 2007: Issues, Perspectives and Challenges*, Ilorin: Faculty of Business and Social Sciences, University of Ilorin.

Alabi, M.O., 2009, 'The Legislatures in Africa: A Trajectory of Weakness', *African Journal of Political Science and International Relations*, Vol. 3 No.5, May.

Alemika, E. E., 2007 Quality of Elections, Satisfaction with Democracy and Political Trust in Africa, Afrobarometer Working Paper No. 84.

Ali, W.O., 1998, 'Development of Legislative Practice in Nigeria', in Tyoden, S ed. *Legis- lators and the Legislature,* Jos: Sikitse Consults.

Anifowoshe, R. and Babawale T., 2003, *2003 General Elections and Democratic Consolida- tion in Nigeria*, Lagos: Fredrich Ebert Stiftung (FES).

Bratton, M., 2008, Do Free Elections Foster Capable Governments? The Democracy Governance Connection in Africa, *Afrobarometer* Working Paper No. 104.

Dudley, B. J., 1982, *An Introduction to Nigerian Government and Politics,* London: Macmillan.

Fawole, W.A., 2005, 'Voting Without Choosing: Interrogating the Crisis of Electoral Democ- racy in Nigeria', In Lumumba-Kasongo T., ed., *Liberal Democracy and the Critics in Africa: Political Dysfunction and the Struggle for Social Progress,* Dakar: CODESRIA.

Hamalai, L., 1996, The Legislative Process and the Political Empowerment of the Masses in Nigeria, *Nigerian Journal of Policy and Strategy*, Vol II, Nos. 1 & 2, June/ December.

Ibrahim, J., 2007, 'Nigeria's 2007 Elections: The Fitful Path to Democratic Citizenship', United States Institute of Peace, Special Report 182 January. (http//: www.usip.org) 13 June, 2008.

Ibrahim, J., 2003, *Democratic Transition in Anglophone West Africa*, The CODESRIA Monograph Series, Dakar: CODESRIA.

Kurfi, A, 1983, *The Nigerian General Elections of 1959 and 1979 and the Aftermath*, Lagos: Macmillan Nigeria publishers.

Kurfi, A., 2005, *Nigerian General Elections 1951–2003: My Roles and Reminiscences*, Abuja: Spectrum Books.

Mohammed, S.B, 2001, 'Mismanagement, Leadership Crises and Instability in Nigeria's National Assembly, June 1999-May 2001', A Paper Presented at a Conference on 'Democracy and Democratisation', organised by CDRT Mambayya House, Kano 28-30 May.

Nwabueze, B.O, 1993, 'The Electoral Process and the 1989 Constitution', in Umezulike, I.A. ed., *Democracy: Beyond the Third Republic*, Enugu: Fourth Dimension Publishers.

Obi, C., 2008, *No Choice but Democracy: Pricing the People out of Politics in Africa?* Claude Ake Memorial Papers, No. 2. Nordic Africa Institute Uppsala.

Obiyan, A.S., 2007, 'An Evaluation of the Role of the Legislature as an Institutional Actor in Nigeria's Democratic Process in the Fourth Republic (1999-2006)', in Anifowose, R and Babawale, T. eds. *Nigeria Beyond 2007: Issues, Challenges and Prospects*, Lagos: Concept Publishers.

Okoosi-Simbine, A. T., 2008, 'Elections and Development: Nigeria and Indonesia in Comparative Perspective', Paper presented at the *First Plenary Meeting of Tracking Development*, Leiden, 25-28 June 2008.

Osaghae, E. E., 2002, *Crippled Giant: Nigeria since Independence*, Ibadan: PEFS.

Sha, D. P., 2005, 'Too Much Politics, Too Little Democracy: Assessing the Quality of Nigerian Democratic Transition Project', *Nigerian Journal of Policy and Strategy*, Vol. 15, Nos. 1 and 2, December.

Sha, D. P., 2006a, 'Election Observation Missions and the 2003 Nigerian Elections: Successes, Challenges and Lessons for 2007', in Olawale, A. I., Marco, D. and Adetula, V. O., eds, *Towards the 2007 Elections: Perspectives on 2003 Elections in Nigeria*, Abuja: Institute of Democracy.

Sha, D. P., 2006b, 'Vote Buying and the Quality of Democracy', Adetula, V. O et.al eds. *Money, Politics and Corruption in Nigeria*, Abuja: International Fund for Electoral Support (IFES).

Tamuno, T.O, 1972, *The Evolution of the Nigerian State: The Southern Phase, 1898-1914*, London: Longman.

The 1999 Constitution of the Federal Republic of Nigeria, Abuja: Federal Ministry of Information.

TMG 2003, *Do Votes Count? Final Report of the 2003 General Elections in Nigeria*, Abuja: TMG.

TMG 2007, *An Election Programmed to Fail: Final Report of the April 2007 General Elections in Nigeria*, Abuja: TMG.

Yaqub, N., 2004, 'The Military, Democratic Transitions, and the 1999 Elections', in Olurode L. and Anifowose R. eds., *Issues in Nigeria's 1999 General Elections*, Lagos: Rebonik Publications.

6

A Review of the National Assembly Elections

Sharkdam Wapmuk

Introduction

The legislature is a crucial institution of democracy. Its function is defined in terms of lawmaking, representation and oversight responsibilities, all of which are necessary for democratic governance. This chapter examines the conduct of elections for the legislature at the national level and the implications for governance in Nigeria between 1999 and 2007. It argues that the problems associated with the electoral process and elections have direct impact on the performance of democratic institutions such as the legislature. The nature and character of the elections conducted in 1999, 2003 and 2007 for the legislature, as well as other elective positions, have raised serious questions about democratic governance in Nigeria. It has raised questions about the character of individuals purportedly elected to represent the people and the need to hold the executive accountable.

The legislature, no doubt, occupies a central position in the process of governance. This is more so for a democratic polity where the legislature is supposed to provide the most comprehensive platform for citizens' participation in the governance of their own affairs. However, the legislature has been described as 'a trajectory of weakness' (Alabi 2009: 233; Tyoden 1998: ii). This situation is not only peculiar to Nigeria, but has also been observed in other African countries and many other countries of the world. Alabi (2009) argues that the weakness of the legislature in terms of powers to act is evident when compared to the powers of both the executive and judicial arms of government. While colonialism and military rule contributed in no little way to the weakening of the legislature as an institution of governance in Nigeria, the quest for political power, which is seen by the dominant class as a guarantee for unlimited and uncontrollable access to the resources of the state, which in turn is appropriated for personal use, has produced questionable characters as legislators, governors, as well as other political office holders. This has significantly diluted the intended purpose of representative democracy. The manner in which politicians in Nigeria conceive of it is in the Hobbessian art of capturing state power and using it in a domineering manner, and not necessarily for public good. This is the characteristic nature of politics in the post-colonial Nigerian state.

Some have argued that Nigeria's post-colonial state is under the control of a dominant class which inherited political power from the colonial powers at independence (Ake 1981). The dominant class has subordinated the state to its class interest. This class does not only subordinate the state in order to build its own economic power, but also has used its position to control the state. Onuoha (2003: 48) argues that 'the dominant instrument for controlling the state is political power and that the acceptable avenue for winning political power is through elections'. This, to a large extent, explains why the dominant political class views elections as a 'do-or-die' affair in order to maintain control of state power. Ake (1994) further notes that activities of the state have become over-politicised and political stakes have become too high and state activities are thus defined in this context in terms of political power and elections. The postcolonial state, by its very nature, is therefore not disposed to democratisation and the conduct of free and fair elections. Instead, as observed by Joseph (1991), the state is deeply entrenched in the politics of prebendalism. This was particularly observed during the era of military rule when the leadership was surrounded by a small circle of civilian cronies who largely served the interest of the military elite that had no interest in democratic rule and good governance. This military elite and the dominant class, did everything within its power to prevent the institutionalisation of elections and democracy in the country. It is against this background that we critically examine the conduct of National Assembly elections of 1999, 2003 and 2007.

We begin by exploring the theoretical perspectives and some concepts on elections and governance. We also discuss the methodology and proceed to examine the electoral system, legal framework and the electoral playing field, including the legislative election campaigns which exposed the way politicians struggle to occupy political offices in Nigeria. In addition, we examine the participation of the electorate in the elections of 1999, 2003 and 2007 and the performance of the legislators. Issues such as participation in the campaigns and elections, level of participation, representation of political parties, and whether the electorate was given any form of inducement to vote as well as problems encountered during the elections of 1999, 2003 and 2007 are examined. These form the subject of the first part of the assessment. The second part dwells on the performance of representatives in governance. We focus on the access of electorates to the legislators after elections, knowledge of legislation(s) sponsored/supported by the legislators since assuming office, availability of constituency offices, number of constituency projects and the rating of performance from 1999 to 2003, 2003 to 2007 and 2007 and beyond.

The case studies were drawn from three states in the country. These are Plateau State in the North Central, Borno State in the North East and Lagos State in the South West. The main justification for the purposive selection of these states is the desire to engage the stakeholders as closely as possible. This enabled us to do a critical examination of the elections conducted in these states with a view to gaining deeper understanding of the character of elections conducted in Nigeria in 1999, 2003 and 2007. This is with particular reference to the elections into the national assembly. The second reason for the choice of the three states is financial constraints, which limited our selection of not more than three states for the study.

The legislative institution was suffocated out of existence by past military regimes in the country. Among the first actions of military regimes in the country was the dissolution of pre-existing democratic structures, of which the legislature was the greatest casualty. The judicial arm of government is allowed to exist, even though as an instrument of state coercion, to give some semblance of commitment to governance under the law. On the other hand, the executive arm of government tends to gain strength under military administration (Alabi 2009:233). The military rulers through the Supreme Military Council (SMC) or by whatever other name called, wielded both legislative and executive powers, and sometimes even judicial powers. In such a situation, the legislatures could not but be weakened as a key governance institution.

Ideally, the legislature should offer the most comprehensive platform for citizens' participation in the governance of their own affairs. This is made possible only through the election of candidates of their choice to represent them at various levels such as in the National Assembly as 'Representatives' or 'Senators'. Kurfi (1983:259) observed that a representative democracy 'absolutely depends upon the integrity of elections'. Thus, elections and their outcomes have implications for democratic consolidation and governance. Problems associated with the electoral process and elections, therefore, has direct impact on the performance of democratic institutions like the legislature.

The majority of Nigerians are often called out, intimidated and even blackmailed into voting for specific candidates at elections, including representatives, who have been pre-selected for them, which may not necessarily reflect their choices (Fawole 2005:149). Once elected into office, members of the legislature become remote and distanced from the people that elected them and operate conveniently without them. After many years of military rule, Nigerians expected that with the return to democratic rule in 1999, the political space would be widened for their participation in governance and that, through elections, they could genuinely choose their representatives. They also expected their representatives to advance the interests of the electorate, ensure social justice and ensure a more equitable distribution of resources to the ordinary people through a transformational process that empowers them.

While the broad theme of this study is elections and governance in Nigeria, this chapter specifically focuses on the actual conduct of elections into the National Assembly. It seeks to understand the role of the state, the challenges of conducting the elections and the implications for governance.

Methodological and Theoretical Perspectives

Sources of Data and Information

This study draws extensively from primary and secondary materials/data to examine elections and governance in Nigeria, particularly the conduct of National Assembly elections. The study combines opinion sampled from face-to-face interviews with lawmakers, officials of INEC, individuals, and FGD with voters. The assessment of the participation of the electorate in the 1999, 2003 and 2007 elections as well as the performance of the legislators were based largely on (but not limited to) data drawn from the FGDs. The latter were held in three states, namely, Plateau State in the North Central, Borno State in the North East and Lagos State in the South West.

Three local government areas were also selected in each of the states – Plateau State has 17 Local Government Areas (LGA) and is ethnically and religiously diverse. Jos-North, the administrative capital fits into this description more than the other local government areas. Three LGAs were selected for FGDs. In Plateau State they include: Jos-South (Urban), Jos-North (Urban) and Barkin Ladi (Rural). The FGD for Barkin Ladi LGA were held with 14 participants in attendance: eight males and six females out of which twelve were farmers and two workers with the LGC. The FGD for Jos-South LGA had 16 participants in attendance, out of which 10 were males and 6 females, 2 Muslims and 14 Christians. The FGD for Jos-North LGA had in attendance 12 persons, 8 were males and 4 males; 3 were Muslims and 9 Christians. Borno State which has 27 LGAs is also ethnically and religiously plural. The FGD was held in three local government areas: Maiduguri (Urban), Bama (Urban) and Konduga (Rural). The FGD held in Konduga LGA had in attendance 10 participants, mostly farmers (6) local traders (2) and local government workers (2). The FGD for Bama LGA had in attendance 10 participants out of which 9 were males and 1 female. The FGD for Maiduguri LGA had in attendance 12 participants. Ten of the participants were male, while two were females, all of whom were civil servants. Lagos State has 20 LGAs and is the most ethnically and religiously diverse State in the country. Lagos State was the administrative capital of Nigeria before it was relocated to Abuja. The FGD for Lagos State was held in Somolu, Lagos Mainland and Eti-osa LGAs. The FGD held in Somolu LGA had in attendance 10 participants – 6 males, 4 females. The FGD for Lagos Mainland LGA had 11 persons in attendance – 9 males and 2 females. All were within the voting age of 18 years and above. The FGD for Eti-osa LGA had in attendance

10 participants – 5 males and 5 females (made up of civil servants, businessmen, women and students). Discussions were also held with individuals, journalists, civil society activists   and community groups. Information derived from the review of relevant texts, journals, magazines, newspapers, official publications and historical documents were analysed through content analysis. Each of these methods provided us with deeper understanding of the efforts by the people to choose their representatives, their participation in elections, expectations from legislators and the performance of the legislators. It also revealed the character of elections management by INEC and the competition, intrigues, and methods employed by politicians to secure and retain power at various levels, including the National Assembly.

Democratic Theory

This study finds its theoretical anchorage in the popular democratic theory as the preferred form of democratic governance. This is opposed to the liberal or just social democratic theory, which could equally be non-inclusive; it is people-centred in a way that is rooted in the ethos and culture of the people and able to meet the needs and material conditions of the people. Nevertheless, at the heart of the democratic theory lies the notion of a system of rule and authority that is derived from the people and also accountable to them. Generally, democratic theory denotes the idea and practices of democracy to include some continual mediation between collective self-determination and individual self-determination of particular citizens (O'Donnell 2001). It follows that some kind of equality of participation and discourse is needed for this mediation, so that citizens can feel that their own agency in political matters can potentially have an effect in the larger society. Individuals possess political will which they seek to actualise through active participation. With respect to the legislature, the democratic theory argues that the people should be the authors of the laws that apply to them, and not just be at the receiving end. Obviously, if conditions are such that citizens feel that they can make no impact, and that laws are made by those who in no way seem to take heed of their views, then the ideals of such democratic government are called to question.

Actually the literature on democracy offers a wide range of competing explanations on what democracy ought to be. While some view democracy as a form of government, others see it from the perspective of procedure of arriving at decisions that have implications on individuals and the society. These issues are amplified by the liberal and participatory theories. While liberal democratic theories advocate the idea of decision-making powers to representatives, participatory theories advocate that citizens vote directly on political issues. Ake (1993a:243) was particularly critical of liberal democratic emphasis on individualism as against the African democracy which, according to him, offers a form of political participation that is based on the social nature of human beings (Obi 2008). He further observed that since liberal democracy and the market share the same values, liberal democracy has been trivialized to the extent that real participation has lost its pride of place and is thus reduced to a form of dictatorship of the bourgeoisie. He was most critical of 'electoralism' which, he argues, disempowers African people. While Ake's thoughts on liberal democracy are apt, the reality however is that the direct form of democracy, which he subscribes to, is quite complex and difficult to operate due to the nature of modern society (Agbaje and Adejumobi 2006:27).

Unlike the liberal democratic theory which places much emphasis on individualism, participatory theory of democracy places emphasis on the principle of majority participation. Essential principles such as political equality, majority rule, 'common good', fall into the tradition of participatory democracy. Hence the focus of this study is on elections of the legislature at the national level. Here, a discussion on representation is imperative. The idea of political representation may be found in social contract theories, in which the governmental power was justified in terms of the delegation of powers by individuals to a representative(s). This brought about representatives as the link between 'the will of the people' and 'the will of the state'. According to this theory, individual citizens transfers their governmental power to a representative who then votes on legislation according to the will of the majority or the common good. To ensure that the representative actually follows the will of the people, representative democracy developed the practice of electoral accountability that holds representatives responsible for their actions during elections. However, the idea that elections serve to hold representatives accountable has been refuted by scholars (Ake 2000; Fawole 2005:150; Adejumobi 2000). In the words of Ake, voting does not necessarily amount to choosing. As observed in the Nigerian environment, electoral choices are made outside the orbit of electoral norms, rules and procedures. It is against this background that the study will examine the elections into the legislature at the national level in 1999, 2003 and 2007.

Definitions of the Key Concepts: Elections and Governance

Elections

It is important to clarify the meaning of the key concepts as used in this study. Elections are properly regarded as the core institution of any democratic government. This is because in a democracy, the authority of the government derives from the consent of the governed and not the other way around. Elections are, therefore, the primary mechanism for obtaining and translating the consent of the governed into governmental authority. Elections involve a complex set of activities with different variables that act and feed on one another. Key (1978) defined elections as a 'formal act of collective decision that occurs in a stream of connected antecedent and subsequent behaviour'. The study adopts the submission of Nwabueze (1993) that democratic elections are expected to be not only competitive, periodic, inclusive, and definitive, but also free and fair. The significance of election is that it provides an avenue for the concrete expression of the attributes of democratic governance, which includes choice, participation and accountability. It involves the choice of people in the act of electing their leaders and their own participation in governance. Elections are not necessarily about the Election Day activities, although they form an important component. Elections include activities before, during and after elections. They include the legal and constitutional frameworks of elections, the registration of political parties, party campaigns, the activities of the electronic and print media in terms of access; they include campaign financing, the activities of the security agencies and the government in power. They also include the authenticity and genuineness of the voters register, and the independence, or lack of it, of electoral agencies and organs. of course, they also include the liberalism or otherwise of the political process in the country and the independence of adjudicating bodies of elections.

Governance

Different definitions and concepts of governance exist. Governance may be broadly defined as a process that facilitates the use of political power or collective power for the management of public affairs. Kaufmann, Kraay, and Mastruzzi (2004:4) defined governance as 'the traditions and institutions by which authority in a country is exercised'. Governance therefore include: the process by which governments are selected, monitored and replaced; the capacity of the government to effectively formulate and implement sound policies; and the respect of citizens and the state for the institutions that govern economic, political and social interactions among them. The process of governance takes place within a geographical setting and is shaped by many factors such as the historical realities, traditions and values, resources, competition and ethnic composition of the geographical area. Just as there is good governance, there is also bad governance. While there are universally accepted principles of good governance especially as articulated by donor institutions such as the World Bank and IMF, the same cannot be said of bad governance. The study adopts an operational meaning of governance as the means by which power is acquired and used in the management of public affairs in a most effective and efficient manner. The legislature is an institution that ensures effective governance by lawmaking and by maintaining a system of checks and balances on government. It does that by checking public expenditures, appointments, articulating the views of the people, and compelling the government to ensure accountability to the people. The manner in which collective power is acquired affects the legitimacy of governance. Our concern here is the acquisition of collective power through democratic elections and its use by representatives of the people.

History of Elections and Development of the Legislature in Nigeria

Elections and the legislative institution in Nigeria grew side-by-side out of agitations against non-involvement of Nigerians in the governance of their country. The British colonial power was not interested in giving franchise to Nigerians until various Pan-African movements started demanding for equal rights for the people of the colonies (Tamuno 1972:127). The activities of bodies such as the National Congress of British West Africa (NCBWA), formed in Accra in 1920, the West African Students Union (WASU), as well as the role played by pan-African nationalists such as Caseley Hayford, W.E.B Du Bois, Marcus Garvey and many others were instrumental in inspiring nationalist agitations in Nigeria. From the outset the British did not grant limited franchise for altruistic reasons but to douse the agitations that were growing across the country. The emergence of the first Legislative Council in Nigeria dates back to the pre-World War I period. The first of such was the Nigerian Council that was brought about by the Supreme Court Ordinance of 1913, which was composed of wholly European appointees of Sir Frederick Lugard. This Council possessed almost no legislative powers because it was largely constituted to advise the governor (Alabi 2009:235).

The lack of involvement of Nigerians led to agitations for inclusion. Their demands were for greater representation based on population and election. All these led to the introduction of Elective Representation in the Legislative Council for Lagos and Calabar in 1922 by Sir Hugh Clifford. That notwithstanding, the elective principle of 1922 was very restrictive, as it was not based on universal adult suffrage. It was rather based on income suffrage, as only adult males with a gross income of not less than £100.00 could vote. Despite its shortcomings, the introduction of elective principle in Nigeria in 1922 encouraged the formation of political parties. For instance, the Nigerian National Democratic Party (NNDP) that was formed by Herbert Macaulay and other leading nationalists participated in the first elections into the legislative council in 1923.

The next elections in the country took place in 1947 following the introduction of Arthur Richards Constitution which established, for the first time, a Central Legislature for the country. However, out of the 24 members of the Central Legislative body, only four were elected, three from Lagos and one from Calabar. The rest were either appointed or nominated by either the colonial authorities or the regional local authorities. A notable feature during this period was that ethnic groups and communities were used by the colonial governments, thus giving these groups or individuals a sense of ethnic consciousness (Nnadozie 2008: 50). This was part and parcel of the British policy of divide and rule or indirect rule (Okafor 1981). It was not long after that the interest and enthusiasm generated by the introduction of limited franchise began to wane when it became clear to the electorate and the African elected members that they could do very little by way of fulfilling election promises.

The Macpherson Constitution of 1951 introduced slight changes to that of Arthur Richards. In the 1952 elections, popular franchise was restricted at the regional level where voting took place only in the primary electoral colleges. Different electoral laws were applied in the regions. It was only in the East and North where every adult male tax payer was entitled to vote. In the West, acclamation was used to choose candidates at the primary college. The Central Legislature which was composed of 136 members was chosen through the Electoral College System. Though the Macpherson Constitution of 1951 did not formally recognize political parties, the leaders of political parties with the greatest followers in the respective regions had stronger advantage in taking the seats provided for the regions by the Constitution (Okafor 1981).

The Lytleton Constitution of 1954 recognized political parties and introduced the party system. It also provided for separate elections into the regional and central legislature, but continued the system of operating different electoral laws for the three regions. In the east, universal adult suffrage for persons over 21 years was stipulated; in the north, voting was by indirect college system and only for adult male tax payers; and in the west, only adult males who paid taxes could vote. During this period, the emerging political party and support were ethnically and regionally inclined. This was noted in the regional drawn support of the three major political parties – the National Council for Nigeria and Camerouns (NCNC), Northern People's Congress (NPC) and the Action Group (AG) – led, respectively, by Dr Nnamdi Azikiwe, Alhaji Tafawa Balewa and Chief Obafemi Awolowo. The 1959 federal elections was the last to be conducted under the direct supervision of the British colonial authorities. In the East, the NCNC won 58 seats and the AG 14; while NPC won a seat. In the West, the AG won 33 seats; the NCNC won 21 and the Independent 8. In the North, the NPC won 134 seats, the AG 25, NEPU 8 and Independents 7. The result of the elections showed that out of a total of 312 seats in the Federal House, the NPC won 134; the NCNC 81 and the AG 73, Northern Elements Progressive Union (NEPU) 8, the Niger Delta Congress (NDC) 1 and other independent candidates 15. The elections witnessed not only intense campaigns by the various political parties to assert their dominance in their respective regions and at the federal House of Representatives, but also the results revealed the decisive role of ethnicity in Nigerian politics (Nnadozie 2008:55; Okafor 1981:224).

The colonial legislatures lacked independence and autonomy and this affected their effectiveness. In the circumstances, legislative chambers became mere avenues for articulation of anti-colonial and nationalist sentiments and not a platform for governmental accountability. The legislatures were treated by the colonial administrators as 'anti-government' and not as partners in the making of good governance. These perceptions have subtly coloured the executive-legislative relations in the post independence politics. This is simply a carry-over, however, in reality the ruling party, PDP have numerically dominated the

National Legislature, hence, one does not really expect a serious opposition to the Executive.

Constitutional development after independence largely reflected the pattern of the 1957 independence Constitution. Between 1960 and 1966, the Parliamentary System was practised in Nigeria. This system was described as weak. As observed by Alli (1998), the parliament in the first republic had no clear-cut role in policy making, instead, it seems Parliamentarians 'met seldom and merely approved what had already been decided rather than take part in meaningful debates' (Ali 1998: 15). After the seizure of power by the military in January 1966, decrees and edicts replaced the legislative acts at the federal and state levels. The federal parliament was replaced by the Supreme Military Council (SMC). This arrangement was adopted by the General Yakubu Gowon, General Murtala Muhammed and the General Olusegun Obasanjo regimes.

After thirteen years of military rule, the 1979 general elections were held and power transferred to civilian rulers in a transition that lasted from 1975 to 1979 From 1979 to 1983, the legislature existed under a new environment – the presidential system. In a sharp departure from the parliamentary system inherited from the British, the legislature – made up of the two chambers of the Senate and House of Representatives – was separate from the executive branch. However, on 31 December 1983, it was disbanded in a putsch headed by Major General Muhammadu Buhari. The regime, following the termination of civilian administration of Alhaji Shehu Shagari, adopted the Supreme Military Council as its legislative arm. It wasn't long after that General Ibrahim Babangida came in August 1985 and changed the Supreme Military Council to Armed Forces Ruling Council (AFRC). Under intense pressure to return the country to democratic governance, the military government under General Ibrahim Badamasi Babangida organised a series of elections in 1991. The elections saw the inauguration of state governors, state legislative houses and the National Assembly. The State Houses of Assembly were answerable to the governor, who reported to the military president. The National Assembly was answerable to the military head of state, who had earlier given instructions on what the Assembly could discuss and what it could not. Shortly before the Assembly was disbanded in 1993, the military, which had handed over power to a group of civilian nominees called the Interim National Government (ING), took over the reins of power again.

General Abacha who dislodged the Interim National Government of Chief Ernest Shonekan renamed the ruling organ as the Provisional Ruling Council (PRC). On the whole, the various military regimes have over the years undermined the development of the legislature as an institution of lawmaking, representation, accountability and the promotion of good governance. It is against this background that Nigeria's return to democratic rule on 29 May 1999 was generally seen as a landmark development. However, the conduct of elections for not only the parliamentarians, but also other elective positions, and their performance resulted in people asking more questions about the prospects of democracy in Nigeria.

The Structure and Functions of the National Legislature

The legislature at the federal level is made up of a National Assembly with two chambers, the Senate and House of Representatives. The Senate consists of 109 members and the House of Representatives has 360 members. Both houses are elected for a period of four years. The Senate consists of three Senators from each of the 36 states of the federation and one from the Federal Capital Territory (FCT), Abuja. Each state is divided into three senatorial districts to produce one senator per district. The 360 members of the House of Representatives are elected from 360 federal constituencies.

The Legislature in modern democracies performs four core functions that distinguish it from other arms of government. First, legislatures are the institutional mechanism through which societies realise representative governance. The main function of individual legislators and the body, to which they belong, is to represent the varied and conflicting interests extant in society as a whole. Secondly, the legislatures also legislate. This occurs at two levels – they pass laws and contribute to the making of public policy by crafting legislation in partnership with or independent of the executive. The third function is that of oversight of the executive to ensure that policies agreed upon at the time they are passed into laws are in fact implemented by the state. Fourthly, legislators acting individually are expected to perform the function of constituency service. Constituency services are in different forms and include regular visits by legislators to their districts to meet constituents and assist some with their individual needs. These could include involvement in small-to-medium-scale development projects that provide various forms of public goods roads, water supply systems, schools, health clinics, meeting halls, etc., to the residents of their district (Barkan 2007: 16). Among the four functions mentioned, the fourth presents the most daunting challenge where legislators have been found wanting by the electorate.

The Electoral System and Campaigns for the National Assembly Elections

The electoral system of Nigeria is historically patterned along the British system. This has been sustained since independence with minor adjustments. Based on the principle of First Past the Post (FPTP), the winning candidate is the person with the highest number of votes. The 1999 Constitution provides for the FPTP system for all levels of election, apart from the presidential and gubernatorial levels, where each must have a clear majority win of two-third of electoral areas (states or local government areas) (Sections 134 and 179 of the 1999 Constitution).

Those seeking legislative positions mostly staged their campaigns at party offices in their respective constituencies and reach out to a network of influences and institutional support. Some placed high premium on religious, ethnic and group affiliations to mobilise voters. Campaigns also entailed visiting traditional rulers and demonstrating loyalty to persons that could be of support either financially and/or in the mobilisation of political support. Most of the state governors as well as political godfathers were particularly targeted for such support. Compared to the 1999 and 2003 campaigns, the 2007 campaigns were quite active, characterised by public rallies, gathering at party offices, and at public centres in local governments. Campaigns also featured the use of billboards, posters, and mobilisation through the print and electronic media. Some media houses organised debates for candidates seeking elective positions. However, these debates tended to concentrate on the governorship aspirants than on those seeking legislative positions. In Plateau State, campaigns through the public and private media outlets included the call for peaceful co-existence among the different ethnic and religious groups in the state. This approach to campaign was against the background of several ethnic and religious crises that have occurred in the state since the return to democracy in 1999. Cases of violence were reported during the campaigns in Plateau, Borno and Lagos States, though with varying degree of intensity. During political campaigns, political thugs made up of mainly youth gangs, were reportedly recruited by some persons seeking elections to the National Assembly. On the whole the campaigns tended to focus more on the personality of the candidates seeking legislative positions than on critical policy and ideological issues about how to improve the wellbeing of their constituencies.

The National Assembly Elections

The period before the 1999 elections was characterised by uncertainty and intrigues following the past experiences when democratic experiments failed, and transitions were shifted and elections annulled (Akinboye 2004:136). However, the sustained efforts by the Abubakar government gave some assurance that the transition programme would usher in an elected government in 1999. Abubakar also kept faith by releasing a new political transition programme. Amongst others, the transition programme stipulated the date for National Assembly elections as 20 February 1999. Only three political parties that succeeded after the local government elections of 1998 and were officially registered presented candidates for elections for 109 senatorial seats. The results released by INEC showed that PDP had 59 seats, APP 24 and AD 20. In some areas, the National Assembly elections witnessed low voter turnout. For instance, some of the Igbo residents around Apo legislative quarters and mechanic village in Abuja refused to vote in protest of the presidential primaries of the PDP held in Jos, Plateau State. The primaries witnessed the emergence of a former military Head of State, Chief Olusegun Obasanjo as the PDP presidential candidate in 1999 (Agugua 2003:122).

The National Assembly election for the 2003 elections took place on 12 April 2003. Among other issues, the endless crisis and struggle between President Olusegun Obasanjo and the national legislature had set the stage for the texture of elections of 2003. After the 1999 elections, the legislative and executive arms of government were engaged in the contestation of power, with the legislature accusing the executive of interfering with its work. There was a determination by most of the incumbent legislators to remain in power at all cost, probably because of the perquisites of power (Onuoha 2003:57). Beginning with the registration process to the display of voters register, several problems were encountered such as outright lack of registration materials; lack of proper training of supervisory assistants, registration officers and assistant registration officers; insufficient registration centres; underage registration; hoarding and selling/buying of voters cards; late release of voters' lists as a result of problems encountered during the registration of the voters in 2002. As a result of the problems encountered during the registration of voters, the process had to be repeated in January 2003. At the end of the exercise, INEC had received 67.7 million applications for registration. However, only about 60 million voters were accepted due to the cancellation of cases of double registrations. Among the many problems encountered on election days were the late distribution of voter cards, late opening and sometimes early closure of polling units, interference by party agents who sometimes influenced voters and the direct involvement of state officials in some cases. The result declared by INEC shows that of 2,156,019 registered voters in Borno State for the 2003 National Assembly elections, total votes declared for the Senate stood at 886,742, while that of the House of Representatives stood at 877,875. For Lagos State, number of registered voters stood at 4,558,216, out of which 1,434,730 was for the Senate and 1,397,650 was for the House of Representatives; out of this result for Lagos, two representative constituency results remained outstanding. The national assembly elections in Plateau State showed that of 1,391,594 registered voters, total number of voters declared for Senate stood at 955,371 while that of the House of Representatives stood at 922,749.

The 2007 elections were the third elections to be held since the transition from military to civilian rule in 1999. The 2007 elections were considered a test case for Nigeria's commitment to strengthen and consolidate democracy. This was against the background of the problematic elections of 1999 and 2003. The National Assembly elections of 2007 took place on the 21 April on the same day (Ibrahim 2007). Election management proved to be a challenge for INEC which failed to draw lessons from the 1999 and 2003 elections. The administrative lapses on the part of INEC began right from the voters' registration exercises and permeated the entire conduct of the 2007 election. The introduction of the Direct Data Capture (DDC) system proved to be a difficult exercise for INEC, which required a total of 33,000 DDC machines for the registration exercise. However, the failure to secure the required number of machines to cover the exercise as well as the malfunctioning of the machines during the registration process due the mechanical and power problems led INEC to abandon the approach. INEC also failed to address problems observed in the previous elections such as underaged voters in several parts of the country and also problems of partisanship of some of its staff. It was alleged that INEC officials collaborated with party agents to thumb print unused ballot papers where the turn out for elections was low. The presence of security agencies such as the police, civil defence corps and others failed to deter these negative activities and behaviour. Angry citizens resorted to the blockage of INEC building and preventing INEC and presiding officers from delivering results.

The PDP was accused of rigging the election in several parts of the South West. Chief Abraham Adesanya, the AD/Afenifere leader accused former President Olusegun Obasanjo and the PDP of rigging the National Assembly elections in the South West and asked INEC to consider changing the electoral officials who were card-carrying members of the PDP. The outcome of election to the legislative houses in the 1999, 2003 and 2007 revealed the dominance of the PDP. The PDP, being in the majority in both the Senate and House of Representatives, produced the Senate President and Speaker of House of Representatives and their deputies (Akinbobola 2003:102). Many political parties did not grasp the importance of the legislature in an emergent democracy.

Assessment of the Conduct of the National Assembly Elections and Performance of the Legislature in Plateau State

Barkin Ladi LGA: Participation in National Assembly Elections

There were reports of low participation in the National Assembly elections in 1999 in many parts of Barkin Ladi LGA. The electorate was not sure that the transition programme would be concluded. This happened against the background of previous experiences where elections and transition programmes were either cancelled or shifted *ad infinitum*. Those who did not take part in the 2003 and the 2007 legislative elections observed that their votes would hardly make any difference, since the candidates they never voted for would still emerge winner. People participated less actively in the campaigns of 1999, than in 2003. Low participation during political campaigns was reported in 2007. Though some people participated as members of political parties, majority participated as voters. Some changed political parties in the 1999, 2003 and 2007 elections. The participants in the FGD in Barkin Ladi observed that all political parties were represented in the 1999 elections; however, not all were represented in the 2003 and 2007 elections. Some of the political parties had no candidates seeking election for legislative positions at the national level. Voter turnout was said to be higher for the 2003 elections than the 2007 elections for the National Assembly.

In some cases, politicians sought to use monetary inducemens to get voters to vote for them. The FGD observed that not all the national legislators declared as winners in elections of 1999, 2003 and 2007 actually won the elections. The most doubtful were candidates declared as winners in the 2007 elections which was said to have been extremely flawed. The elections were characterised by late arrival and shortage of materials, as well as the interference by state officials and political thugs.

Assessment of the Performance of the Legislators at the National Level

Most of the electorate interviewed said they had no access to their legislators. Some legislators who had constituency offices hardly visited theoffices. The offices only become vibrant during election campaigns or when political rallies are held. Most people had no knowledge of legislation sponsored/supported by their elected lawmakers that could improve their lives. Participants at the FGD were unaware of constituency projects executed by the elected legislators at the national level. Even though views differed on the actual performance of individual legislators, they were said to have performed below expectation by the electorate from 1999 to 2007.

Jos-South LGA: Participation in the National Assembly Elections

Though participation in the National Assembly elections was low in the elections of 1999, some people did not take part because they lacked interest. Some who participated and did not win believed that they were rigged out. Most people, who participated as voters, were not card-carrying members of any political party. Some reported leaving the PDP because it was hijacked by the state government and supporters of the state governor. The FGD in Jos-South observed that politicians seeking elective positions as national legislators were quite desperate for the office and would do anything to get there. Consequently, most of them devised different means to win at all costs, including the use of monetary inducement and employment of political thugs. Some candidates, especially women, complained of being denied party tickets after spending so much money on campaigns and mobilisation of the electorate. The women pointed out that the men held nocturnal meetings and this timing constrained the women from active participation in political party activities. Some of the women also accused the male politicians of using them to mobilise voters and to sing their praises only to dump them after campaigns. Some decided to team up with the candidates selected by the party, while others switched to a different political party. The FGD agreed that some of the legislators declared winners in the 1999, 2003 and 2009 elections did not actually win the elections. Some argued that the elections held in 2007 were characterised by competitive rigging. The elections of 1999, 2003 and 2007, in varying degrees, were characterised by problems of poor management, interference by state officials and clashes among political groups and parties supporting different candidates.

Assessment of the Performance of the Legislators at the National Level

The FGD noted that performance of the legislators at the national level was below the expectation of voters. Most voters lacked knowledge on how to access the law makers. Those who attempted to seek audience with them were rebuffed.

Political associates and cronies were said to have more access to the lawmakers than other voters. Most people were also unaware of the constituency projects executed by the lawmakers at the national level. Most were also unaware of legislation sponsored by the lawmakers that could be said to improve their lives.

Jos-North LGA: Participation in the National Assembly Elections

Discussions revealed that most people participated in the 1999, 2003 and 2007 elections as voters. While some reported not participating because of lack of interest, others said they did not know the candidates to vote for. Some voters that belonged to certain political parties switched political camps between 1999 and 2007. Whereas all political parties participated in the 1999 elections, however not all political parties participated in the 2003 and 2007 elections. Some of the political parties did not have candidates seeking elective positions on their platforms. The FGD observed that not all legislators declared winners at the national level actually won. Some seeking re-election in 2003 and 2007 were said to have rigged the elections with the support of the officials of the elections management body – INEC. The elections themselves were characterised by several problems, including political violence in some centres, especially where the supporters of PDP and ANPP clashed. The presence of security agencies made little or no difference to the activities of party agents who sought to influence voters, especially those seeking assistance during elections.

Assessment of the Performance of Legislators at the National Level

The electorate reportedly lacked access to the legislators and so made no input into the law making process. Some said they only saw the legislators when they came to seek re-election. Most electorate was also unaware of the sponsorship and/or support of legislation(s) by lawmakers representing them at the national level that could improve their welfare. As such, they were rated to have performed below expectation by the electorate especially in the area of consultation and constituency services.

Assessment of the Conduct of the National Assembly Elections and Performance of the Legislators in Borno State

Konduga LGA: Participation in the National Assembly Elections

The people in Konduga LGA participated in the 1999, 2003 and 2007 legislative elections for national level elections. However, more participation was reported in 1999 and 2003 than in 2007. Some said that they wanted nothing to do with 'democracy' and politicians because of their experience with politicians who failed to keep their promises. Several problems were encountered during campaigns and on election days. Politicians used money to buy votes from the people especially the youth who participated actively in the political rallies and campaigns. The youth was the most vulnerable because most of them were unemployed. Some electoral officials were reported to be members of the ruling party posted to do the bidding of the government in the local government. There were also clashes in some areas between the supporters of the PDP and the ANPP. The people expressed doubt whether the legislators declared winners in the 1999, 2003 and 2007 elections actually won. More problems were encountered in the 2007 elections than in the previous elections because some of the law makers wanted re-election by all means possible, including using political thugs and security officials to intimidate voters that were not willing to do their bidding.

Assessment of the Performance of the Legislators at the National Level

Most of the electorate did not know the number of constituency projects executed by their lawmakers. They lamented that the lawmakers hardly came to Konduga to consult with, and interact with them. Supposedly elected members at the national level were mostly at Abuja where people could hardly reach them, and they did not make themselves available to their constituencies. However, the legislators at national level were said to visit their constituencies more frequently during campaigns and when seeking re-election. Most people also had no knowledge of any legislation sponsored/ supported by their legislators since coming into office. Some legislators were said to have bought motorcycles for the youth and also distributed money to some women who supported and campaigned for them. Some were said to have supported the less privileged; however, only few people were able to access these benefits.

Bama LGA: Participation in the National Assembly Elections

With the exception of those who contested for political offices and party members, most of the people in Bama LGA participated as voters in the 1999, 2003 and 2007 elections. However, not all political parties were represented in the 2003 and 2007 elections. Some reported that their names were omitted in the voters register even though they were properly registered as voters. The participation of voters was reported to be higher in 2003 and 2007 than in 1999 because of the mobilisation of the youth in the area. Some of the youth that participated in the elections were reported to be under-aged and vulnerable to the manipulations of politicians. Some of the youth were also used as political thugs by those seeking legislative and other elective positions within the state. The INEC officials did nothing to prevent the under aged voters from voting during the elections. The

FGD observed that there was no need debating whether the candidates declared winners in the elections for legislative positions actually won or not because it was a case of competitive rigging. The candidates with more financial resources to mobilise and attract the support of voters, and/or who rigged most, were declared winners. Apart from monetary inducement, some of the youth were given motorcycles and women were equally mobilised through material inducements like, soap, salt, and clothes to support certain candidates. Several problems were encountered during campaigns and during elections. These included frequent clashes by supporters of political parties and candidates, late arrival of election materials, and the partisanship of some INEC officials.

Assessment of the Performance of the Legislators at the National Level

Some people claimed to know some of the legislators at the federal level, but had no means of reaching them. As such, they made little or no input into the laws initiated by their representatives. Most people in the local government were not aware of the number of constituency projects executed by legislators at the national level since the return to democracy in 1999. Against this background, the legislators were said to have performed below expectation.

Maiduguri LGA: Participation in the National Assembly Elections

Most people of voting age in Maiduguri participated in the 1999, 2003 and 2007 elections as voters and less in the campaigns. Apart from the political parties that were active in terms of the mobilisation of voters, there were a number of smaller groups that identified with candidates seeking elective positions. These groups that were mostly formed by the youths and women groups, participated actively in the campaigns and rallies organised by the candidates and political parties. The smaller groups were either financed by the political party or the candidate seeking a particular position. Some of these groups identified with those seeking elections into the legislature at national level. However, it was noted that most of these groups became moribund after the elections. Most people that were within the voting age (18 and above) and also those below the voting age (below 18) claimed to be members of political parties. All the political parties were represented in the National Assembly election in 1999. However, not all political parties were represented in the 2003 and 2007 elections. Some described the elections for the legislators and other positions in Maiduguri as a game of competitive rigging. Numerous problems were also encountered during the elections, including the late arrival of voting materials, under aged voting, the activities of political thugs and even the involvement of INEC officials in some cases of electoral irregularities.

Assessment of the Performance of the Legislators at the National Level

The FGD in Maiduguri was of the view that not all people actually knew their representatives in the National assembly nor had access to them. Most of the lawmakers connected with the people only during campaigns, but failed to sustain a line of interaction with the electorate after the election. The national legislators were particularly said to be far from the people, who, coincidentally, were ignorant of how to make inputs into the laws that affected their welfare. People were also unaware of any legislation sponsored by their representatives at the national level that could improve their lives. Overall the performance of the legislators was rated low by the FGD in Maiduguri LGA.

Assessment of the Conduct of the National Assembly Elections and Performance of the Legislators in Lagos State

Somolu LGA: Participation in the National Assembly Elections

Most people reported taking part in the 1999 elections because they were desirous of the military returning to the barracks. However, some did not participate in the elections especially in 2003 and 2007 because of disappointment with 'democracy' and the performance of the politicians. The majority reported participating in the elections, but not in the campaigns. Some pointed out that they did not know the candidates to vote for on election days. The campaigns by politicians seeking election into the national assembly were said to be low keyed compared to the gubernatorial and presidential elections. Some candidates seeking election as legislators at the national level were desperate and used every means to achieve their goals. Some argued that it was better to leave politics for the politicians who were desperate to be in office at all cost. They also argued that the actual candidate they voted for in previous elections was rarely declared the winner.

The 2007 elections were seen as the worst elections since the return to democratic governance in Nigeria in 1999. In addition to using monetary inducement, some politicians seeking election as legislators and other elective positions were said to have used political thugs to intimidate not only their opponents but also INEC officials in order to actualize their goals. It is questionable whether those declared winners in the 1999, 2003 and 2007 elections for the national assembly elections actually won. Many problems were encountered during the campaigns and on the election days. These included violence, activities of political thugs, the partisanship of state officials and some security agencies, particularly the police.

Assessment of the Performance of the Legislators at the National Level

People reported knowing some of their legislators and following some of the debates in the National Assembly. However, they argued that since they did not have access to the law makers, they could not contribute directly by making suggestions on how to improve the laws that affect them. The FGD in Somolu argued that though some of the lawmakers were said to have constituency projects such as scholarships schemes and other forms of support for the people, very few people knew about these and how they could access them due to poor communication between the legislators and the people.

Lagos Mainland LGA: Participation in the National Assembly Elections

Even though many participated in the 1999 elections, they were not very sure that the Abubakar transitional military government would be committed to handing over to a democratically elected government. The case of the annulled June 12 1993 elections and the lack of commitment on the part of previous military regimes to transition programmes, which they midwived only to abort at some point were cited as responsible for such doubt. However, more participation was reported in 2003 than in 2007. Most people participated more during elections than during campaigns. Some argued that since the campaigns are the activities of politicians and their supporters, they have no business being part of them. All political parties were represented in the 1999 National Assembly elections. Most political parties participated in the elections of 2003 and 2007 even through some of these political parties did not have candidates seeking elections for the National Assembly. The FGD observed that politicians used monetary and other forms of material inducement to solicit the votes of the electorate. There was scepticism about the authenticity of those declared winners in the elections as legislators at the national level in the 1999, 2003 and 2007 elections. Numerous problems were encountered in all three elections. These included poor management of elections by the electoral body, partisanship of some INEC officials, political intimidation by thugs and the interference of some influential persons and political financiers.

Assessment of the Performance of the Legislators at the National Level

People reported knowing some of their legislators but not having access to them. Those at the national level were particularly said to be distant from the people. Not many knew the number of legislations sponsored/supported by the legislators that could improve their lives. The legislators were said to have performed below the electorate's expectation.

Eti-osa LGA: Participation in the National Assembly Elections

Some people were reluctant to participate in the 1999 elections because of the previous experiences where the elections were either annulled or the transition programs shifted several times. The 2003 and 2007 elections witnessed lower participation because people were dissatisfied with the performance of the politicians. Some who contested but lost argued that they were rigged out by the richer and more influential candidates backed by political godfathers. Politicians, including those contesting for the elective positions, used various forms of inducement to secure votes. Several problems were equally encountered during campaigns and during elections, including the partisanship of some INEC officials, poor conduct of the elections and politicians that used political thugs to intimidate the electorate.

Assessment of the Performance of the Legislators at the National Level

The legislators hardly reach out to communicate with the people. Some people reported only seeing their representatives on TV. Most of them do not hold consultations with their constituencies to ascertain the views of the electorate concerning issues that affect them. Most people also reported lacking knowledge of legislations sponsored/supported by the legislators at the national levels that could improve their lives.

Conclusion

We have attempted in this chapter to examine the conduct of the 1999, 2003 and 2007 elections into the National Assembly and the implications for governance. This we have done against the background of the realities that led to the re-emergence of the legislature as an institution of democratic governance in Nigeria's fourth republic. The past military regimes in the country undermined institutions that were capable of checking their powers. The legislature suffered from reccurrent military bans, and emerged as a very weak institution as observed in the nature of electoral competition for the national legislature in 1999, 2003 and 2007. More attention tended to be focused on the gubernatorial and presidential campaigns and elections than those of the legislature. The study generally revealed the manner of competition among politicians struggling to occupy public offices by focusing on elections into the National Assembly. The politicians employed every possible means to achieve their political goals. These included manipulating the electoral process to increase their chances of emerging as party candidates, manipulating the registration of voters and the actual elections through brazen rigging, and influencing the election management body with the machinations of political godfathers and party financiers to achieve their goals.

The assessment of the participation of the electorate and the performance of the legislators in Plateau, Borno and Lagos States was quite revealing. The study noted from responses of the FGDs, interviews and discussions with major stakeholders that the electorate had low opinion of the elections and also questioned the outcome of the elections in respect of representatives that emerged from the process. The elections into the National Assembly held in 1999, 2003 and 2007 were described as anything but free and fair. The dissatisfaction of the electorate with the elections, as gleaned from the responses of the FGD, interviews and discussion, particularly implicated the 2007 elections describing it as the worst election conducted for the National Assembly since Nigeria returned to democratic rule in 1999. Findings of the study also revealed that unlike the elections of 1999, not all the political parties participated in elections of 2003 and 2007 because some of the political parties had no candidates contesting for seats in the National Assembly on their platforms. It also revealed that most voters in Nigeria do not participate in either the election of their representatives or in the governance of their own affairs by making inputs to the decision making process. The expectations of the electorate from the national legislators were not in concurrence with the tenets of democratic theory that people should own the process and participate actively in the governance of their own affairs. Voter expectations from the national legislators included good representation, the making and/or support of legislation that could improve the peoples' wellbeing, the involvement of the legislators in some form of constituency development and provision of constituency services – all of which turned to be pipe dreams.

Arising from this study is the realisation that politicians are yet to take the issue of legislative elections and their implications for governance of the country seriously, especially in respect of the representative and oversight functions the legislature is expected to perform. By realising that the character of election and the people elected to represent the people in the National Assembly are important for ensuring effective democratic representation and governance in the areas of law making, accountability, and efficient utilisation of resources, perhaps key political players and social actors will take the election of members of this institution more seriously. Since governance on the part of the legislators involve acting on behalf of the majority, the input of the people in the governance of their own affairs by ensuring their active participation in elections and thereafter in the democratic process will go a long way in the achievement of a more democratic polity.

References

Adejumobi, S., 2000, 'Elections in Africa: A Fading Shadow of Democracy?', *International Political Science Review*, Vol. 21, No. 1.

Agbaje, A., 2004, 'Prospects for the Fourth Republic', in E. Gyimah-Boadi, ed., *Democratic Reform in Africa: The Quality of Progress*, Boulder: Lynne Rienner Publishers.

Agbaje, A. and Adejumobi, S., 2006, 'Do Votes Count? The Travails of Electoral Politics in Nigeria', *Africa Development*, Vol. XXXI, No. 3.

Agugua, A., 2004, 'Elections Day', in Olurode, L. and Anifowoshe, R. eds., *Issues in Nigeria's 1999 General Elections,* Lagos: Rebonik Publications.

Ake, C., 1981, A Political Economy of Africa, London: Longman.

Ake, C., 1993a, 'The Unique Case of African democracy', *International Affairs,* Vol. 69, No. 2.

Ake, C., 1993b, 'Is Africa Democratising?' Guardian Annual Lecture, Guardian on Sunday, 12 December.

Ake, C., 1994, Democratisation of Disempowerment in Africa, CASS Occasional Monograph No 1.

Ake, C., 2000, *The Feasibility of Democracy in Africa*, Dakar: CODESRIA.

Akinbobola, A., 2003, 'The Nigerian Political Party System and the 2003 General Elections', in Anifowoshe, R and Babawole, T eds., *2003 General Elections and Democratic Consolidation in Nigeria*, Lagos: Fredrich Ebert Stiftung.

Akinboye, S., 2004, 'Nigeria's 1999 Multiparty Elections: An Overview of Electoral Conduct and Results', in Olurode, L. and Anifowoshe, R. eds., 2004 *Issues in Nigeria's 1999 General Elections, Lagos:* Rebonik Publications.

Alabi, M.O., 2008, 'The Electoral Act 2006 and the Conduct of 2007 Elections in Nigeria', in Saliu, H.A. et al eds., *Nigeria Beyond 2007: Issues, Perspectives and Challenges*, Ilorin: Faculty of Business and Social Sciences, University of Ilorin.

Alabi, M.O., 2009, 'The Legislatures in Africa: A Trajectory of Weakness', *African Journal of Political Science and International Relations*, vol. 3, No.5.

Ali, W.O., 1998, 'Development of Legislative Practice in Nigeria', in Tyoden, S. ed., Legislators *and the Legislature*, Jos: Sikitse Consults.

Ashanfa, A. A., 2009, 'Experimenting Separation of Powers and Oversight Functions in Nigeria's Democracy, 1999-2007'. *Development Review*, Volume 1, Number 1. Barkan, J.D., 2008, 'Legislative Development in Africa, in Conference Report, *Democratisation in Africa: What Progress toward Institutionalisation?*' US State Department/US Embassy Ghana and the Centre for Democratic Development (CDD).

Chukwu, P., 2007, 'The 1999 Constitution and the Independent Electoral Commission (INEC): Prospects for Impartial Supervision and Conduct of Elections', in Jega, A and Ibeanu, O eds., *Elections and the Future of Democracy in Nigeria*, Nigerian Political Science Association (NPSA).

Electoral Act, 2006 Electoral Act 2006, Lagos: Federal Government Printer.

European Union Report (Nigeria, 2003), Nigeria: Final Report of National Assembly Elections, 12 April 2003, Presidential and Gubernatorial Elections, 19, April 2003, and State Houses of Assembly Elections, May 2003, European Union Election Observation Mission.

European Union Report, Nigeria, 2007, Nigeria: Final Report of Gubernatorial and State Houses of Assembly Elections, 14 April 2007, and Presidential and National Assembly Elections, 21 April 2007, European Union Election Observation Mission.

Fawole, W.A., 2005, 'Voting Without Choosing: Interrogating the Crisis of Electoral Democracy in Nigeria', in Lumumba-Kasongo T. ed., *Liberal Democracy and the Critics in Africa: Political Dysfunction and the Struggle for Social Progress,* Dakar: CODESRIA.

Jinadu, L. A., 1997, 'Matters Arising: African Elections and the Problem of Electoral Administration', *African Journal of Political Science*, Vol. 2, No. 1.

Ibrahim, J., 2003, *Democratic Transition in Anglophone West Africa*. The CODESRIA Monograph Series, Dakar: CODESRIA.

Joseph, R., 1991, *Democracy and Prebendal Politics in Nigeria: The Rise and Fall of the Second Republic,* Lagos: Spectrum Books.

Kaufmann, D. Aart, K. and Massimo, M., 2004, 'Governance Matters III: Governance Indicators for 1996, 1998, 2000, and 2002', *World Bank Economic Review*, 18.

Key, V.O., 1978, '*A Theory of Critical Elections'* in Abbott, D and Rogowsky, E.T. eds. *Political Parties,* Chicago: McNaccy College Publishing.

Kurfi, A., 1983, *The Nigerian General Elections of 1959 and 1979 and the Aftermath,* Lagos: Macmillan Nigeria publishers.

Lewis, P., 2003, 'Nigeria: Elections in a Fragile State', *Journal of Democracy,* Vol. 14, No. 3.

Mazrui, A., 2000, 'The African Legislature: Constitutional Functions and Political Experience', *Africa Quarterly,* Volume 40, No. 2.

Mohammed, S.B, 2001, 'Mismanagement, Leadership Crises and Instability in the Nige- ria's National Assembly, June 1999-May 2001', A Paper presented at a conference on 'Democracy and Democratisation', organised by CDRT Mambayya House, Kano, May 28-30.

Obi, C., 2008, *No Choice but Democracy: Pricing the People out of Politics in Africa?* Claude Ake Memorial Papers, No. 2, Nordic Africa Institute Uppsala.

Obiyan, A.S., 2007, 'An Evaluation of the Role of the Legislature as an Institutional Actor in Nigeria's Democratic Process in the Fourth Republic (1999-2006)', in Anifowose, R and Babawale, T. eds., *Nigeria Beyond 2007: Issues, Challenges and Prospects,* Lagos: Concept Publishers.

O'Donnell, G. A., 2001, 'Democratic Theory and Comparative Politics', *Studies in Comparative International Development* Vol. 36, No. 1, Spring 2001.

Okafor, S.O. 1981 *Indirect Rule: The Development of Central Legislature in Nigeria,* Hong Kong: Tomas Nelson and Sons Ltd.

Olurode, L. and Anifowoshe, R. eds., 2004, *Issues in Nigeria's 1999 General Elections,* Lagos: Rebonik Publications.

Onuoha, B. 2003, 'A Comparative Analysis of General Elections in Nigeria' in Anifo- woshe, R and Babawole, T eds., *2003 General Elections and Democratic Consolidation in Nigeria,* Lagos: Fredrich Ebert Stiftung.

Tamuno, T.O., 1972, *The Evolution of the Nigerian State: The Southern Phase, 1898-1914,* London: Longman.

The 1999 Constitution of the Federal Republic of Nigeria, Abuja: Federal Ministry of Information.

7

Presidential and Gubernatorial Elections in the Fourth Republic

Ogaba Oche

Introduction

One of the key features of an emergent democratic system is the institutions that are established and constitute the respective parts of the entire system. Elections and institutions that carry out electoral processes are not only central to the entire democratic system, but also attract significant attention because they facilitate the process of legitimising leadership. This they do through voting processes and through also facilitating the systematic acquisition and transfer of political power. This chapter focuses on the presidential and gubernatorial elections that have taken place since Nigeria returned to civil rule in 1999, and the governance impacts of the emergent administrations. In doing this, the chapter is divided into two broad sections with the first focusing on an overview of elections from 1999, and the second examining the impact of the civilian administrations in respect of governance.

Elections 1999-2007

Following the death of Gen. Abacha, the military strongman who seized power from the Interim National Government in Nigeria in November 1993, the pace of political change in the country became very rapid. The country witnessed the legalisation and creation of political parties, vast improvements in the level of press freedom and political competition and the completion of four rounds of elections. Indeed, the initial transition toward civilian rule, which was completed with General Obasanjo's swearing in as elected President on 29 May 1999, took less than a year from the day the transition began.

The 1998-99 transition occurred without a constitutional framework or a genuine public debate about the nation's constitutional future.

On assumption of power in June 1998, Abubakar had announced that a new Constitution would be made public before the December local government elections. It was to be based on the 1995 Constitution drafted under the Abacha administration, but never released to the public. Abubakar later announced the setting-up of the Constitution Debate Coordinating Committee (CDCC) to organise a public debate, and recommend a new Constitution. General Abubakar also handpicked the members of CDCC which conducted all of its work behind closed doors (Momoh and Thovoethen 2001:4-9).

In December, the CDCC recommended the adoption of the 1979 Constitution with some amendments based on the 1995 draft Constitution. The Abubakar administration, however, never formally announced that the CDCC's recommendations would be implemented. Calls from civil society groups and political leaders to hold a public constitutional debate were ignored. The government also dismissed widespread calls to hold a Sovereign National Conference (SNC) that would address fundamental political issues undermining the Nigerian state.

Throughout the election period the military government relied on decrees and ad-hoc regulations to guide the transition process. In August 1998, Abubakar issued Decree No. 17 which established the Independent National Election Commission. At the national level during the transition, INEC appeared to have developed some reputation for neutrality and fairness, despite the fact that its members were appointed without public input or scrutiny. At the state level however, some of its officials were seen as partisan supporters of the military government or a given political party. Also while INEC issued rules to guide the electoral process it often released rules governing each round of elections just days before the vote, and never adequately addressed many important issues (Momoh and Thovoethen 2001:19).

The first major task carried out by INEC was to conduct a national voter's registration exercise. Registration held from 5 to 19 October and experienced logistical problems which would later hamper INEC's election efforts at virtually every stage. Shortages of materials, delays in the opening of registration centres, poorly trained officials, and attempts by political party agents to manipulate the process were rife. The poor registration exercise lay at the root of many subsequent problems during the transition and created opportunities for fraud.

With respect to political parties, INEC established strict registration conditions. To compete in local elections, political parties were required to set up and maintain offices in 24 of the 36 states and demonstrate an ethnic and regional mix in each party's leadership. To continue the transition process, parties initially were required to obtain at least 10 per cent of the vote in 24 states during local government elections. This figure later changed to 5 per cent, with a caveat that at least three parties would advance to the later three rounds of elections. This set of regulations actually set the stage for intense competition between parties to attract and retain prominent politicians, potential candidates, and financial backers, especially in parts of the country where support for the parties was weak. With no regulations for campaign finance, parties competed vigorously for wealthy, well-connected, and sometimes dubious individuals to fund campaigns out of their own pockets (Momoh and Thovoethen 2001:19).

Most of the parties were hastily formed and suffered from a general lack of experience and ideological clarity. Perhaps the lack of ideological disputation amongst them subsequently could be attributed to the fact that they all more or less subscribe to the neo-liberal ideology. As a result, carpet crossing and shifting allegiances emerged during the transition process. However, the more established parties such as the People's Democratic Party (PDP) and the All People's Party (APP) drew upon political machinery that were already in place from past elections to give them some advantage in mobilising financial and political support.

1999 Gubernatorial Elections

On 9 January 1999, Governorship and Houses of Assembly elections were held nationwide. The results largely reflected the pattern that the local government elections had taken earlier in which the PDP had the vast majority of chairmanship and councillorship seats nationwide. In the gubernatorial elections, the PDP maintained its lead by winning twenty governorship seats. The APP won nine governorship seats and the Alliance for Democracy (AD) dominated the southwest by winning in six south-western states. Elections into the State Houses of Assembly also showed the same pattern of victory by the political parties.

This was followed by the National Assembly elections which took place on 20 February 1999. The PDP also maintained its lead thereby winning 69 senatorial seats and the majority of the seats in the House of Representatives elections. It was followed by the APP which won 21 senatorial seats and had a considerable number of seats in the House of Representatives. The AD maintained its third position by winning 19 senatorial seats and the least number of seats in the House of Representatives. The major upset came with the AD winning two senatorial and two House of Representatives seats in Enugu State, one of the PDP strongholds in the eastern part of the country (Momoh and Thovoethen 2001:25).

The 1999 Presidential Elections

As a result of the electoral dominance of the PDP in all the elections held, the scene was set for an easy victory for any presidential candidate presented by that party. In anticipation of this the AD and APP developed an alliance to checkmate the antics of the PDP. Chief Olu Falae was selected as the joint presidential candidate of the AD and the APP hoping that he would be the right candidate to counter the stature of Obasanjo, the PDP flag-bearer. As it turned out, both presidential candidates were from the south-western part of the country, a novel development in Nigeria.

The presidential election took place on 27 February 1999. There was a low turnout in most parts of the country. The day after the election, international observers invited by the government to allay fears of bias estimated the voter turnout to be about 20 per cent. The election results announced by INEC, however, placed the turnout at between thirty and 40 per cent. A number of the election observer groups such as those from the United States, the European Union and the Commonwealth, reported that they observed a wide discrepancy between voters seen at the polling stations and results that were announced. Although this was indicative of rigging and inflation of voters, it was not assumed to have been serious enough to affect the overall outcome of the election.

However, the result of the presidential election confirmed the trend that had emerged since the inception of the transition programme which was the dominance of the PDP in most states and zones of the federation. At the end, the PDP candidate, General Obasanjo, won 18,738,015 votes representing 62.78 per cent of the votes cast. On the other hand, Chief Olu Falae of the AD/APP alliance won 11,140,287 votes representing 37.22 per cent of the total votes cast. An analysis of the outcome of the 1999 presidential election shows that the PDP won in five of the nation's six geopolitical zones, conceding only the south-western to the rival APP/AD alliance. This distribution did not elicit surprise, though, because in all the previous elections of the transition programme the PDP had consistently lost the southwest by a wide margin to the AD (Momoh and Thovoethen 2001:29).

In the post-election analysis, electoral observers reported a number of irregularities that had been seen. For example, observers reported instances of ballot box stuffing, including polling sites where INEC officials or party agents illegally printed multiple ballots with their own thumbs. In some states in the South South zone, actual voter turnouts were significantly lower than the official tally. In some states delegates estimated that less than 10 per cent of registered voters cast ballots, but official turnout rates for those same states exceeded 85 per cent. Many individual polling sites recorded that all 500 registered voters had cast ballots when observers actually saw fewer than 100 people there during the day.

Other significant developments included the altering of results. In many instances observers recorded low numbers of accredited voters at polling stations, sometimes less than 10 per cent of the registered voters. During the counting or collation process later in the day, they found that these same polling stations reported considerably higher numbers, sometimes even 100 per cent of the registered voters. Usually the voters at these polling stations were mainly or entirely for a single party. At many polling stations it appeared that the party agents and polling officials were involved in the malpractice. As a consequence of the numerous discrepancies detected by observers, widespread criticism of the entire electoral process was generated. Indeed, Chief Olu Falae, using this as basis for contention, rejected the results of the election which he eventually challenged in a court of law. This did not stop the outcome of the presidential election from being upheld and General Olusegun Obasanjo from being sworn in as President on 29 May 1999 (Momoh and Thovoethen 2001:6-9; Ihonvbere 1999; Enemuo 1999:3-7).

Given the sophistication of the Nigerian electorate (Mackintosh, 1966), it could be argued that the PDP may have retained central power all these years largely through systematic, large-scale election rigging and by manipulating INEC.

The 2003 Elections

With the 1999 elections having successfully taken place and provided a starting point for Nigerian democracy, there were heightened concerns over the prospects of an election that would constitute the basis for leadership succession given that second elections tend to be problematic on the African political terrain. Thus the 2003 elections were seen as an important step on the path towards the consolidation of democracy in Nigeria.

However, from inception questions were raised about the ability of INEC to accurately register millions of voters, administer well over 100,000 polling stations, and supervise and train roughly half a million election workers. This was in view of the fact that INEC had failed to make adequate use of the preceding four years, after the previous elections, to improve its organisational capabilities. INEC started late and carried out what was regarded as its most important task, that of voter registration, in a very shoddy manner. A complete computerised registry of voters which would serve as a basis for all subsequent elections in Nigeria would have been a major accomplishment in the strengthening of the country's electoral system. Instead, the entire exercise was marred with allegations of fraud, manipulation and poor organisation (IRI 2003:12 – 20).

The entire registration process was an exercise that stretched the organisational capabilities of INEC to breaking point. As at the time of the first election on 12 April 2003, INEC had yet to compile a comprehensive national voters' registry from which citizens could confirm their registration. The absence of such a registry delayed the distribution of permanent voter registration cards. Confusion, therefore, surrounded the initial registration process in September 2002, thereby leaving room for fraud, chaos and various forms of malpractices. Out of an estimated 80 million registration forms that were distributed to 120,000 registration centres, only 67 million could be accounted for at the conclusion of the process. Indeed, it has been argued that the poorly administered registration process was a contributory factor to the eventual low voter turnout in many parts of the country on election days (IRI 2003:12 – 20).

In addition to the shoddy manner of election administration, INEC could not escape accusations of not maintaining standards of impartiality. By law, INEC officials are not supposed to exhibit any particular political affiliation. According to the Federal Government of Nigeria, qualified and unbiased personnel were sought for appointment into INEC; however, given the heated nature of the political campaign period, it was difficult for INEC to escape accusations of partiality and bias in favour of the ruling political party, PDP. Matters were not helped by the fact that only a week before the National Assembly election, President Obasanjo and leaders of the PDP had a meeting with INEC officials which did not have members of the opposition parties in attendance. The absence of opposition leaders further fuelled speculation and criticism regarding the true motives behind the meeting (IRI 2003:12 – 20).

The political environment that enveloped the campaigns at that time was becoming increasingly characterised by a breakdown of public order. There were numerous incidents of criminality, ethnic and religious strife as well as acts of political thuggery. In the weeks preceding the elections, major international oil companies operating in Nigeria evacuated all their personnel from the country and shutdown nearly 40 per cent of Nigerian oil production in response to attacks by armed groups of militant youth, which continued despite the deployment of federal troops. All these were happening at the same time as communal conflicts between some ethnic groups. Newspapers regularly reported on violence between various ethnic communities that resulted in loss of lives. Some of the states within the federation were declared by President Obasanjo as being politically volatile, thereby necessitating the deployment of troops.

The fact that politically motivated forms of violence and killings persisted during the campaign period was of serious concern to many. The killing of Dr. Marshall Harry, a regional campaign coordinator for the ANPP, was an incident that shocked the country as a whole. Harry's death was one among a number of killings that were politically motivated and occurred during the period of election campaigns. Party offices were often destroyed and opposing party members hounded or killed. Quite interesting was the fact that police appeared to be completely incapable of solving the murders. It was in response to the growing incidence of violence that the Federal Government instructed that leaders of at least 23 political parties should sign an electoral code of conduct compelling the parties to refrain from engaging in electoral violence during the campaign and election. The need for such an agreement, however, was an indication of the extent to which violence had influenced and marred the country's political process (NLC 2003; Iyayi 2003; Jeter 2003; Nwabueze 2003; Akpan 2003; Yusuf 2003).

Despite the relatively unsettled political environment, the election campaign was vigorously conducted in many parts of the country. Parties advertised widely through the use of print and electronic media, regardless of the fact that many opposition parties complained of biased treatment from state-owned media outlets. The presidential and gubernatorial elections took place on 19 April 2003. It was observed that relatively few problems emerged that were directly related to voter registration lists or voter identification. During the elections, however, cases of electoral irregularities regarding ballot box security were reported. The ballot boxes were not mechanically locked or sealed and could easily be tampered with. In a number of states, incidents of ballot box stuffing and the falsification of results were reported. The incidence of electoral malpractices continued right up to the point of collation of results where, in some cases, voting workers entirely ignored their responsibility to count their ballots and record their results, instead filled ballot boxes were delivered directly to the collation centres. Nevertheless, the results of the 19 April 2003 presidential election secured another four-year term for Obasanjo and Atiku Abubakar, his deputy. The PDP, the party under whose banner they contested, won a total of 24,456,140 votes nationwide, making up 61.99 per cent of the overall votes according to overall Presidential Election Result (*see The Guardian* of 23 January 2003).

The 2007 Elections

The 2007 elections were the third to be held since the reintroduction of democracy in 1999. The elections were considered to be very critical because, apart from providing a platform to test the commitment of the Nigerian authorities to the strengthening and consolidation of democracy, it was also the second time that power would be transferred from one civilian president to another, after the botched transfer in 1983, when General Buhari and his supporters removed Shehu Shagari through the 31 December *coup d'etat*.

The build-up to the election, however, was not helped by a number of factors that featured in the polity at the time. Chief among these was the political feud between President Obasanjo and his Vice-President Abubakar Atiku which featured exchanges of accusations and counter-accusations of various forms of wrongdoing. INEC had initially disqualified Atiku from participating in the elections but this was later overturned by the Federal High Court only five days before the elections. The immediate effect was to create added logistical problems for INEC. However, with very strong political support from Obasanjo, Umaru Yar'Adua, the Governor of Katsina State, won the PDP nomination as the party's flag bearer (EU 2007; Human Rights Watch 2007; Ibrahim 2007).

The ANPP contested the elections with Muhammadu Buhari as its presidential candidate, just as it did in 2003. The presidential candidates representing the major parties all came from the north while their vice-presidential candidates werefrom the southern part of the country (Goodluck Jonathan for PDP from Bayelsa State; Ben Obi for AC from Abia State; and Edwin Ume-Ezeoke for ANPP from Anambra State).

As with earlier elections, organisational problems weighed very heavily on INEC. Increasingly, it became clear that INEC was not operating in an autonomous capacity, away from federal government influence. This contributed towards undermining confidence in INEC among political parties, civil society and the wider public. INEC lacked transparency and failed to provide information on a number of important issues such as the final number of candidates, the final number of voters per constituency, and the final number of ballot papers that had been printed and distributed.

The decision by the Supreme Court on 11 April to allow Abubakar Atiku to participate in the election only five days to the election meant that INEC had to print and redistribute some 70 million ballot papers before the 21 April election. Indeed, the ballot papers, which were printed in South Africa, arrived in Nigeria only one day before the election, triggering a logistical nightmare of delays, disruptions and cancellations in some wards (Iwu 2008a; Iwu 2008b).

The campaign process was quite vibrant, sending the respective candidates and their supporters to different parts of the country. An intrinsic problem with the entire campaign process, however, was the absence of a level playing field among the parties with specific access to resources. While the Electoral Act 2006, in Article 103, stipulates that 'state apparatus, including the media, shall not be employed to the advantage or disadvantage of any political party or candidate at any election', incumbent parties at federal and state levels took advantage over other political parties by using state resources that were attached to their offices to support their campaigns. The abuse of state resources covered the use of state finances, media, civil servants, aid programmes and infrastructure. The Electoral Act also provides for the allocation of annual public funds to political parties. However, it was claimed by a number of the small parties that the distribution of grants was not made in accordance with criteria specified in the law. In some cases, the claim by the parties was that they did not receive the correct amounts of money that was due to them while in others the claim was that they were not given grants at all.

In addition to the abuse of resources, violence had been a recurring decimal in Nigeria's political terrain and the 2007 elections proved to be no different in this regard. Violence was a major issue of concern throughout the election process. In several states, incidents of violence increased as the elections drew nearer. There were numerous reports of killings resulting from political violence perpetrated by thugs. Most parties were united in accusing the PDP of being the main party using the financial resources to hire thugs. However, it was in fact a practice that was carried out by virtually all the parties. Overall, however, the violence experienced in the build-up to the 2007 election seemed to be much less in terms of spread and intensity than what was experienced in the 2003 election Makanju 2007: 65; Human Rights Watch 2007:67; Nwabueze 2007: 20 -24).

Overview of Democratic Governance in Nigeria 1999-2009

From 1999, when Nigeria returned to democracy, 'good governance' has been the operational mantra upon which successive civil administrations, at both federal and state levels, have hinged their governance. The civilian administration of President Olusegun Obasanjo took a step towards halting social and political degradation which the country had been subjected to due to the military incursion in governance. The years of military rule were characterised by arbitrariness, massive corruption, abuse of human rights, gagging of the press, favouritism and enthronement of mediocrity (Igbuzor 2005:78). In trying to do this, the new civilian administration decided to introduce a number of programmes and strategies to reform the political, economic and social spheres of Nigerian life which were in various states of decay and disintegration (Aligan 2008). There have been visible gains to the Nigerian polity as a consequence of these initial efforts. There is now increased respect for civil and political rights, improvement in the remuneration of public sector workers, improvement in some public utilities such as telecommunications, access to internet facilities, access to health care facilities through the National Health Insurance Scheme (NHIS), improved road networks in some states of the federation, improved funding of the education sector and a sustained investment in the power sector. Others are in the areas of tackling corruption, improved economy, sustained fight against HIV & AIDS and other deadly diseases, increased level of security, increased employment opportunities, etc. Some of these issues will be discussed in turn in an attempt to give a sweeping assessment of the gains of democratic governance in Nigeria since 1999.

Since the return of democracy, the country has witnessed remarkable gains in its fight against corruption, which is not only one of the major hindrances to development in many countries but also antithetical to good governance (Adefuye 2008: 8). In its fight against corruption, the government established the Economic and Financial Crimes Commission (EFCC) in 2000 to combat the activities of fraudsters and public office holders who enrich themselves with public funds. This institution and others such as the Independent Corrupt Practices and other Related Offences Commission (ICPC) and the Code of Conduct Tribunal are fighting and gradually, but steadily making an impact in the anti-corruption war which has not only enhanced the credibility of the country, but has also marginally improved the quality of governance and curtailed the wastage of government resources (Aligan 2008:90).

The administration also set up its home-grown strategy for eradicating poverty by establishing the National Economic Empowerment and Development Strategies (NEEDS). These strategies were replicated at the state and local government levels as SEEDS and LEEDS, respectively, which are all aimed at improving the level of development and reducing poverty in Nigeria. However, with the benefit of hindsight, and the increase in population growth in Nigeria, this does not appear to have significantly reduced poverty in the country.

The banking sub-sector of the economy received a turn-around with the banking reforms embarked upon by the Central Bank of Nigeria (CBN) under the auspices of the bank consolidation exercise. In this reform, the capital base of each commercial bank was increased to a minimum of N25 billion. This was aimed at increasing investor confidence in Nigerian banks and also boosting the capacity of the banks to guarantee loan facilities to both individuals and corporate entities. The insurance sub-sector also got a turnaround but with a smaller capital base of N5 billion.

Within this period the country also witnessed another round of privatisation. Series of policies were introduced such as liberalisation of the downstream sector of the petroleum sub-sector, as well as privatisation and monetisation policies. Under the privatisation policy, the telecommunications sub-sector became privatised with the licensing of three major Global Systems Mobile telecommunication (GSM) companies in February 2000. This privatisation exercise saw the subscriber base grow from about 400,000 lines to about 21 million lines (Aligan 2008:90). Other government-owned companies that were privatised saved the country money and brought money into the coffers of the government. In 2005 alone, the Bureau for Public Enterprises (BPE) contributed N20 billion in earnings into the Federal Government account.

In the health sector, the fight against HIV & AIDS and other diseases has received a tremendous boost since 1999. The prevalence rate of HIV & AIDS rose from 3.8 per cent in 1993 to 4.5 per cent in 1998. The civilian administration from 1999 ensured that HIV prevention, treatment and care became one of the government's primary concerns. The National Agency for the Control of HIV & AIDS (NACA) was established in the period under review, specifically in February 2000 and in 2001 the government established the HIV & AIDS Emergency Action Plan (HEAP). Through these efforts, the prevalence rate fell to the current level which is now about 2.5 per cent. This is low when seen in relation to the size of the population of the country. There has also been an increase in the number of medical centres all over the country. Health pandemics such as polio have received great attention. The government was able to mobilise international donor organisations to assist in the fight against polio with the most recent and prominent being the Bill and Melinda Gates Foundation. This foundation pledged the sum of US$75 million for2009 alone for the eradication of polio in Nigeria (Daily Trust 17 February 2009).

The Security sector has also been given a boost with the establishment of the Police Equipment Fund (PEF). This fund was meant to cater for the proper equipping of the Nigeria Police Force and other security agencies. The PEF is known to have equipped security agencies like the police, military, state security service, among others with state-of-the-art equipment. These, however, have not translated into improved security for the country. In fact, in the period under review, the country witnessed high profile cases of assassinations and killings, to the extent that an incumbent Attorney General and Minister of Justice, Chief Bola Ige, was killed in his house. Added to this list is Marshall Harry, Chief Dikibo and the incessant breach of peace and communal conflicts in Kaduna, Plateau, Kano and Bauchi States where thousands of lives were lost and properties worth millions were also destroyed. There was a reported increase in the rate of highway robberies due to the influx of small arms into the country.

The Niger Delta crisis is being addressed with the establishment of the Niger Delta Development Commission (NDDC) and the creation of the Ministry for Niger Delta Affairs. These two organs have increased the tempo of development in terms of infrastructure, employment and rehabilitation in the Niger Delta. Also, the recent grant of amnesty by the Federal Government to the militants in the creeks is an added bonus for democracy and good governance in the country. The amnesty granted the Niger Delta militants in particular has significantly reduced the extent of militancy in the region, and may have helped finally in charting a path to development in the region in the short term. This notwithstanding, overall, many Nigerians have not had any experience of the dividends of democracy .

In spite of the above measures characterised by the establishment of a host of new institutions, it is important to point out that in broad terms, the performance of the two civilian regimes of Presidents Olusegun Obasanjo and Umaru Yar'Adua did not meet the wishes and aspirations of Nigerians. Events and circumstances, such as the invasion of Odi, the continued militarisation of the Niger Delta, the killings of innocent civilians in the Jos crises, widespread poverty and unemployment have left much to be desired. The murder of innocent people, assassinations, robbery and general sense of insecurity in the country are deficiencies in the country's governance. The government needs to do more in the areas of social provisioning in terms of security, food, potable water, fuel, electricity, good transport system, and affordable education for its citizenry.

The Way Forward

For Nigeria and indeed Nigerians to feel the impact of democracy or the much-talked about dividends of democracy, certain fundamental issues need to be addressed more vigorously and sincerely. These include the following: Corruption – Corruption is perhaps the greatest problem confronting Nigeria. Since the advent of this democratic dispensation, as noted earlier, efforts have been made to fight corruption without this yielding the desired results. The establishment of the EFCC has been a step in the right direction but unless there is a sincere and sustained fight, the problem of corruption will continue to spread deep into the fabric of the Nigerian society. Indeed in many quarters there is doubt about the sincerity of the fight against corruption. The question people ask is whether the campaign against corruption is targeted against the opponents of the ruling elite or whether it is applicable to all who fall foul of extant anti-corruption laws. The recently removed Attorney-General and Minister of Justice practically sought to paralyse the EFCC by asking it (EFCC) to obtain approval from his office before embarking on the prosecution of offenders. This gives the impression that the anti-corruption crusade is a platform for public posturing and grandstanding.

Transparency in Governance – Closely linked with corruption is transparency in governance. According to democratic ethos, the process of governance should be transparent and open. This will help to curtail sharp and unethical practices. The era in which governance is shrouded in secrecy should be done away with. In this regard, Nigerians continue to canvass that the Freedom of Information (FOI) bill before the National Assembly be passed into law despite veiled opposition from the executive itself. The FOI Bill was finally passed into law on 28 May 2011, but the challenge has remained its implementation at the various levels of governance.

Strengthening of Institutions – Because of the long years of military rule, certain institutions were affected. Worst hit are the legislature, which is antithetical to military rule and has been non-existent, as well as the judiciary. Other institutions such as the electoral commission, human rights, police and even the armed forces were severely compromised during the long years of military rule. These institutions, in addition to others that have been weakened through corrupt and unconventional practices, need to be developed to help entrench a sound system of democracy and good governance.

Infrastructure – The state of infrastructural decay all over the country is lamentable. Policies need to be formulated and implemented to solve the issues confronting the people. The era of paying lip service to these issues must stop forthwith. Words need to be matched with action. Roads, schools, transportation, security, housing and employment needs of the people must be addressed.

Conclusion

Despite the problems that have underpinned elections in Nigeria, the fact is that a democratic political system has been introduced and efforts should be made to consolidate it primarily by way of ensuring good governance. This is the only premise upon which development can be attained. Democracy upholds the tenets of good governance. These include public accountability, transparency, predictability of government behaviour, adherence to the rule of law, and the sound management of national resources, among other things (Obadan and Edo 2007: 38). So far, some of the signs, although not all, are encouraging; back-to-back elected civilian leadership, prospective educational reforms, an increasingly independent judiciary and economic gains, increase in foreign reserves, debt cancellation, rising GDP and sound fiscal management; all these are good signs, although unemployment still remains high. Also, Nigeria is strengthening the rule of law. There has been a concerted action by the government in recent times, strongly supported by the vocal civil society, against corruption and backed by determined leadership. If these actions are sustained, then, Nigeria is on the march towards achieving good governance and reaping the benefits of democratic elections.

References

Abraham, Isaiah, 1999, 'Assessment of the Presidential Election', *Daily Times*, 4 March. Adefuye, A., 2008, *Good Governance and Accountability in Nigeria*, Lecture delivered at the National Defence College, 17th November.

Akpan, Felix, 2003, 'Truth as Casualty in 2003 Elections,' *Daily Champion*, 23 April. Aligan, I. Z., 2008, 'Seven Years of Democracy in Nigeria: The Pains and Gains, in Hassan Saliu et. al eds., *Perspectives on Nation Building and Development in Nigeria: Political and Legal Issues*, Lagos: Concept Publications Limited. *Daily Trust*, 2009, 17 February.

Enemuo, C. Francis, 1999, 'Elite Solidarity, Communal Support, and the 1999 Presidential Election in Nigeria', *Issue: A Journal of Opinion*, Vol. 27, No. 1.

European Union Election Observer Mission Nigeria, 2007, *Final Report: Gubernatorial and State Houses of Assembly Elections 14 April 2007 and Presidential and National Assembly Elections 21 April 2007, European Union*.

Human Rights Watch, 2007, 'Election or "Selection?', Human Rights Abuse and Threats to Free and Fair Elections in Nigeria, No. 1, 2007, April.

Human Rights Watch, 2007, 'Nigeria: Polls Marred by Violence, Fraud', *The Guardian*, 19 April. Nwabueze Ben, 2007, '2007 Election Violated Our Constitution, So No body Can Legitimately Govern us Based on Them, *Sunday Champion*, 3 June.

Ibrahim, Jibrin, 2007, *Nigeria's 2007 Elections: The Fitful Path to Democratic Citizenship*, United States Institute of Peace, Special Report 182, January.

Igbuzor, O., 2005, *Perspectives on Democracy and* Development, Abuja: Joe-Tolalu and Associates.

Ihonvbere, O. Julius, 1999, 'The 1999 Presidential Elections in Nigeria: The Unresolved Issues', *Issue: A Journal of Opinion*, Vol. 27 No. 1 1999.

International Republican Institute (IRI), 2003, *Nigeria Election Observer Report*, (http://aceproject.org/ero-en/regions/africa/NG/nigeria-final-report-general-elections-iri-) 2003, 18 September.

Iwu, Maurice, 2008a, 'Nigeria's 2007 Elections; What Went Right', *The Guardian*, 2 May.

Iwu, Maurice, 2008b, 'Reflections and Lessons from 2007 Nigerian Election, Daily *Champion*, 19th August.

Iyayi, Festus, 2003, 'Before and after the 2003 Elections', *The Guardian,* 16[t] July.

Jeter, F. Howard, 2003, 'Reflections on the 2003 Elections: A Historic Moment, *This Day,* 16th April; '2003 Elections; Matters Arising,' *The Guardian*, 28 April 2003.

Labour Election Monitoring Team, 2003, *Nigeria: Balloting for Democracy – a Report of the 2003 General Elections*, 2003, Abuja: Nigeria Labour Congress.

Mackintosh, P. John, ed. 1966. *Nigerian Government & Politics, Prelude to the Revolution*, London: Allen & Unwin.

Makanju Olatunde, 2007, '2007: An Unacceptable Larceny', *The Guardian*, 7 May.

Momoh, Abubakar and Paul-Sewa Thovoethen, 2001, 'An Overview of the 1998-1999 Democratisation Process in Nigeria, *Development Policy Management Network Bulletin*, Vol. xiii No. 3, September.

Nwabueze, Ben, 2003, 'Nature and Forms of Election Rigging', *The Guardian*, 8 May. Obadan, M.and Sam Edo, 2007, 'An Overview of the Reform Programme', in Hassan.

Saliu, et al eds., *Nigeria's Reform Programme: Issues and Challenges*, Ibadan: Vintage Publishers Limited.

The Carter Centre, 2001, 'Observing the 1998-99 Nigeria Elections – Final Report', (http://www.cartercentre.org/documents/1152.pdf), 18 September 2001.

The Guardian 2003,'Overall Nigerian Presidential Election Result', Wednesday, 23 April.

Yusuf, Afolabi, 2002, 'Election 2003 and Ethnic Militias', *Daily Champion*, 23 January.

8

Consolidation of Democracy and Good Governance in Nigeria: The Role of the Civil Society

Ogaba Oche

Introduction

It is axiomatic that the withdrawal of the military from governance in Nigeria and the subsequent enthronement of an American-style presidential democracy came about largely as a consequence of the agitations and efforts of civil society. Civil society, especially those groups that had an explicitly pro-democracy and pro-human rights focus, were at the forefront of the tortuous struggle for the removal of the military from the helm of state affairs.

It is the position of this chapter that the immediate aftermath, and even beyond, of the transition to democracy, which is commonly referred to as a learning period, is possibly the most crucial period in the whole transition experience. This is for the critical reason that the foundations for a lasting democracy and good governance are established with the process of consolidation which, in itself, is one that should commence in the immediate aftermath of transition from autocratic to democratic governance. With the establishment of political structures and institutions that define pro-forma democracy, the manifest role of pro-democracy civil society groups in Nigeria seemed to recede, although, civil society still has a central role to play in the cultivation of the necessary behavioural underpinnings of democracy and the overall cultivation of a democratic political culture which are pivotal necessities for democratic consolidation.

In undertaking an analysis of the role of civil society in democratic consolidation and good governance in Nigeria, this chapter is divided into six sections, the introduction being the first. The second and third sections will focus on the defining characteristics of civil society, and an explication of the concept of democratic consolidation and governance. The fourth section will examine the problems and dilemma of Nigeria's young democratic project around which efforts towards consolidation will have to gravitate. The fifth section will focus on the roles of civil society in the process of consolidation which will entail an analysis of their weaknesses and strengths while the final section will be the conclusion.

Civil Society Organisations

As stated earlier, it is virtually impossible to provide any analysis of the struggle for democracy in Nigeria without a commentary about the vanguard role played by civil society. Indeed, the activism it displayed on the Nigerian political terrain came into conspicuous light under the authoritarian era of General Ibrahim Babangida and his convoluted transition programme that culminated in the annulment of the June 12 presidential election. The democratic transition of 1998 has been the outcome of protracted agitations on the part of civil society, which gathered momentum from the political injustice of the June 12 annulment, with pro-democracy and human rights civil society groups playing a leading role.

For the purposes of this chapter, therefore, a very broad definition of civil society has been adopted. This is primarily because a broad range of such organisations with a wide diversity of functions are in operation today. Essentially, civil society groups are not based on government, and the motives for their operation do not include profit making. The defining characteristics of civil society are useful in this respect. Civil society groups are:

i.   Non-profit making, voluntary, service-oriented organisations either for the benefit of its members or of members of the society.

ii. Organisations of private individuals who believe in certain basic social principles and who structure their activities to bring about development to communities that they are serving.

iii. Organisations that assist in the empowerment of people (politically, socially and economically).

iv. An organisation or a group of people working independently of any external control with specific objectives and aims to fulfil tasks that are oriented to bring about desirable change in a given community or area or situation.

v.   An organisation not affiliated to political parties and engaged in work for aid, development and welfare of the community.

vi. An organisation committed to the root causes of the problems, be they political, social, economic or environmental and trying to better the quality of life for the poor, the oppressed and the marginalised.

vii. An organisation that is flexible and democratic and attempts to serve the people without profit for itself (Chalmers 1997:1-4; Maslyukista 1999:6 – 70.

Democratic Consolidation and Governance

A discussion of the role of civil society in the process of consolidating democracy would be lacking in focus without an elucidation of the meaning of democratic consolidation. While some scholars regard it as an illusory concept that fails to offer any new insight into the process of democratisation (O'Donnell 1996:34 – 51), others perceive democratic consolidation as being descriptive of an identifiable phase in the process of transition from authoritarian to democratic systems that is critical to the establishment of a stable, institutionalised and lasting democracy (Clinz and Stepan 1996:14 – 33). This chapter takes the latter position.

Juan Linz and Alfred Stepan argue that democratic consolidation can only be said to take place after a transition to democracy has taken place. They define a consolidated democracy as a political regime in which democracy, as a complex system of institutions, rules and patterned incentives and disincentives, has become, in a phrase, 'the only game in town' (Clinz and Stepan 1996:15).

The idea of perceiving democratic consolidation as being consonant with 'the only game in town' is itself predicated on a trifocal operationalisation comprising behavioural, attitudinal, and constitutional dimensions.

In behavioural terms, a democratic regime can be regarded as consolidated when no significant actor (national, social, political, economic, institutional) will attempt to achieve its objectives either through the creation of a non-democratic regime or by attempting to break off from the existing democratic community. In attitudinal terms, a democracy is consolidated when the overwhelming majority of public opinion is consistently supportive of democratic procedures, processes and institutions as being the only appropriate method of conducting governance and public affairs. In constitutional terms, a democracy can be said to be consolidated when government and non-governmental actors become subject and habituated to the resolution of conflict within the bounds of the specific laws, procedures, and institutions sanctioned by the new democratic process (Clinz and Stepan 1996:16).

Thus, in order to be regarded as being consolidated, a democracy must develop behavioural, attitudinal and constitutional dispositions and qualities that are completely supportive of the democratic way of life. The emphasis on human dispositions in the forms of attitude, behaviour and the willingness to uphold the dictates of the constitution, which is more or less coterminous with upholding the rule of law and the corresponding de-emphasis of the structural and institutional dimensions of democracy, highlights the centrality of the human factor in consolidating democracy. In other words, democratisation and the consolidation of democracy go beyond the elaborate formalities of fashioning constitutions and establishing institutions. As a process, democratic consolidation lays emphasis on the development and cultivation of the critical behavioural and attitudinal underpinnings that are necessary foundations for a viable democratic system.

refers to that aspect of politics that aims to formulate and manage the rules of the political arena in which state and civil society actors operate and interact to make authoritative decisions. In more operational terms, governance refers to those measures that involve setting the rules for the exercise of power and setting conflicts over such rules. Such rules translate into constitutions, laws, customs, administrative regulations, and international agreements, all of which in one way or the other provide the framework for the formulation and implementation of policy decisions. The actors involved in governance may also be involved in other political arenas, be they in the state or in civil society (Hyden 1999:185).

However, a better grasp and understanding of the concept of democratic consolidation and governance is obtained when consideration is given to possible alternative scenarios. Andreas Schedler argues that the alternatives to the processes of completing transition, as well as deepening and consolidating democracy lie in the possibility of democratic breakdown and democratic erosion (Schedler 1998:95 – 98). The concept of democratic breakdown, one with which Nigerians are all too familiar, denotes dysfunctionality and failure of the democratic system leading to the supplanting of the system through a *coup d'état* or any other anti-democratic process that culminates in the establishment or restoration of an authoritarian system. Seen in this light, therefore, a major goal of democratic consolidation is to avoid a breakdown of democracy. An equally possible scenario is captured by the concept of democratic erosion. As the term suggests, this is a process that involves the slow and gradual decay and disintegration of democracy. Not being as sudden as a complete breakdown of democracy, it involves a gradual relapse to old authoritarian ways characterised by a steady re-emergence of anti-democratic forces, attitudes and behaviour. The danger of democratic erosion lies in the possibility of its growing and developing completely unnoticed and undetected. In their struggle to consolidate, young democracies such as Nigeria's, face this critical impediment. While it can be overcome if detected early, there is also every possibility that democratic erosion can eventually lead to a complete breakdown of democracy.

The Problems and Dilemma of Governance in Nigeria's Democracy

Any discussion about the prospects of democratic consolidation in Nigeria must be predicated on the problems and dilemmas that have arisen with the country's transition to democracy. The introduction of democracy has given vent to a litany of demands and agitations which have led to fears in some quarters that the system could be overwhelmed. Some of the major problems of the current democratic dispensation will be discussed in turn. The first problem area stems from the political institutions that constitute Nigeria's young democracy. The importance of political institutions cannot be overstated because they provide the structural foundations of a democracy and are central to the persistence and stability of democracy. It is common knowledge that effective and properly functioning institutions structure behaviour in stable and predictable patterns, thereby reducing uncertainty over role functions; tend to perform well even under circumstances of economic adversity; will produce more workable and sound public policies; and as a consequence of the above, will go a long way to limit the likelihood of military incursion into governance.

The reality, however, is that after the withdrawal of the military in May 1999, Nigerians have been witnesses to protracted disputes between the executive and the legislature at the federal level and within a number of states. Disputes and quarrels have also become virtually permanent features of political life within the national and state legislatures and within each of the three political parties. Attempts were made on different occasions by federal legislature to impeach President Olusegun Obasanjo, while the twilight of his second term (2003-2007) witnessed a fierce political fight between President Obasanjo and his Vice-President, Atiku Abubakar all of which had deleterious effects on the process of governance. Observers, both local and international, began to question the character of a democracy that seemed to be in perpetual conflict with itself (Maiyaki 2006:3).

A second problem relates to the evolution of a democratic political culture. A democracy introduces freedoms and rights which were suppressed under authoritarian systems, and if the pursuit of these freedoms and rights are not to degenerate into extremism and violence, it is important to cultivate mechanisms to contain such tendencies. One of the most important means of supporting and sustaining the 'democratic way of life' is through the evolution of a democratic political culture. As was alluded to earlier, such a culture involves beliefs, values, behavioural and attitudinal dispositions held by both the elite and the masses that are supportive of democracy. Beliefs and values such as tolerance for opposing views, willingness to compromise and demonstrate moderation in political positions, among others, are critical to the consolidation and development of democracy. In a young democracy like Nigeria, it is all the more important that such values are upheld by the elite primarily because they have a role to play in providing an example for the rest of society to follow. On some critical national issues, however, members of Nigeria's political class still need to exhibit these values that are so critical to the consolidation of democracy and improving the process of governance. Issues such as the introduction of the Islamic legal code of the Sharia in 12 northern Nigerian states and the persisting demands for enhanced autonomy of southern states have fractured the political elite and by extension, polarised the polity (Nzeshi 2010:6; Ibrahim 2007).

The third problem revolves around socio-economic development which is undoubtedly one of the most powerful factors that enhances the prospects for a consolidated democracy and legitimises governance. Evidence has shown that advancement in socio-economic development tends to strengthen belief in democracy which in turn helps to consolidate it. Socio-economic development leads to greater economic security and more widespread education, a lowering of socio-economic inequality and a reduction in feelings of deprivation and injustice on the part of the lower class as well as groups that may feel marginalised. This in turn will lead to a reduction in the high premium and stakes that politicians attach to the acquisition of government office as well as a movement away from extremist politics.

One of the consequences of prolonged military rule in Nigeria has been the virtual destruction of the Nigerian economy. Nigeria, today, is classified as one of the poorest nations in the world with the vast majority of its citizens living below the poverty level. As a result of this, democracy has been superimposed on a fragile economic base. Although one of the cardinal objectives of the successive administrations of Obasanjo and Yar Adua had been poverty alleviation, the welter of competing demands that the government had to cope with in addition to its obligation to service Nigeria's external debt has made this commitment a very difficult one. This situation was also equally compounded by endemic corruption in the system. These circumstances have not been helped by massive expenditure that have been incurred by legislators and elected government officials on fabulous salaries, unnecessary perquisites and frivolous purchases. Indeed, one of the expected dividends of democracy has been the yearning for an improvement in the socio-economic conditions of the ordinary man which, quite unfortunately, has failed to come about (World Bank 2010).

The fourth problem area is the persistence of corruption. The monumental heights to which corruption was carried by the military and the corrosive effects that it has had on the polity, economy and society is well known and does not need to be dwelt upon at any length. What is at issue is the persistence of corrupt practices on a large scale under the present democratic dispensation. Despite the professed intention of the Obasanjo administration to combat corruption and its initiation of an anti-corruption bill which was eventually passed into law by the legislature, the formation of the Independent Corrupt Practices and Other Offences Commission (ICPC), and the Economic and Financial Crimes Commission (EFCC), the fact that corruption and financial mismanagement still occurs at the apex of government was brought to light by the self-investigation that was undertaken by the Senate. Although the exercise was lauded by the public as an exercise in self-cleansing, a number of questions arose, not least of which was the punishment to be meted out to the erring members of the legislature. The cogency of this question is brought to light by the collective denial made by all the senators even after incriminating evidence against them had been unearthed. The demonstration effect of their actions for the rest of the Nigerian society and the seeming impunity of their escapades even when due consideration is given to thestringency of the anti-corruption law which the legislators themselves passed was indicative of a gradual erosion of the rule of law which the legislators have sworn to uphold. Furthermore, the potential of the 'probe' to be used as a weapon of political vendetta is a regrettable twist that the exposure of corruption at the highest levels has taken (Ibrahim 2007:2 – 3; Fine 2007). Indeed, the nexus between Nigeria's electoral democracy and its critical corruption, as the impact on governance and development, cannot be overemphasised.

The final major problem area has been the maintenance of security and the management of internal conflicts. Democracy has been described as the best political mechanism for the management of conflicts. This is principally because, unlike authoritarian and centralised systems of government, democracy is broadly inclusive in theory; however the Nigerian experience up to 2007 leaves much to be desired. The principle of majoritarianism, which is upheld by democracy, ensures to a much greater degree than any other political system the involvement and participation of the plurality of individuals and groups in a given society. The equality of citizenship regardless of race, ethnicity, religion or language is upheld and protected by democracy. As a result of this, feelings of marginalisation and deprivation on the part of groups and individuals are expected to be reduced to a minimum.

Paradoxically however, the liberalisation of Nigeria's political space and the freedoms that have attended the establishment of democracy opened a Pandora's Box of conflicts that have provided appropriate cause for serious concern. Such conflicts have been occasioned by factors such as the introduction of Sharia law in parts of northern Nigeria; violent activities perpetrated by ethnic militia in various parts of the country; and vicious clashes occasioned by differences between indigenous and settler communities in the central Nigerian city of Jos, among others. These conflicts have occurred alongside earlier persistent and strident demands for a restructuring of the federation in order to provide greater autonomy for its component states (Oche 2004:74 – 90).

The above constitutes a major problem of governance that Nigeria's current democracy is faced with. They represent the primary impediments to the entrenchment of good governance and cultivation of behavioural, attitudinal and constitutional underpinnings that are required for democratic consolidation. What then can civil society do to help in improving this circumstance?

Civil Society and the Consolidation of Democracy and Good Governance in Nigeria

As stated at the beginning of this chapter, the importance of civil society in the process can be gleaned from the role they played in the ferment that led to the eventual withdrawal of the military in 1999. Civil society engaged in agitations and protests that led to the eventual demise of military rule. A good number of them had an explicitly pro-democracy and pro-human rights agenda (Schmitter 1991). This was in contrast to other groups, such as professional and religious bodies, that eventually joined the agitation for democracy but ordinarily pursued and advancedalternative interests. With the enthronement of democracy in 1999 and the formation of democratic institutions, pro-democracy groups, and civil society at large, seemed to have lapsed into suspended animation. Members of civil society that are still active seem to advance parochial interests that revolve around ethnic, religious and regional demands. The quest for the economic dividends of democracy and the pursuit of the national welfare seem to have been abandoned.

While the aftermath of the transition should attract concerted efforts towards the consolidation of Nigeria's hard-won democracy, this seems not to be the case as much of civil society is in pursuit of narrow agenda and the consolidation of democracy seems not to be in the consciousness, discourse or agenda of the politically attentive and active public. The dangers and possibility of democratic erosion, which may have already started, and breakdown seem to have been entirely discounted. The avaricious and self-serving disposition of Nigeria's political class has been made apparent within the past ten years. The quest by the various political parties at times of elections is more for the acquisition of political office and power that would facilitate financial accumulation than for the ultimate betterment of the average Nigerian. An observable feature of Nigerian political parties has been the absence of discourse anchored upon ideological leanings. The ruling party, the People's Democratic Party (PDP), contested the 2007 elections without a political manifesto that would commit them towards achieving specific objectives. It, therefore, leads to the question of the possible role that civil society can play in promoting good governance and consolidating Nigeria's democracy. In answering this question, a realistic assessment of the weaknesses and strengths of civil society must be made.

Weakness of the Civil Society

One of the main weaknesses of civil society lies in urban-rural dichotomy to the extent that most, if not all, pro-democracy civil society groups are based in urban areas. Even the urban areas that are home to pro-democracy civil society are situated largely in the southern parts of the country. Cities like Lagos, Ibadan and Port Harcourt were hotbeds of pro-democracy agitation in the years that led to the withdrawal of the military. The argument here is that for purposes of governance and democratic consolidation in a country with a predominantly rural population, the spread of the activities of civil society, in terms of a watchdog role and engendering active rural involvement in governance is circumscribed and limited to urban areas. The impact and effectiveness of representative institutions at the local government level, for instance, is not an issue that should be ignored by civil society. While issues regarding corruption at the state and federal levels are given publicity, corruption at the local level goes unheralded and uninvestigated to a very large extent. Thus, the prospects of illegal financial accumulation provide a powerful incentive for corrupt politicians to seek office at the local government level.

The second weakness lies in the divisions that have occurred among the ranks of civil society immediately after the withdrawal of the military. The coalitions of human rights and pro-democracy civil society such as the National Democratic Coalition (NADECO) and the Joint Action Committee on Nigeria (JACON) have shown that they are not immune to the ethnic, religious, social divisions and biases that affect the wider society. The latter group, JACON, split up almost immediately after the transition. However, what one cannot be sure of is the overall impact of this split on their subsequent objectives. The undemocratic organisational structures, which a number of civil society groups possess, is the third problem. Severely afflicted by funding and other resource constraints, a number of civil society organisations became simply a 'one-man show' or 'Portfolio NGOs' with authoritarian decision-making processes revolving around one individual, and expenditure of funds also restricted to individual diktat. These factors restrict the growth and structural differentiation of these groups as well as their ultimate ability to become institutionalised, entrenched and effectively contribute to the consolidation of democracy and good governance.

A fourth problem area is the inadequacy of funding for most civil society groups. In fact, most civil society organisations have serious financial problems. Many of them lack the financial capacity to give life to their fervent organisational objectives. Some are constrained by lack of decent office abodes as well as equipment for their work. The ability to monitor the country's politics or even play an effective monitoring role during elections is seriously limited unless they are supported by external funding. The donor community in a country like Nigeria is quite small and efforts by civil society to raise funds locally are usually met with limited success. The result has been an ever increasing dependence on foreign donor agencies by CSOs, leaving them vulnerable and restricted to the implementation of agenda established by the donors.[15] The problem of dependence on foreign donors is itself tied to the broader and more fundamental problem of economic development, if any at all, and a weak private sector that is still ultimately dependent upon government for contracts and business. If civil society is to remain autonomous of government, then their resource base within the country, severely circumscribed by a weak private sector, which compels civil society to continue depending on foreign donors, must be expanded.

Lastly, a major weakness of civil society derives from the gender-imbalance displayed by a number of civil society groups. There is a dearth of women in professional positions in pro-democracy and human rights organisations as well as those that are specifically focused upon women's issues. If good governance and democratic consolidation are all about cultivating the attitudinal and behavioural dispositions that are supportive of democracy, then the exclusion of women from civil society activities would really amount to losing focus from the very beginning.

Although these weaknesses exist, they really should not forestall these civil society groups from playing an active and effective role in consolidating democracy and promoting the pattern of governance that would be beneficial to the plurality of Nigerians. The fact that they were central to the initial, and presumably more difficult, task of compelling the withdrawal of the military presupposes their value and utility in consolidating the system that has already been established. To this end, human rights and pro-democracy civil society possess a number of strengths and advantages (Mwmakumbe 1998:314 – 316). First, civil society provides an independent means of monitoring the activities of government and ensuring the accountability of elected officials. This is a very important role for civil society in Nigeria to play especially in view of the direction that elected officials are already taking at various levels of government. Side by side with the media, the civil society can play the role of impartial, independent and non-committed watchdogs of the activities of government and help reduce corrupt tendencies which have become characteristic of the post-1999 era.

Second, the activities of civil society help to stimulate the interests of the citizenry at large in politics and also to promote their involvement. To this end, they supplement the functions of political parties. Their activities in this regard can only help to promote proper governance and consolidate democracy if the proper messages are communicated to the public by the civil society. Communications that promote the rule of law and help to build attributes that are supportive of democracy are very important.

Third, a vigorous community of civil society is especially well placed to help in the long-term cultivation of a democratic political culture (Oyebode 2009:3). The importance of such a culture towards consolidating democracy and ensuring proper governance has already been mentioned but cannot be over-emphasised. The culture of authoritarianism that attended years of praetorian rule still pervades the Nigerian society and polity. The overt attempt by Obasanjo at tenure elongation during his second term in office was a carryover of this culture.[17]

Any attempt to strengthen the attitudinal and behavioural bases of democracy must address the problem of the hangover of praetorianism. As an attitudinal disposition that is borne out of a militaristic culture, praetorianism directly militates against the nurture and growth of a democratic political culture.

Fourth, civil society groups, side by side with the academia, are adequately suited for carrying out research into problem areas of Nigeria's nascent democracy. Such research and their findings could be documented and disseminated to members of the public as well as the government. Lastly, an active community of civil society groups could help to enhance the representative function of democracy by providing outlets for the expression of diverse views, opinions and interests. It is very important however, that such expressed interests should be constructively critical and not subversive of the democratic project as a whole. Indeed, the entire democratic enterprise would be meaningless if the interests and views that are purveyed by civil society eventually result in the destruction of the system which they so arduously fought for.

Conclusion

It is evident from the foregoing that what Nigeria has experienced so far is nothing more than a transition from military to civil governance in democratic guise. The style of governance being displayed by elected functionaries of the federal and state governments, the persistent face-off between the legislature and the executive, the use of the processes of probes and impeachments, the recrudescence of religious, ethnic and factional conflicts, the pervasiveness of corruption, all denominated by further downturns in the economic fortunes of the country provide very strong suggestions that Nigeria was really not yet on the track of good governance or consolidation of democracy. One explanation for this was that the leading lights and groups that were at the forefront of the struggle are, today, not in power. Most of those in power now are yesterday's military apologists for whom democracy is no more than a strategy of winning and retaining power, and not fundamentally for public service. Indeed, the experiences of Nigeria in the present circumstances may be better captured by the concept of democratic erosion in several areas, denoting the slow and gradual decay of democracy, rather than democratic consolidation and the entrenchment of good governance. This was indeed, the case up to 2007, when the country's democratic process picked up with the fairly satisfactory conduct of the 2011 elections, and the goodwill this brought to the country.

In the face of this perceptibly uninspiring scenario, civil society has an important role to play in consolidating a hard-won democracy. Civil society can play a more pro-active role in propagating what Peter Ekeh refers to as 'the republican principle' which simply means that the state belongs to its citizens (Maslyukivsta 1995:8-10; Diamond, Linz and Seymour 1995:27; Ekeh 1998). The arrogant perception, widely held by elected officials and politicians, that the powers and institutions of state are now theirs to use for purposes of primitive accumulation, rather than held in public trust, should be the focus of unrelenting attack. Civil society should communicate and cultivate values and attitudes that can help to support and consolidate Nigeria's democracy. A major plank in this endeavour should be a focus on upholding the rule of law as the administration of the late President Umaru Yar' Adua emphasised. This will facilitate a movement towards a strong state and a strong civil society.

References

Chalmers, A. Douglas, 1997, 'What is it About Associations in Civil Society that Promotes Democracy?', Paper prepared for *Project on Civil Society*, Princeton University.

Clinz, Juan and Alfred, Stepan, 1996, 'Towards Consolidated Democracies', *Journal of Democracy*, Vol.7, No.2.

Diamond, Larry, Linz Juan, and Seymour, Martin Lipset, 1995, 'Introduction: What Makes for Democracy?' in Larry Diamond, Juan Linz, and Seymour Martin Lipset eds., *Politics in Developing Countries: Experiences with Democracy (2nd ed)*, Boulder, Colorado: Lynne Rienner Publishers.

Diamond, Larry, 1995, *Promoting Democracy in the 1990s: Actors and Instruments, Issues and Imperatives,* New York: The Carnegie Commission.

Ekeh, Peter, 1998, 'Civil Society and the Construction of Freedom in African History', Paper presented at the *Wilberforce Conference on Civil Society in Africa*, Central State University, Ohio, U.S.A., July.

Guillermo, O'Donnell, 1996, 'Illusions About Consolidation', *Journal of Democracy*, Vol.7, No.2.

Human Rights Watch, 2008, 'Chop Fine: The Human Rights Impact of Local Government Corruption and Mismanagement in Rivers State, Nigeria', *Human Rights Watch Report*, January, Vol. 19, No. 2(A).

Hyden, Goran, 1999, 'Governance and The Reconstitution Of Political Order' in Richard

Joseph ed., *State, Conflict, And Democracy In Africa*, Boulder, Colorado: Lynne Reinner, Ibrahim, Jibrin, 2008, 'Nigeria's 2007 Elections: The Fitful Path to Democratic Citizenship', United States Institute for Peace Special Report. (http://www.usip.org/print/resources/nigerias2007 elections-fitful-path-democratic-citizenship), 16 April.

Maiyaki, Eben, 2006, 'Obasanjo is Playing God', *This Day Newspaper*, 26 December. Makumbe, John, 1998, 'Is There a Civil Society in Africa', *International Affairs*, Vol.74, No.2. Maslyukivska, P .Olena, 1999, *Role of Nongovernmental Organisations in Development Cooperation*, Research Paper for UNDP-Yale Collaborative Programme.

Nzeshi, Onwuka, 2010, 'Bankole Canvasses Attitudinal Change to Elections, *This Day*, 16 April.

'Nigeria: Poverty in the Midst of Plenty: The Challenge of Growth With Inclusion', *World Bank Report.* (http://web.worldbank.org/WBSITE/EXTERNAL/TOPICS/EXTPOVERTY/EXTPA/0, contentDK:20204610~isCURL:Y~menuPK:435735~pagePK:148956~piP K:216618~theSitePK:430367,00.html), 18 April, accessed 11 March 2010.

Oche, Ogaba, 2004, 'Democracy: Conceptual and Theoretical Issues' in Hassan A. Saliu ed., *Nigeria Under Democratic Rule, 1999 – 2003 (Vol. I)*, Ibadan: University Press PLC.

Oyebode, Olayinka, 2009, 'the Resurrection of Tenure Elongation', *Punch Newspaper*, 19 July.

Schedler, Andreas, 1998, 'What is Democratic Consolidation?' in *Journal of Democracy*, Vol.9, No.2, 1998.

Schmitter, C.Philips, 1991, 'Dangers and Dilemmas of Democracy', *Journal of Democracy*, Vol.5, No.2.

9

Impact of the Elections on Governance: Lessons Learned

Osita Agbu

Introduction

Being in politics can be seen as the most lucrative profession in Nigeria today. Somehow, the country must find a way to make political office less attractive compared to other professions. This may ensure that the public gets the type of services it deserves from political office holders. There is no gainsaying that the pressure of the international community on Nigeria and its leaders to democratise has helped the nation to embrace democracy, if only to be seen to conform to international requirements of civilized political leadership. Leadership is critical to improving public governance, and good leaders are needed at all levels of the society – the presidency, state level, military and security agencies, public service, private sector and within families. Reducing corruption and primitive accumulation in Nigeria, which obviously has implications for elections and governance, demands that positive fundamental societal values be re-emphasised as the basic norm of good governance.

With respect to building and strengthening political institutions and enthroning the rule of law, these more often than not derive their legitimacy from long-term usage. While it is good that Nigeria successfully held three consecutive elections between 1999 and 2007, it is also disheartening that all three elections were adjudged not to be free and fair. The Nigerian electorate is currently disenchanted with politicians and their politics and the poor quality of public service delivery. It is not surprising, therefore, that many Nigerians were apprehensive of the outcome of the 2011 general elections in the country against the backdrop of the shortcomings that characterised the last three elections. As we saw later, the

2011 elections were better organised and declared credible by the international community. President Jonathan did promise that he would not interfere with the work of Attahiru Jega's INEC, and it did appear that, indeed, there was very little interference in the management of the elections by the different agencies involved. The Presidency and the leadership of INEC were instrumental to the success of this election, and INEC, in particular, must be commended this time around for its integrity and unbiased management of the elections. Unrepentant politicians found it difficult to subvert the electoral process, and many who had hitherto benefitted from rigged elections failed in the elections. The opposition parties to the PDP also made substantial gains in electoral votes.

Impact of the Elections on the Democratisation Process

A representative democracy is representative to the extent that it 'absolutely depends upon the integrity of elections' (Kurfi 1983; 259). When the integrity of the processes leading up to the elections, and the elections proper are compromised, then democracy is in jeopardy. The inability to conduct free and fair elections acceptable to all in the 1964/65 and 1983 led to the collapse of the First and Second Republics (Dudley 1982; Osaghae 2002). Osaghae (2002:152) has enumerated four related reasons why elections have been problematic in Nigeria, namely:

(a) The ethno-regional character of the political parties and the zero-sum nature of politics which compel politicians to seek to win by any means, fair or foul.

(b) The manner in which electoral commissions are constituted which does not insulate them from partisanship.

(c) The misuse of state-owned media by incumbent parties to the disadvantage of rivals and;

(d) The partisan use of the police and other security forces.

A critical examination of the reasons given above for electoral shortcomings show that while some effort has been made to make the present parties, namely, the PDP, ANPP, APGA, CPC etc. broad-based, very little has been achieved with respect to changing attitudes to politics, the misuse of the media and the police and other security agencies. However, it is only with respect to INEC that one could venture to say that perhaps, the body is becoming relatively independent from the control of the Executive and other forces in society. Again, while we will like to see the building of a stronger INEC institutionally, the reason for its success now is committed leadership, and a leadership with integrity. Nigeria surely needs leaders with integrity to guide the state.

Against this backdrop and examining the three previous elections held before 2011 in the country from 1999, we find that indeed little changed, as each election instead of improving on the previous one became worse. This position is evident from the various studies carried out by scholars in this volume, whether at the local, state or national level. In short, it was a miracle that the country did not implode before 2011. Perhaps, the reason for this could be attributed to the collective memory of a people that had gone through three years of an excruciating civil war (1967 – 1970), and seen the devastating effects of war on development. Nigerians wanted no more of this. Within the period under study, Nigeria, rather than enjoy democratic consolidation, actually experienced democratic erosion, making many to question the veracity of democracy as an organising principle of governance.

Having said this, the Local Government elections of 2007, for example, as local as it was supposed to be, did not afford Nigerians the opportunity of freedom of choice as their votes did not count. The desire of politicians to win at all costs, the open partisanship of the police and the electoral management authorities constrained citizens' freedom of choice from the available political alternatives. Indeed, both local and international observers and monitors generally agreed that the elections were fraught with serious irregularities and that they fell short of international standards and expectations (TMG 2008a:13).

The elections were regulated by the 1999 Constitution, the Electoral Act adopted in 2006 as appropriate, as well as regulations and guidelines issued by INEC. The Electoral Act 2006 was an improvement on the Electoral Act 2002 which regulated the conduct of the 2003 general elections. The 2006 Act contained measures aimed at strengthening the independence of INEC, including the appointment of the Secretary of the Commission by INEC and the creation of a fund to provide INEC with financial autonomy. Nonetheless, this was not established for the 2007 elections. A number of problems were not addressed in the 2006 Electoral Act, especially relating to the independence of INEC. The President continued to be involved indirectly in the appointment of INEC Commissioners. Also, at the federal level, all Commissioners were still appointed by the President, after consultations with the Council of State and confirmation by the Senate (dominated by representatives from the PDP). At the state level, all 37 Resident Electoral Commissioners (RECs) were appointed directly by the President (TMG 2008b:3). Nigeria, a federal republic, has aggregated enormous amount of powers to the presidency via the 1999 Constitution, which many believe is a hangover of military rule.

Other significant lacunae which later came to haunt the 2007 elections included the lack of requirement for results to be announced at the polling station and for a breakdown of polling station results to be displayed at all superior levels of the election. There was also a lack of adequate procedures for the handling of complaints and appeals before Election Day, and the lack of time limits for the publication of results and for the determination of election petitions. Significantly, there was no provision on the use of state resources during campaigns or provisions to promote transparency in the appointment of polling staff or access to INEC decisions. Notably, petitions could only be filed by candidates and political parties (TMG 2008b:3). This effectively derogates the rights of the electorate to challenge any electoral outcome.

In effect, the 2007 state and federal elections fell short of basic international and regional standards for democratic elections. They were marred by poor organisation, lack of essential transparency, widespread procedural irregularities, significant evidence of fraud, particularly during the result collation process, voter disenfranchisement at different stages of the process, impersonation of voters, under-aged voting, vote solicitation by party agents, thumb-printing of ballot papers by INEC officials, no level playing ground for contestants and numerous incidents of violence. The elections did not meet the expectation of the Nigerian people. The politicians had learned nothing, so politics remained a do-or-die affair which shut decent Nigerians out.

Impact at the National and State Levels

The conduct of the 1999, 2003 and 2007 elections in Nigeria did not have positive impact on the polity and its development. Although grudgingly accepted by the international community amidst vociferous condemnations by local monitors and civil society organisations, the elections did not contribute to the advancement of the Nigerian democratic project, but rather created doubts in the minds of many. Rather than change the attitude of people towards politics in the country, these elections only succeeded in creating apathy and strengthening the resolve of many not to participate in the political process, especially since the people's votes often do not count in deciding who wins an election.

Related to this is the corruption of the entire political process before, during and after the elections. Politics in Nigeria has always been a game of money, with politicians bribing themselves, party stalwarts, government officials and INEC staff to gain advantage over others. This situation was so bad that party primaries were so bastardized that incompetent individuals were thrown up and eventually became local government chairmen, members of state Houses of Assembly, 'selected' members of the National Assembly and Ministers. Ultimately, good governance suffered as some of these individuals neither had the experience nor qualifications to occupy the positions they did; in short, many of them lacked legitimacy. Some were alleged certificate forgers, people of questionable background and character, impersonators and touts. These were the days of the 'political god-fathers' who superintended over their territories and rode rough-shod over anyone who dared to challenge their overlordship. They selected those who would occupy political positions in their domains. Although the phenomenon of 'god-fatherism' is on the decrease, it is yet to abate in Nigeria's political landscape. In fact, one can say that this phenomenon, although less brazen now, has become even more sophisticated to the extent that the violence associated with it although less visible or physical, is now more psychological. It is psychological in that it makes the average Nigerian sceptical and docile about competitive politics and elections in the country.

Prior to 2011, beatings, kidnappings and murder were not unheard of. Again it appears that the politicians have decided not to learn from history. The PDP National Convention of 8 March 2008 saw the 'selection' (not election) of officers based on zoning and the parochial interests of the 'Governors' Forum'. This scenario repeated itself in the internal politics of the party and of other parties toward the 2011 general elections. At a convention purportedly called to elect a new national executive, no ballot was cast for any candidate – those that emerged as national executive members did so by 'consensus', the party's nomenclature for imposition (TMG 2008c). This trend appears particularly ingrained in the ruling PDP, where more often than not, qualified candidates are not given the opportunity to contest freely during the party primaries. Hence, it is the case that those who indicated interest in contesting the party's nomination for the 2015 general elections were persuaded otherwise by the party machinery, with President Goodluck Jonathan emerging as the 'adopted' candidate through 'consensus'. This may not be good for the party in the future, as transparency is sacrificed on the altar of expediency. It is obviously not good for the growth of democracy in the country. Again, this practice has implications for the war against corruption, both in cash or kind.

Closely associated with this was the corruption of members of the police and security services. This greatly aided corrupt politicians to rig the elections. In Nigeria, this has given rise to the focus on electoral security as critical to the conduct of free and fair elections. Indeed, it is difficult to find any election in Nigeria that was not manipulated or rigged without the purported cooperation, through action or inaction of security personnel. For the governorship and presidential elections of 2007, although overtly the majority of security personnel appeared to have conducted themselves according to the INEC guidelines and the guidelines of the Police Service Commission, certain inadequacies impeded the performance of the security personnel that included inadequate number of security personnel at the polling stations, dearth of communication equipment, lack of vehicles for movement and lack of arrangement for the feeding of the security personnel (NHRC 2007). This again laid them open to being compromised by party agents and politicians. However, we should not lose sight of the fact that the problem of corruption in Nigeria is more structural than this. The penchant for the acquisition and retention of power by any and all means because the state is everything creates a conducive environment for corruption to thrive. Although beyond the scope of this work, this immediately takes us to the issue of Nigeria's practice of federalism; a federalism in which the centre has incrementally arrogated to itself immense constitutional and political powers, to the extent that the states and local governments have become mere political appendages to whosoever controls the centre. Perhaps, this is why Nigeria's fiscal federalism is so problematic, especially against the backdrop of an economy largely sustained by oil revenues, distributed from the centre. Nigerians have rightly alluded to the process of sharing this revenue as steeped in 'distributive politics'. Indeed, this is why the call for a Sovereign National Conference or National Dialogue was so loud. It was basically to discuss this defective federal structure and, through consensus, agree on how the polity should be organised to make progress. It is said by many that Nigeria has been making movements, but in a circle, never forward, because the immense energies of her people are trapped in the contraption of a defective federal structure. While a section of the elected politicians and elite are afraid of losing their privileged positions in the pecking order, others are simply afraid of the consequences of a political reform gone wrong. In other words, they are simply scared! The energies of Nigerian peoples and the Nigerian state need to be released to enhance its development, and this is only possible through struggles from below, as the elite have proven incapable of initiating this change.

And what of the body expected to organize and supervise the elections – INEC? This is a body that has been much maligned by the electorate. Often, it has fallen prey to its officials being corrupted by the political parties and wealthy individuals. It has been suggested that some INEC officials may have been planted by politicians or parties for the purpose of influencing the work of the body or for providing critical information about what the body was planning (Onu and Momoh 2005:9). Nigeria needs to begin to think more seriously of how best to assure the integrity of the administration of elections and the electoral process. Perhaps, it is with a view to addressing this matter that the late President Umaru Yar'Adua set up an Electoral Reform Committee on 28 August 2007 to revisit the history of elections in Nigeria and the Electoral Act of 2006 and make recommendations on possible amendments. The Reform Committee was chaired by Justice Muhammadu Uwais (rtd).

The Committee submitted what could be regarded as novel recommendations to the government on electoral reforms. For a long time, the House of Representatives and the Senate bickered over whether to accept all the recommendations or not, or even to include new, but largely selfish amendments in the original report before they could pass it into law. This was after a Review Committee had gone through the Report. On the key issues addressed by the Uwais committee, they included that of appointment of the INEC Chairman, which was recommended as per section 153 of the 1999 Constitution to be amended to have this removed from the list of federal executive bodies. In addition, the Chairman and members of the INEC Board may only be removed by Senate on the recommendation of the National Judicial Council (NJC) by two-thirds majority of the Senate which shall include at least 10 members of the minority parties in the Senate. In other words, the Committee made it difficult to have the INEC Chairman removed by anybody. On the funding of INEC, it recommended that section 84 of the 1999 Constitution be amended to read that 'the election expenditure and the recurrent expenditure of the INEC Commission offices (in addition to salaries and allowances of the Chairman and members mentioned in Subsection 4 of this section) shall be first charge on the Consolidated Revenue Fund of the Federation' (Alliance for Credible Elections n.d). This was to make INEC financially independent from an incumbent government. Again, on electoral offenses, the Committee recommended the establishment of an Electoral Offenses Commission and a penalty of 10 years disqualification from contesting for any election for all offenses relating to registration of voters, in addition to other penalties in the Act. It recommended that the disqualification period for any candidate, upon conviction, for corrupt practices under section 31 of the Electoral Act 2006 should be increased to ten years.

Also, on the issue of elected persons remaining in office pending determination of appeal, the Committee recommended that section 149 of the Electoral Act 2006 be repealed, and that no elected person should assume office until the case against him or her in the Tribunal or Court is disposed of. Furthermore, on the determination of election petitions, it recommends that the Electoral Act 2006 be amended to shift the burden of proof from the petitioners to INEC to show on the balance of probability that disputed elections were indeed, free and fair and candidates declared winners were truly the choices of the electorate (Alliance for Credible Elections n.d). Most interestingly, the Uwais Committee recommended the retention of the Open Secret Ballot System for the country, which basically allows a voter to go into a polling booth to mark his/her ballot in secrecy and drop it in the ballot box in the open. However, in all these recommendations, and after the work of the Review Committees, the House of Representatives and the Senate were expected to pass the Act into law. However, the 2006 Electoral Act was subsequently replaced by the 2010 Electoral Act as Amended which sought to redress some of the shortcomings of the 2006 Act. This Act was used in the conduct of the much appreciated 2011 elections. However, if we are to go by the views expressed by the then Chairman, Justice Muhammadu Uwais that 'the will to bring change is not there' (Coalition of Democrats for Election Reforms 2010), then we do not have much hope for optimism. For him, politicians are usually reluctant to modify the existing electoral system because there tended to be significant transitional costs that accompany the move from one system to another. Of critical concern to politicians is that the reforms may lead to their losing upcoming elections or losing electoral dominance. The process and outcome of the 2011 elections were therefore instructive, as they indicated some progress.

The elections under survey also brought out the best and worst from the public and the civil society. While some were willing to be used by corrupt politicians as thugs and instruments of disenfranchisement of the populace, others organised to challenge high-handed government officials, corrupt parties and politicians as well as the various human rights abuses associated with stolen mandates. On the whole, while the civil society remained weak, it showed flashes of potency often led by a few individuals who over the years acted as bastions or strong defenders of democracy. These included individuals like the late Gani Fawhenmi, the late Chima Ubani, Wole Soyinka, Pat Utomi, Olisa Agbakoba, Ayo Obe, Shehu Sani, Tunde Bakare, Reuben Abati, Col. Abubakar Umar (rtd), Kayode Fayemi and Abubakar Momoh. Worthy of mention are also organisations like NADECO, and to some extent the G34. These were individuals and organisations that sacrificed in different ways to ensure that Nigerians enjoy democracy and progress today. We cannot but salute their tenacity in the midst of intimidation and a decadent political culture.

Lessons Learned

What lessons have we learned from the conduct of the 1999, 2003 and 2007 elections and the aftermath from Nigeria? It is that bad elections invariably produce poor or bad governments. Why? The resulting government will not only lack legitimacy, it will spend a disproportionate amount of time and state resources trying to prove its legitimacy, or ensuring regime survival. Here, public service delivery is not the object of governance, but regime survival, and the accumulation of resources to ensure this survival. Invariably, what suffers is good governance as the people continue to look for and yearn for the forever elusive good roads, clean water, decent housing, qualitative education, basic health services and personal security. Infrastructural development is critical to the development of democracy anywhere. Without the minimal provision of good roads, housing, clean water, telephony and power for example, it will be difficult to effectively sensitise the people and organise people-friendly elections. The provision of these infrastructure has to do with good governance, which has much to do with the relationship between the governments and the governed. This is generally the process of steering the state and society towards the realisation of collective aspirations. Key actors in the governance project therefore include the state, the private sector, the people and the civil society; however the state remains pivotal in this project. But, to what degree has governance in Nigeria been effective to the extent that collective good has been upheld and attained? The answer to this is logically linked to the quality of the democratic and electoral processes that produced those who governed Nigeria from 1999 to date. The overwhelming verdict is that the processes had been compromised and deleterious to good governance.Governance can only be 'good' when operated in accordance with legal and ethical principles as conceived by society (Adejumobi 2004).

The experience from these elections and the aftermath is that the social contract remained wobbly, the dividends of democracy remained undelivered, while the people generally remained apathetic praying that one day it shall be well. In other words, a key lesson from the elections is that incumbent governments should not be allowed to superintend electoral reforms or the processes leading to elections, or organise elections aimed at changing governments. The people are important in the political equation to the extent that they are able to organise from below in the form of social movements to contest and challenge policies considered detrimental to them and the country. This is not just for Nigeria, but applicable to all countries under the stranglehold of autocracy, be it military or civilian. Electoral reforms are important to the extent that they emanate from informed practices in the political and electoral processes found to be defective and needing amendment for the conduct of freer and fairer elections. Any country not ready to embrace electoral reforms is not ready for change and is a willing candidate for political and social uprising.

Conclusion

That democracy is the transcendent system of government in the world today is not in doubt. While liberal democracy is popular, the preference is for popular democracy from below through representation, in which the people remain the focal point of governance and not the market. As earlier opined, popular democracy for a country like Nigeria entails that the basic principles of democracy has its roots from the culture and norms of the Nigerian society. Since democracy is work in progress, it implies that continuously, there will be challenges to its workings. And in a popular democracy, this is encapsulated in the popular struggles expected from the people. It is a democracy that is focused on meeting the needs and material conditions of Nigerians, not necessarily the market. However, it is enough for us to note that the experiences from the general elections of 1999, 2003 and 2007 in Nigeria show that the country still has a long way to go in approximating any semblance of representative popular democracy. But, what kind of political system does Nigeria need? At the risk of ruffling feathers, we will say that considering the country's level of economic and technological development, it is commonsensical for the country to avoid extreme capitalism, though capitalism encourages competition and efficiency; it is also important for the country to avoid extreme state control of the political and economic spaces, but to thread in between the two extremes. In other words, were the country to embrace popular democracy dictated by the people, it is probable that the state will not only be more relevant to the people, but the people will also be able to claim ownership of the state and protect the state from political opportunists and foreign entrepreneurs that have colluded with the national elite over the years to exploit and undermine the country. Blessed with immense natural and human resources in arable land, good weather, oil and gas resources, a courageous embrace of social democratic governance based on ensuring that the people have access to basic needs of housing, water, food, health, education and security will elicit the right attitude to governance and lead to the protection of people's rights in all spheres. In this scenario, it is only the people, not the rich, not the elite and not foreign interests, that matter. Anything that is not of the public good is not a priority. However, this does not mean that spaces are not left for the blossoming of the creative energies of the people. It is the astute balancing of public good with individual and group creativity that will ensure the progress of the country. In all this, governance and leadership are critical and can only thrive when good leaders emerge from a process that is transparent and determined by the need to protect the general good.

The end of democracy is the provision of security and the good life for the citizens, where this is lacking democracy even if transparent and fair, will still be inadequate. However, Nigeria's democracy remains problematic (TMG 2007), and requires proactive attitude and ingenuity to negotiate the many obstacles it presents. From the several dimensions of the elections addressed in this study, from conceptual issues surrounding the state to the character of the political parties, local and state governance issues, presidential and National Assembly matters, the role of INEC to the role of the civil society, it is in order to say that though Nigeria's Fourth Republic has been problematic, it has also provided us with the ingredients to understand and re-structure the country's politics for the general good.

Instructive is the fact that late President Umaru Musa Yar'Adua at his inauguration actually acknowledged the monumental fraud perpetuated in the election that produced him as President and promised that Nigerians will never witness such fraud again in their history. Unfortunately, he did not live long enough to see this through. Nonetheless he demonstrated his seriousness by inaugurating the Electoral Reform Committee. Since the 2003 elections to date, the country's judiciary has been bedevilled by electoral litigations, with the tribunals under siege to either declare retention or vacation of political offices, a sign that the elections were truly compromised. In short, as a result of judicial interventions, no fewer than 10 states of the federation were affected by technical nullifications or otherwise of election results. The more visible ones being the removal of the purportedly elected Governors of Rivers, Edo, Ekiti, Ondo, Osun, Anambra and Delta States many years after the elections were held. This is simply alarming and calls for drastic measures to ensure that this kind of anomaly never again occurs in Nigeria's electoral process.

The surprising part of the ironies of Nigeria's political and electoral processes is that in spite of the shortcomings, the willingness of the international community to accept the results, reinforced the country's acceptance back into the comity of nations after about sixteen years of unbroken military rule. Nigeria is obviously key in the calculations of the major powers that need it to protect and pursue their interests in the West African region and the continent. In this, the purportedly elected two-time civilian President, Olusegun Obasanjo did not disappoint, and played the role to the hilt. To his credit, however, is the effort he and his team made in getting the country back into the comity of nations and once again giving the country some space to continue its experimentation with democracy. It suffices to opine that whilst democracy as a concept is attractive, there are different types of democracy; and the best type for each country is that democracy that grows out of the experiences and peculiarities of a particular people. Nigeria cannot be different. And thus, the disposition is not to be despondent or dismissive about democracy when it is not yet working well.

Recommendations

Based on the multiplicity of issues raised in this study on Nigeria's politics and government, electoral process and elections, the following recommendations are offered as ways to re-position the country's democracy and improve its electoral process. While some of the recommendations may have been proffered by the Transition Monitoring Group (TMG), others have arisen from the observations and experiences garnered during the elections as discovered in this study:

- Early preparation of a fresh voters register is imperative to having a comprehensive and credible voters list for elections. This will restore confidence in the electoral process.
- INEC should be adequately funded to enable it prepare properly and resist interference from corrupt politicians.
- Voter education and mobilisation of people by the government, political parties and civil society should be embarked upon early enough to elicit a buy-in by the people.
- Internal democracy should be entrenched within the political parties to ensure that credible candidates are presented for elections.
- Court procedure rules should be reviewed to enhance the speed with which electoral matters are addressed.
- Enlightenment is also necessary for the political parties, candidates and the electorate to desist from the culture of disputing every election, of refusing to accept defeat and disrespecting the rule of law.
- Citizens need to be assured that term limits will always be respected as a means of building confidence, as certainty and predictability assures stakeholders that if they lose, they can try again.
- Political parties and individuals who commit electoral offenses should be seriously sanctioned as provided for in the subsisting Electoral Act and laws.

- There is a need to effectively regulate the behaviour and activities of contestants, voters, officials and other stakeholders in the entire electoral process through the framing of rules and their application in order to reduce the chances of having the electoral process compromised.
- There is the need to involve the Non-Governmental Organisations (NGOs), and community based organisations (CBOs) as well as the media as partners in the electoral process. Engaging these bodies is necessary to enhance sensitisation, while drawing attention to instances of potential violence, violence and fraud in the electoral process.
- While public office is to be dignified, it should be demystified through instituting accountability checks to make contestants and the general public realise that winning an elective office is a call to service not a means of self aggrandisement and/or primitive accumulation.
- Political parties should draw up a code of conduct to be subscribed to by candidates standing on their platforms.

  Adequate and early training of security personnel, election monitors and INEC officials is essential for the orderly and successful conduct of elections. Security personnel should provide for the free movement of monitors during elections.
- Adequate arrangements should be made to provide for the welfare of security and electoral officers such that they do not have to leave their duty posts during elections, even as effort is made to improve their attitudinal disposition to electoral duty.
- Political parties should endeavour to grow their parties based on ideology and the need to provide an alternative and capable platform for national stability and development.
- Elections at the local and state levels are as important as those at the centre, and all stakeholders are urged to pay closer attention to the conduct of elections at these levels.
- Sensitisation is necessary for the electorate to know their elected officials at the State and National Assemblies and to collectively call them to order when found wanting.
- Measures should be put in place to comprehensively scrutinise the credentials and health condition of all Presidential aspirants. This is critical to ensuring national stability and progress.
- Political parties, the private sector and civil society are called upon to actively support the passage of progressive electoral bills, as this is the foundation for democratic rebirth and growth in the country.

We conclude by stating that politics remains the master science. If this is not so, why is everybody interested in being a part of it? Politics holds the key to progress in society, perhaps, this is why it is so problematic. Over the centuries, men have striven to master the art and science of politics, of governance and of elections without being able to do so. The reason for this is because politics is the quest to understand human behaviour as we seek power and the use of power. This is a complex game, as men and women exercise their freewill in the struggle for the authoritative allocation of values, limited only by the rules and regulations guiding the process of political interaction. Nigeria is still struggling to have some control over its democratic and electoral processes, a situation made worse by the character of its elite, who are still quagmired in a cesspool of primordial encumbrances. Following the various contributions in this book and the recommendations above, we hope that our efforts will in some way contribute to a clearer understanding of the practice of democracy and to charting the way forward for better politics, better elections, better governance and progress for Nigeria.

References

Adejumobi, Said, 2004, 'Democracy, Good Governance and Constitutionalism in Africa', in S. Odion-Akhaine, ed., *Governance: Nigeria and the World*, Ikeja: CENCOD.

Alliance for Credible Elections, n.d., *Electoral Reforms: Recommendations of the Electoral Reform Committee*. Funded by The International Republican Institute.

Coalition of Democrats for Election Reforms, 2010, *Government Lacks Will to Implement Report on Electoral Reform, says Uwais*. (http://codernigeria.org/2010/12/govt-lacks-will-to-implement-report-on-electoral-re...). 12 December 2010.

Dudley, B.J., 1982, *An Introduction to Nigerian Government and Politics*, London: Macmillan.

Kurfi, A. 1983, *The Nigerian General Elections 1959 and 1979 and the Aftermath*, Ibadan: Macmillan.

National Human Rights Commission (NHRC), 2007, *Monitoring the Conduct of Security Personnel in the April 2007 General Elections*, Abuja: NHRC.

Onu, Godwin and Abubakar, Momoh, 2005, *Elections and Democratic Consolidation in Nigeria*, Lagos: A-Triad Associates.

Osaghae, E. E., 2002, *Crippled Giant: Nigeria Since Independence*, Ibadan: PEFS. Transition Monitoring Group (TMG), 2007, *Mandate Protection: Training Manual*, Abuja: TMG.

Transition Monitoring Group (TMG), 2008a, Vol. 10, No.1, January/February.

Transition Monitoring Group (TMG), 2008b, *April 2007 General Election: An Election Programmed to Fail*, Vol.10, No.4 July/August.

Transition Monitoring Group (TMG), 2008c, *Democracy Watch*, Vol.10, No.2, March/April.

10

Elections in Nigeria: A Select Annotated Bibliography

Pamela Ogwuazor Momah

This chapter presents relevant bibliographic sources on elections in Nigeria. It focuses especially on the 1999, 2003 and 2007 general elections at the Presidential, Gubernatorial, House of Assembly and Local Government levels. What was common to all the elections, according to several local and international observers, was that they were characterised by malpractices in the form of vote rigging, ballot box snatching, ballot box stuffing, violence, including use of political thugs to intimidate voters and opponents, registration of under-aged voters and manipulation of results. There was also the issue of poor logistic support on the part of INEC. The voter registration exercise was marred by irregularities while the conduct of the elections was adversely affected by late arrival of personnel and voting materials. The government apparently did not help matters as INEC often complained of late release of funds. All these problems left majority of Nigerians disenfranchised and unhappy with the elections.

In a democracy, periodic elections of the political leaders and legislators constitute the principal means of making sure that government derives its power from the consent of the governed. Therefore, one can reasonably say that elections are central to the functioning of modern day democracies, and voting is the simplest form of democratic participation, as it is a procedure generally accepted as binding within any political society. Voting is a device through which a citizen makes an explicit choice between alternative candidates in an election.

This annotated bibliography points to the fact that the elections under review fell short of accepted democratic standards.

Elections in Nigeria

Abati, Reuben 2009, 'Electoral Reform and the Federal Executive Council, *The Guardian*, 13, March, p. 51.

The article discusses the decision of the Federal Executive Council on the recommendations of the Justice Uwais-led Electoral Reform Committee (ERC). It concludes that it is important more for what it rejected, rather than what it accepted and in the forefront is the sincerity or otherwise of President Umaru Yar'Adua about electoral reform.

Aborisade, Femi, 2008, 'A Case for Credible Elections in Nigeria: Proposed Agenda for Electoral Reform,' *The Constitution*, vol. 6, no. 1, pp. 112-123.

The article captures the preponderance of a totalitarian character in Nigeria's electoral process and democracy as practised by the ruling class. It avers that since the amalgamation of Nigeria in 1914 up to the fourth republic under Olusegun Obasanjo's administration, electoral dictatorship had been foisted on the people.

Abraham, Isaiah, 1999, 'Assessment of the Presidential Election', Daily Times, 4 March, p. 7.

The article takes a look at the 1999 general elections and discusses how the country witnessed a massive invasion of international observers, some headed by world leaders. The Carter Centre and the National Republican Institute, led by Jimmy Carter, said that there was a wide disparity between the number of voters observed at the polling stations and the final results that were reported from several states.

Adegbuyi, Ayodele, 2002, 'Nigeria at Cross-Roads over Local Government Election?' *Daily Times*, 20 April, p. 7.

The Article takes a look at the controversy surrounding the elections into local government councils across the country, and concludes that if care is not taken, the entire political process in the country could be jeopardized by this.

Adeniyi, Abiodun, 1999, '21.2 million voters Shun Polls, says INEC', *The Guardian*, 8 March, p. 1.

The article points out that the number of registered voters who stayed away from the four elections held in 1999 averaged 21.2 million, according to statistical analysis by INEC. This underscores the level of voter apathy in the country.

Adetayo, Olalekan, 2007, 'Iwu and the burden of flawed poll', *The Punch*, 30 November, p. 48.

Both local and foreign observers have described the 2007 April polls, as far from being free and fair and the call for Maurice Iwu, the electoral umpire, to quit, was heightened especially, by the upturning of some of the results of the last elections by the election petitions tribunals across the country.

Adeyemo, Ademola, 2009, 'Ekiti Rerun: Any Lessons for Nigeria?' *Thisday*, 15 May, p. 22.

The article sees the Ekiti rerun election as an event that left a dark scar on the Nigerian electoral system. The election could have served as a golden opportunity for Nigeria to re-brand itself and send a positive message to the international community about the nation's determination to reform her electoral system. Instead, intimidation of voters, arson, thuggery, hooliganism, harassment of journalists and snatching of ballot boxes, among other things, marred it. It was an electoral war between the PDP and the AC.

Adegbuyi, Ayodele, 2001, 'INEC and Survival of Democracy', *Sunday Times*, 17 Jun., p.5.

Now that Nigeria wants the democratic culture to stay, people are wondering whether INEC has got what it takes to conduct free and fair elections.

Adeniyi, Olusegun, 2006, 'The Role of the Media in the 2007 General Elections', in Proceedings and Communique of the INEC forum on Nigeria's

2007 General Elections: The Challenges Ahead, Abuja, INEC pp. 150-155.

This paper takes a look at the role of the Nigerian media and concludes that the media is not holding the politicians accountable as regards the welfare of the public. The media do not know what many political parties stand for and what they intend to do to improve the lot of the people.

Aderemi, Adewale, 2005, 'Electoral Commissions and Construction of Democratic Rule in Nigeria, 1979 to Date', in *Elections and Democratic Consolidation in Nigeria*, by Godwin Onu and Abubakar Momoh,eds., Lagos: A–Triad Associates, Pp. 326-338.

The paper examines the viability, coherence and complexity of electoral commissions as political institutions in Nigeria's attempt at the construction and reconstruction of enduring democratic rule from the Second Republic.

Aderanti, Adepeju, 2005, 'Women, Politics and Elections in South West Nigeria', in *Elections and Democratic Consolidation in Nigeria*, by Godwin Onu and Abubakar Momoh, eds., Lagos: A–Triad Associates pp,. 510-533.

The paper explores the level of women's participation in politics in Nigeria using the 1999 and 2003 general elections in South West Nigeria as a case study.

Agbaje A.B. Adigun, Diamond Larry; and Onwudiwe Ebere, 2004, *Nigeria's Struggle for Democracy and Good Governance*. Ibadan, Ibadan University Press. 471pp.

The book focuses on the four cardinal points that signpost Nigeria's perennial struggle for democracy and good governance.

Agbu, Osita, 1996, 'External Pressure and the Quest for Democracy in Nigeria'. Nigerian Journal of International Affairs, vol. 22, No. 1 pp. 1-10.

The article examines the international dimensions of Nigeria's democratic crisis, especially since the annulment of the June 12, 1993 presidential elections.

Agboola, J. A. 2006, 'INEC's Preparation for 2007 General Elections: The Research Perspective', in *Proceedings and Communique of INEC Forum in the 2007 General Elections: The Challenges Ahead. Abuja*: INEC pp. 172-179.

The Research and Documentation department of the Electoral Institute is the third tripod of the Commission which was established principally to address the inadequacies of the past when little or no research was done on the myriad of problems which the Commission and other stakeholder's faced.

Agboola, Jimoh, 2008, 'Political Culture in Nigeria'. *The Nigerian Electoral Journal*, vol. 2, no. 1. Pp. 43-57.

The author says that persistent general failures in the Nigerian polity have always been traced to the inadequacies in the evolution of a virile political culture in the nation. Specific failure of political parties, electoral process, the governments at all three levels and the entire political component of the national system were explained in terms of the poor political culture of Nigerians.

Ahmed, Abubakar, 2009, 'Problems of Elections in Nigeria'. *Daily Champion*, 14 Apr. 11.

The article argues that elections in the country have often been characterised by irregularities and fraudulent activities in which electoral competition amongst political parties or candidates take the shape of a Hobbesian struggle.

Akinboye, Solomon O, 2005, 'INEC and the Management of the 2003

General Elections: Lessons and Prospects', in *Elections and Consolidation of Democracy in Nigeria*, by Godwin Onu and Abubakar Momoh, eds., Lagos: A-Triad Associates. Pp. 294-315.

The paper submits that in order to safeguard the nation's democratic system, the electoral process should be completely overhauled, while INEC should be removed from the apron spring of the executive arm of government and allowed to carry out its constitutional roles without hindrance.

Akinterinwa, Bola 2008, 'Validation of Yar'Adua's Election: The International Aspects', *This Day*, 2 Mar., p.4.

The article examines the Court of Appeal's ruling on the Presidential elections and the reasons it gave for upholding the elections in favour of President Yar 'Adua. It concludes that in future, politicians who will be seeking court adjudication on petitions relating to electoral malpractices will need to find more efficient and tangible ways of proving the case of electoral malpractices.

Akogun, Kunle, 2007 'April Polls: Voting for Another Impasse', *This Day*, 6 Mar., p. 18.

The article examines the real implications of a statement allegedly made by

President Obasanjo's statement that: 'the forthcoming election is a do-or-die affair. Winning in the forthcoming election is a matter of life and death for the PDP. I will not hand over to anybody who will not continue with our reform programme'. The conclusion reached in the article is that, with this kind of statement, it would be impossible for INEC to conduct free and fair elections in the country.

Akpan, Felix, 2003, 'Truth as casualty in 2003 Elections', *Daily Champion*, 8 Jul., p.11.

The article looks at all the controversies that the 2003 elections have generated and concludes that what is most disturbing is that none of our leaders, especially those who stand to benefit from the system, can come out and tell the world the truth about the 2003 April elections.

Ajayi, Kunle, 2005. 'Security Forces, Electoral Conduct and the 2003 General Elections in Nigeria', in *Elections and Consolidation of Democracy in Nigeria*, by Godwin Onu and Abubakar Momoh, eds., Lagos A–Triad Associates, pp. 164-180.

The paper investigates the collaborative role of the security forces in allegedly rigging the 2003 elections in favour of the incumbent ruling party.

Arowosegbe, Jeremiah O. 2005. 'Elections and the Politics of Democratic Transition in Nigeria: Lessons from the 2003 Exercise and the Anambra Saga'. In: *Elections and Democratic Consolidation in Nigeria*, by Godwin Onu and Abubakar Momoh. Lagos: A-Triad Associates. Pp. 248-271.

The paper examines the impact of Nigeria's political history, its economic base as well as class property relations in the politics of elections, democratic transition, and the phenomenon of godfatherism in Nigerian politics, especially focusing on the Anambra State saga.

Anifowose, Remi and Babawale, Tunde, 2003, '2003 General Elections and Democratic Consolidation in Nigeria', Nigeria: Friedrich Ebert Stiftung.

The conduct of the 2003 general elections is assessed and the positive areas of the conduct of the elections highlighted. The positive elements are underscored and recommended for strengthening in the future. Recommendations on the observed imperfections are made and suggestions on how they are to be tackled are given.

2009, 'APSA, PDP: A Maze of Legal Tussles', *The Guardian*, 8 Oct. p.8.

The article focuses on how the courts are running the show in Anambra State. The courts stopped the PDP from holding its scheduled primaries for governorship polls. It also stopped the APGA led by Chief Chekwas Okorie from holding its primaries. INEC in the 2010 governorship election in the state did not expect the law courts to play a central role; at least not at the onset.

2005, 'As Abel Guobodia Retires', *This Day*, 22 May, p. 56.

The article states that Guobadia's tenure was marked by electoral infamy. Politicians colluded with INEC officials to hijack result sheets and enter whatever figures they desired, such that the votes recorded, in several instances, were higher than the total number of registered voters. The article also argued that INEC could not produce and carried on as an institution under the direct control and direction of the Presidency and the ruling PDP.

2005, 'As Guobadia Goes', *Daily Champion*, 19 May, p. 10.

Chairman of INEC, Dr. Abel Guobadia in his farewell speech, said that the Executive, and other government officials subjected INEC to a powerless role as far as the ability to conduct free and fair election is concerned by inadequate and late funding due to direct control of such funds by the Executive.

1999 'As US Commends Election', *National Concord*, 9 Mar., p.7.

This article points out that despite claims by some Nigerians who lost the election, as well as by some US observers that the elections were seriously flawed, the election administrators announced that it was pleased that the elections were conducted in an orderly manner, without the intervention of the military.

Ayorinde, Steve 2007, 'Understanding Election as Art of War', *The Punch*, 19 Apr., p.15.

The article is of the opinion that all rules of war are applicable to elections, and the April 2007 election was a simulated battle, that left behind much casualty. He sees a need to question the electoral umpire, before politicians, especially as INEC was unwilling to discuss stolen votes, or deal with statistical monstrosity of the disproportionate relationship between votes secured and seats won in many states. A war it was, because the ruling party had already declared it a do-or-die affair.

Babawale, Tunde. 2003 'The 2003 Elections and Democratic Consolidation in Nigeria', In: Remi, Anifowose, and Tunde Babawale, eds.,, *2003 General Elections and Democratic Consolidation in Nigeria*, Lagos: Friedrich Ebert Stiftung. Pp. 208-230.

The article discusses the 2003 general elections in Nigeria with a view to fashioning out how the elections can be used as a building block for democratic consolidation in the country.

Bamgboye, Adelanwa, 2009, 'Anambra: Confusion Halts PDP Guber Primary Election', *Weekly Trust*, 3 Oct., p.5.

The article focuses on the confusion that arose from the 2 October 2009 primaries of the governorship election of the People's Democratic Party (PDP) in Anambra State, as the Electoral Panel for the exercise, led by the speaker of the House of Representatives, Oladimeji Bankole, acknowledged being privy to the action stopping the congress.

Bello-Barkindo, Abdulrazaque, 2007, 'A New Head of INEC' *ThisDay*, 22

Nov., p.96.

This report takes a look at how courts around the country continue to dismantle the fraudulent structures that the INEC erected throughout the country. The writer notes that all the toppled Governors and the ones that were let off the hook were of the PDP ruling party. The conclusion is that the umpire of the elections was biased in favour of the ruling party.

Benjamin, Solomon A. 2005, 'Comments on Local Government Elections in Nigeria's Fourth Republic', in Elections and Democratic Consolidation in Nigeria, by Godwin Onu and Abubakar Momoh, eds., Lagos: A-Triad Associates. Pp. 330-357.

The paper analyses the series of problems, which arose during the conduct of the 27 March 2004 local government elections.

2003, 'Buhari Insists Polls Are a Charade', The Guardian, 1 May, p. 6. The report examines the unrelenting attitude of the ANPP presidential candidate, General Muhammad Buhari, who, in his quest for justice, called for the cancellation of the presidential and governorship polls of April 2003.

Chukwu, P.C. 2005. 'The 1999 Constitution and the Independence of INEC in the Conduct and Supervision of the Electoral Process in Nigeria', in Elections and Democratic Consolidation in Nigeria, by Godwin Onu and Abubakar Momoh, eds., Lagos: A-Triad Associates. Pp. 357-368.

The paper analyses the provision of the 1999 constitution on the establishment, composition, powers and responsibilities as well as the provisions for the independence of INEC.

Commonwealth Secretariat, 2006 'The National Assembly and Presidential Elections in Nigeria 12 and 19 April 2003': The Report of the Commonwealth Observer Group. London: Commonwealth Secretariat, 57 pp.

This contains the assessment report of the commonwealth observer group on the National Assembly and Presidential elections in Nigeria.

2008, 'Does Iwu still Have a Face to Save', ThisDay, 1 Mar. , p. 14.

The article takes a look at Iwu's first polls as INEC boss, and concludes that they were dismal. Is it a coincidence or an index of his capabilities? Or was he a victim of the mischief of his superiors?

2006, 'Double-Crossed by INEC', ThisDay, 16 Mar., p. 72.

The article is of the opinion that if there is any issue that has exposed the fraud in our electoral system, it is the Anambra debacle where a politician, Dr. Chris Ngige, was installed as Governor by a political godfather, Chris Uba, through the complicity of INEC. The so called political godfather then demanded 'returns on his investment'.

Durojayi, Biodun, Eniseyin, Degi, et al, 1999, '50% Votes Fake: BBC

Correspondent'.

Elizabeth blunt, a BBC correspondent who said she saw rigging in progress in Rivers State where she monitored the election said it was uncertain which candidate won, as half of the votes purportedly cast might have been fake. She further went on to say that because of the Abiola experience, when an election was annulled by the military, Nigerians just wanted the military to go, and so people kept quiet.

Ebome, Victor, 1999, 'Nwabueze backs Falae', *National Concord*, 9 Mar., p. 31. A constitutional lawyer, Prof. Ben Nwabueze observed that the rigging that attended the 1999 Presidential election was worse than that of 1983 and therefore called for investigation and documentation of the irregularities, if for no other reason, at least for record purposes.

Edosa, Ikponwosa, 2007, 'Electoral Crimes: What Legacy for Tomorrow,' *ThisDay*, 17 Jun., p.16.

The article asks how criminal are electoral crimes, especially with the escalation of AK 47 and pump action rifles, which were used in large numbers in broad daylight by PDP party thugs, who were even given police escorts as extra measure.

2003, '2003 Elections: Matters Arising', *The Guardian*, 28 Apr., p. 22.

The article looks at the 2003 general elections and says electoral 'sins' like disenfranchisement of eligible voters by denying them voters registrations, covert and open monetary inducement, collusion of party agents and INEC officials, voting of under-aged minors, multiple voting, intimidating and gangster tactics, stuffing of ballot boxes and falsification of results, were all present in 2003.

The Electoral Institute, 2006, 'Voter Education Training Manual: Building Confidence in the Electoral System', Abuja: INEC, 77pp.

The Electoral Act 2006 categorically provides for civic and voter education. This manual is an outcome of the voter education curriculum developed by INEC.

Ekugo, Andy, 2007, 'Opposition Calls for Mass Action', ThisDay, 26 Apr., p. 6. The coalition of opposition political parties (COPP) states that Obasanjo and INEC chairman, Maurice Iwu, have jointly robbed Nigerians of their mandates and therefore should be rejected and condemned by Nigerians.

Ekwegbalu, Unoaka and Amaedina, Nnaemeka, 2007, 'Triumph of Rule of Law in Nigeria: Historical Judgments Anambra State' , Lagos: UE Communications, 593 pp.

This report chronicles judgments that were given in Peter Obi's numerous journeys to the law court to retrieve and keep his mandate as the elected government of Anambra State.

Emordi, E.C., and Osiki, O.M. 2008, 'The Nigerian 2007, General Elections:

A Balance sheet', *The Constitution*, vol. 8 no. 1 pp. 34-52.

The article examines the April 2007 elections against the backdrop of the country's checkered electoral history. Drawing abundantly from secondary data and personal observation, it argues that the elections were a travesty of Justice.

Eya, Willy, 2007, 'Uncertainty, Apprehension as Tribunals Nullify More Elections', *Daily Champion*, 26 Oct., p. 35.

The article examines the casualties from activities of the election tribunals set up to sift the grain from the chaff and put in place a government that will reflect the true wishes of the people. In Anambra, Kebbi and Kogi, elections have been nullified. It argues that nullification of the elections may not be the solution as those affected are likely to re-emerge if a fresh exercise is conducted, because the structure of the electoral process has not changed and can be manipulated again.

Ezeani O. E. 2005, 'Electoral Malpractices in Nigeria: The Case of 2003 General Elections', In Godwin Onu and Abubakar Momoh, eds., *Elections and Democratic Consolidation in Nigeria*, Lagos: A-Triad Associates, pp. 413-431.

The paper discusses the consequences of electoral malpractices on Nigerians and recommends possible remedies to them.

Fabiyi, Olusola and Soniyi, Tobi, 2007. 'Robbers Hijack Election Materials', 12 Apr., p.2.

Prof. Maurice Iwu raises alarm that three truckload of election materials had been hijacked by robbers. He pointed out that it was the responsibility of the police to make sure that the elections were free and fair. All INEC preparations would amount to nothing if the police did not provide adequate security. It was also revealed that politicians had given their thugs fake police uniforms to use and intimidate their opponents.

Fafowora, Dapo, 2007, 'Electoral Spending Curbs by INEC', *The Nation*, 8 Feb. , p. 48.

INEC put spending limits on all candidates, ranging from N500 million for Presidential candidates to N5 million for states and assembly candidates. This was informed by the fact that money had become the dominant factor in all general elections in Nigeria where poverty has made it easy for voters to be hired by money or some other gifts in kind.

Famoroti, Francis, 'INEC Can't Disqualify Atiku, Others', *The Punch*, 8Mar., p. 2.

A Federal High Court in Abuja declared that the Independent Electoral Commission lacked the power to disqualify any candidate from contesting for political office in the country.

Fawole, Alade, 2005. 'Voting without Choosing: Interrogating the Crisis of Electoral Democracy in Nigeria', In *Liberal Democracy and its Critics in Africa*. Senegal, CODESRIA, pp. 149-171.

This paper traces Nigeria's electoral history from colonial times to the present.

Fidelis, Allen, 2005, 'Electoral Governance in Nigeria: Comparing the Role of the Civil Society and Incumbent Political Parties', In Godwin Onu and Abubakar Momoh, eds., *Elections and Democratic Consolidation in Nigeria*, Lagos: A-Triad Associates. Pp.316-328.

This paper argues that the problem in Nigeria's democracy is that of who determines electoral rules that shape the conduct of elections and their results based on available data on the 2003 Presidential, National Assembly, Governorship and State Assembly and the 2004 local government elections.

2000, Final Report on the 1998-1999 Transition to Civil Rule Elections in Nigeria, Nigeria: Transition Monitoring Group.

The decision to monitor the elections under the Abubakar transition was taken against the background of protracted military rule in the country, and the high public interest in the transition-to-civil rule programme. In response to this, a group of human rights and civil society organisations came together and established the Transition Monitoring Group (TMG) to observe the elections.

2004, 'Gathering Storm of Council Elections', *The Comet*, 9 Feb., p. 13.

The article explains that 774 local government councils were arbitrarily created. They were created at the whims of the military in power; in some cases villages of the military rulers were upgraded to local councils. The unfairness in the process can be seen in the lack of equity, which allows one, or two villages to be constituted into a local government while in other areas 10 towns are lumped together for the same purpose.

Garuba, Dauda, 2005, 'Transition without Change: The 2003 Elections and Political Stability in Nigeria', in Godwin Onu and Abubakar Momoh, eds., Elections and Consolidation of Democracy in Nigeria, Lagos: A-Triad Associates. Pp 181-203.

The paper seeks to examine the threat the 2003 elections pose to transition to positive change and political stability in Nigeria.

2002, 'Guobadia and Election Monitoring', The Punch, 10 Jun., p 14.

The article questions the wisdom of any plan by INEC or the federal government to shut its doors to any foreign observers who may be interested in monitoring Nigeria's elections in 2003. It concludes that such a decision would be straining international relations

Human Rights Watch, 2007, 'Nigeria: Polls Marred by Violence, Fraud', *The Guardian*, 19 Apr., p 67.

The report points out that voting on 14 April in key Nigerian states, including Rivers and Anambra States, was so marred by fraud, intimidation and violence that the results in these states should be cancelled and the polls re-run.

Ibrahim, Jibrin, 2006, 'Legislation and the Electoral Process: The Third Term Agenda and the Future of Nigerian Democracy', *The Constitution*, vol. 6, n°. 2, pp. 46-74.

The article identifies three key challenges facing democratic development in Nigeria, namely; lack of will and capacity on the part of the National Assembly and the Independent Electoral Commission (INEC) to live up their responsibilities, the third term agenda of the incumbent administration, and the electoral integrity of the 2007 election.

Iriekpen, Davidson, 2008, 'The Appeal Court and slow pace of electoral cases', *ThisDay*, 13 Oct., p.20.

The article points out that election petitions were yet to be concluded 17 months after the polls of 2007. It calls on the President and the National Assembly to enact a law to ensure that all election petitions are concluded before the swearing-in of the winner.

Isekhure, Nosakhare, 2005, 'Nigeria's 2003 Fraudulent General Elections, Sowing Seeds of Political Doom', Benin: Oduna Communications Inc. Nig. 536 pp.

The work examines various electoral malpractices, which have done tremendous damage to the credibility of governance in Nigeria in the 2003 general elections.

Iyayi, Festus, 2005, 'Elections and Electoral Practices in Nigeria: Dynamics and Implications', *The Constitution*, vol. 5, no. 2, pp. 1-32.

The article locates the dynamics of electoral practices in the (1) historical context of state formulation in Nigeria; (2) The nature and character of the Nigerian state; (3) The nature and character of the ruling class; (4) Developments in international economy and politics; and (5) The relative strength of the progressive forces in Nigeria.

Iwu, Maurice, 2008, 'Electronic Voting and Future of the Electoral System in Nigeria', *The Nigerian Electoral Journal*, vol. 2, no. 1, pp 1-29.

The INEC Chairman, Maurice Iwu, explains that the Nigerian electronic voting system is an image-based integrated programme, which consists of the electronic voters' register, eligible voters' authentication, electronic balloting i.e. voting machine and electronic transmission of results.

2005, 'INEC after Guobadia', *The Comet*, 1 Jun., p 17.

Guobadia, the outgoing Chairman of INEC, pleads that INEC should have financial and administrative autonomy, pointing out that it is unfair to criticize it without ensuring that it has both the tools and freedom to carry out the expected tasks.

2005, 'Iwu and Growing Controversies', *The Guardian*, 13 Sept., p 8.

The Anambra Gubernatorial Election Petition Tribunal that voided the 2003 election of Ngige confirmed above other things that there were irregularities in the election. The removal of Ngige confirmed that. As the embattled state governor headed for the Appeal Court, INEC also faulted the judgment of the tribunal and sought to appeal the judgment of the tribunal.

2006, 'INEC and Baby Voters', *Nigerian Tribune*, 8 Sept., p10.

The article argues that if babies were registered and ballot boxes found in the hands of politicians, INEC officials who supervised the registration and in whose custody the ballot boxes were kept, should be held liable and prosecuted accordingly.

2007, 'For Improved Conduct of Future Elections', *The Guardian*, 3 Nov., p. 60. The article points out that invaluable lessons and experiences garnered from the circumstances of the 2007 elections should lead to improved conduct of 174 elections in the future. It points out the need for electoral reform and perhaps a total overhaul of the nation's electoral machinery.

2007, 'INEC's Barring of Candidates', *The Punch*, 15 Mar., p. 16.

The article wonders why INEC is insisting on barring candidates after an Abuja High Court had ruled that the electoral umpire has no powers to disqualify candidates seeking elective officers. Sect ion 32 of the 2006 Electoral Act only empowers INEC to verify the claims made by candidates. Only the courts can disqualify candidates.

2007, 'INEC and Council Polls', *The Punch*, 18 May, p.16.

Article says that Iwu's meddling in local government affairs is unjustified and uncalled for and it is clear that the state governments provided INEC with the rope to hang them, because there is no reason why SIEC's should rely solely on INEC for the compilation of the voters register.

INEC, 2007, 'The Official Report on the 2007 General Election', Abuja: INEC, 140 pp.

The 2007 General Elections in Nigeria was not an isolated event. The election may have had certain peculiarities and distinct challenges, but it remains, without doubt, one more juncture in the stretched and eventful stride of the country towards political development.

2008, 'In the Court of Appeal Holden at Abuja Judicial Division on Tuesday,

26 February 2008', *The Constitution*, vol. 8, no. 1, pp. 95-139.

The petitioner, General Muhammad Buhari, is not satisfied with the return and declaration of Alhaji Musa Yar' Adua as the winner of the April 2007 election. The petitioner prayed the court to nullify the election because of many irregularities.

Jega, A. M. et al 2003, 'Strategies for Curbing Election-related Political Violence in Nigeria's North-West Zone', Kano: Mambayya House.

Looks at election-related political violence and proffers solutions for stopping it.
Jega, Attahiru, M. 2006, 'Towards a Strategy for Curbing Violence in the 2007 General
Elections', in *Proceedings and Communique of INEC National Forum on Nigeria's 2007
General Elections: The Critical Challenges Ahead*, Abuja: INEC pp. 1-9.

The author is of the opinion that violence related to election is a significant
aspect of the culture of corruption in Nigeria, saying when or if money fails to
provide the desired outcome for the political entrepreneurs, violence is deployed.
Violence is used to muzzle opponents in what can be termed as the 'politics of the
stomach' i.e. an engagement in politics by the rich to keep stoking their bulging
stomachs and for the poor to seek means of assuaging the rumblings of their
hungry stomachs.

Jinadu, Adele, 2007, 'Elections and Democratic Transitions in Nigeria', *The
Comet*, 6 Aug., p. 32.

The article is of the opinion that before an Electoral Commission can be
analysed, it has to be located more concretely in its political environment,
complementing desk research with more empirically grounded methodology,
like participant observation and survey research, thus looking beyond its formal
institutional arrangement and day-to-day operations.

Johnson, E.A., 2006, 'Method of Election', in *Proceedings and Communique of
INEC Forum on the 2007 General Elections: The Challenges Ahead*, Abuja: INEC
pp. 166-168.

This takes a look at the open-secret system of voting, adopted for the 2007
General Elections, and how it works.

Karunwi, Aderonke, 2003, 'Gender, Politics and the 2003 Elections', in Remi,
Anifowose, and Tunde, Babawale, eds., 2003 *General Elections and Democratic
Consolidation in Nigeria*, Lagos: Friedrich Ebert Stiftung, pp. 188-207.

The article is of the opinion that if democracy allows for diverse opinion and
participation of different groups, then it cannot grow by excluding women, who
effectively constitute half of the world's population and half of each and every
single national population.

Koleosho, Ogun, 2008, 'OBJ, Iwu and the Evils of 2007 Elections', *Nigerian
Tribune*, Feb. 25, pp 16.

The article points out that elections in Nigeria is a most sensitive issue because
it cuts across the entire social strata, and is pinned to resource allocation. The
bizarre conduct of the April 2007 polls in Nigeria is, however, being remedied
by the fearless election tribunals which are rehabilitating the fatal damages that
Obasanjo and Iwu inflected on Nigeria's democratic project.

Komolafe, Kayode, 2009, 'Democracy without Democrats?' *ThisDay*, 29
Apr., p 72.

The article states that the ugly events in the Ekiti rerun election constitute a national embarrassment. INEC leadership, Maurice Iwu, that flaunts its capability to conduct national elections any day, failed to declare results in 64 wards of the state, four days after the exercise. The Nigeria Police, under Mike Okiro who boasted, could not make Oye-Ekiti local government area safe for the elections. So the election in that area is kept at abeyance. The police allegedly looked the other way while some politicians intimidated voters.

Kukah, Mathew, Hassan, 2006, 'The Politics of Money and Elections in Nigeria', In *Proceedings and Communique of INEC National Forum on Nigeria's 2007 General Elections: The Challenges Ahead, Abuja*: INEC, pp. 60-70.

The paper examines the role of individuals in politics, and how they have devolved their resources into politics and consequently affected and influenced political outcomes, and also how money is a lubricant in politics. It concludes that money can take its proper place in the politics of Nigeria.

Madu-West, Augustine, 1999, 'Military Aided PDP to Win Election', *The Punch*, 10 Mar. , p 7.

The article alleges that the military aided PDP to win the 1999 general elections by supporting them with massive military state apparatus and huge sums of money to ensure victory at all cost.

Madunagu, Edwin, 2003, 'Elections as Civil War', *The Guardian*, 17 Apr., p 63. The article takes a holistic look at the Nigerian elections, and concludes that

elections in Nigeria can be seen as a civil war, where power has to be grabbed by all means by politicians.

Muhammed, Safiya, 2006, 'Enhancing Women Participation in Politics and Governance', in *Proceedings and Communique of INEC National Forum on Nigeria's 2007 General Elections: The Challenges Ahead*; Abuja: INEC, pp. 46- 55.

The paper takes a look at the trait and the trend of women's marginalization in party politics, which runs through the political history of Nigeria, and concludes that it is perhaps the most critical factor in the political underdevelopment of Nigerian Women.

2007, 'Nigeria: EU Final Election Report', *The Constitution*, vol. 7, no. 4, pp 79-137.

The report was produced by the EU election observation mission and presents the EU Election Observation Mission's (EOM) findings on the 14 April 2007 Gubernatorial and State House of Assembly Elections, and the 21 April Presidential and National Assembly Elections in Nigeria. A comprehensive assessment of the electoral process in accordance with international standard for democratic elections is reported.

Nigeria Final Report, Gubernatorial and State House of Assembly Elections 14 April 2007, and Presidential and National Assembly Election 21 April 2007. European Union Election Observation Mission.

2003, 'Nigeria's Pretty Good Election', *The Punch*, 25 Apr., p 3.

This article talks about the irregularities recorded in the April elections in Warri, Delta State, where nearly four-fifths of the voters in a particular ward were too frightened to vote because of insecurity, as heavily armed youths, waving sub-machine guns paraded the streets. Some armed youths even drove in their cars to one polling station and demanded for the ballot papers, boxes and result sheets, which were handed over to them.

Nkwachukwu, Orji, 2005 'Civil Society and Elections in Nigeria: Reflections on the 2003 General Elections', In Godwin Onu and Abubakar Momoh, eds.,, *Elections and Democratic Consolidation in Nigeria*, Lagos: A-Triad Associates pp. 555-570.

This paper discusses the role of the civil society in the electoral process of Nigeria. Nnadozie, Uche O. 2005, 'History of Elections in Nigeria', In Godwin Onu and Abubakar Momoh, eds., *Elections and Democratic Consolidation in Nigeria*, Lagos: A-Triad Associates pp. 112-132.

The paper traces the origin, the development and mechanism of elections in Nigeria, including the analysis of the features of these elections from colonial period to date.

Nwabueze, B. O, 1993, 'Democratisation', Ibadan: Spectrum, 304 pp.

This work argues that democratisation is more than multi-partism, it requires that the society, the economy, politics, the constitution of the state, the electoral system and the practices of government be democratised.

Nwabueze, Ben, 2007, '2007 Elections Violated our Constitution so Nobody can Legitimately Govern us based on them', Sunday Champion, 3 Jun., p. 20.

Prof. Ben Nwabueze (SAN), an expert in constitutional law, takes a retrospective look at the eight-year administration of ex-President Olusegun Obasanjo, and insists that the process that produced President Yar' Adua is a subversion of the Nigerian Constitution.

Obegolu, Charles, 1999, 'Free and Fair Elections in Nigeria: Hindrances and Remedies'. Enugu: Jimken, 154 pp.

The work chronicles the author's experience on election malpractices in Nigeria after participating as a member of the local government council election tribunal at Onitsha in1997.

Odita, Frank A. 2006, 'The Role of Security Agencies in Ensuring Peaceful Conduct of Elections', in *Proceedings and Communiqué of INEC National Forum on Nigeria 2007, General Elections: The Challenges Ahead*, Abuja: INEC pp. 119-123.

This paper interrogates whether security agents can ensure peaceful elections in Nigeria. The author is of the opinion that they can, only if the others involved in the electoral process – the public, politicians, government and judiciary all resolve to be respecters of law and politics played according to the rules, thus eliminating the Nigerian factor.

Oji, George Akunna, Chuks et al, 2003 'EU Observers: Police Stuffed Ballot for PDP: INEC Calls for Proof ', *ThisDay*, 23 Apr., p 1.

The reports examines the observations of the European Union Election Observation Mission, who alleged that in the 2003 general elections in Nigeria, policemen stuffed boxes with ballot papers. They also alleged that some officials of the INEC were seen thumb-printing ballot papers for the ruling PDP. INEC has challenged the observers to substantiate their claims with proofs.

Okoroafor, Chris, 1999, 'Abubakar Admits Polls Fraud, But… Counsels Obasanjo', *Daily Champion*, 9 Mar., p. 1.

Head of State, General Abdulsalami, Abubakar said that the rigging noticed in the February 27 Presidential election did not make any substantial difference in the entire result, even as he exonerated the federal government from the irregularities.

Okocha, Chuks 2007, 'Elections: Fifty killed, 1093 Offenders for Prosecution', *ThisDay*, 30 Apr., p. 3.

INEC declares 50 people killed during the 14 April elections, while 1093 electoral offenders were arrested and would be prosecuted for their various electoral offences during the governorship elections.

Okolie, Aloysius-Michaels, 2005, 'Electoral Fraud and the Future of Elections in Nigeria: 1999-2003', in Godwin Onu and Abubakar Momoh, eds., *Elections and Democratic Consolidation in Nigeria*, Lagos: A-Triad Associates pp. 432-447.

The study examines the incidence of electoral fraud particularly in the 2003 general elections and the implications for voting behaviour in future elections.

Okoosi-Simbine, Antonia 2005, 'Political Vagrancy and Democratic Conso-lidation in Nigeria', in Godwin Onu and Abubakar Momoh, eds., *Elections and Democratic Consolidation in Nigeria*, Lagos: A-Triad Associates, pp 17-33.

This article highlights the drift of politics in the Nigerian State, and examines some of the factors that encourage carpet crossing, while highlighting some of the adduced reasons for political prostitution and the effects of political vagrancy on democratic consolidation and the negative impact of the phenomenon.

Okwechime, I. 2005 'The West and Politics of Election Monitoring: A Case Study of the 2003 General Elections in Nigeria', in Godwin Onu and Abubakar Momoh, eds., *Elections and Democratic Consolidation in Nigeria*, Lagos: A-Triad Associates pp 534-554.

The paper focuses on the politics of election monitoring with particular emphasis on the 2003 general elections in Nigeria.

Olaitan, Wale A., 2005, 'Elections and he Making and Unmaking of

Democracy in Nigeria', in Godwin Onu and Abubakar Momoh, eds., *Elections and Democratic Consolidation in Nigeria,* Lagos: A-Triad Associates, pp 43-54.

The paper assesses the contribution of elections to the working of democratic practice and looks at the possibility of it also contributing to the unmaking of democracy.

Ologbenla, Derin 2003, 'Political Instability, Conflict and the 2003 General Election', in Remi, Anifowose, and Tunde, Babawale, eds., 2003 General Elections and Democratic Consolidation in Nigeria, Lagos: Friedrich Ebert Stiffung pp 69-102.

Takes a look at how Nigeria has found it difficult to conduct a free and fair election, with all sorts of election malpractices, fraud, partiality, bribery, stealing of ballot paper and ballot boxes, rigging and even murder of opponents being carried out by the political class.

Olagunju, Sunday, 2007, 'Hurdles to Peaceful Elections', *Nigerian Tribune,* 23 Jan., p 7.

This article points out that most Nigerians who watched the conduct of the April political parties' primaries, expressed disappointment and disbelief, especially at the level of fraud and dishonesty perpetrated by the leadership of most of the political parties, in their desperate attempt to elect their favourites as presidential nominees of the parties.

Olasupo, Ruth 2003, 'Electoral Violence in Nigeria: Issues and Perspectives' Lagos: Friedrich Ebert Stiftung, 407 pp.

Proceedings of the six zonal workshops held in the respective zones of Nigeria, on electoral violence between September 2002 and April 2003.

Olise, Alex and Nwannekanma, et al, 2007 'Civil Groups May Begin Protest Over Polls May 1', *The Guardian*, 26 Apr., p1.

A coalition of 17 Civil Society Organisations across the country and the African Democratic Congress (ADC) have called for the cancellation of the April elections, and threatened to begin a nation-wide protest on 1 May.

Olukotun, Ayo, 2003, 'Observers, the Media and the 2003 General Elections in Nigeria' in Remi Anifowose, and Tunde Babawale, eds., 2003 *General Elections and Democratic Consolidation in Nigeria,* Lagos: Friedrich Ebert Stiftung, pp. 155-187.

The article states that in determining the character of elections in the current world order, observers, external and internal, as well as the media, have emerged as part of the apparatus for vetting and legitimising elections. Thus, the EU the Commonwealth, international and national human rights bodies regularly observe elections and issue reports on the viability of the elections.

Ojelabi, Kolawole, 1999 'Assembly Polls: Monitors Confirm 10% Turnout, Fraud', *National Concord*, Feb. 23, p1.

The article states that just about 10 per cent of the 60 million registered voters exercised their franchise at the National Assembly elections. According to the US-based Carter Centre, there were widespread irregularities and electoral fraud.

Omatseye, Sam, 2009 'Election Arithmetic for Dummies', *The Nation*, 11 May, p 11.

This article takes a look at how the figures of the votes were obtained and wonders what kind of arithmetic was used in arriving at the final figure. According to Solomon, the personal assistant to Mrs. Ayoka Adebayo, the collation on 26 April was to begin by 5pm, but at about 11am that morning she received a phone call, ordering her on what figures to announce.

Omoyefa, Paul, 2007, 'Iwu's INEC-Threat to Democracy', *The Nation*, 13 Jan. , p 12.

Describes INEC as injurious to the health of the nation in the present Nigerian democratic experience.

Onuoha, Browne, 2003 'A Comparative Analysis of General Elections in Nigeria', in Remi, Anifowose, and Tunde, Babawale, eds., *2003 General Elections and Consolidation in Nigeria*, Lagos: Friedrich Ebert Stiftung, pp 46-68.

The article seeks to comparatively examine general elections in Nigeria since 1960, with the aim of identifying the common thread that exists, and also determine to what extent the electoral process in Nigeria has been free, fair and credible, and thus enhanced or impeded democratic consolidation.

Oyedele, Akin 2007, 'How we Discovered Registration Machines in Adedibu's house', *The Punch*, 24 Jan., p7.

INEC in Oyo discovered six direct data capture machines in the residence of Alhaji Lamidi Adedibu. It was found that no fewer than 800 names had been registered on the six machines. It was also discovered that six assistant registration officers conveyed the machines to the residence of Adedibu for illegal registration.

The Punch, 2004, 'Ogunlewe, Criticizes LG Elections in Lagos', 30 Mar., p 8. The article points out that the local government elections held in Lagos contravened section 113 of the 2002 Electoral Act, because most of the local governments are not recognized by the Constitution.

The Guardian, 2003, 'Proposed Reforms and Delayed Council Elections', 19 Nov., p 18.

The technical committee on local government set up by Olusegun Obasanjo, recommended that the existing system of 774 councils should be retained, and abolished use of state joint local government accounts, amongst other things.

The Punch, 2003, 'Reforming the Electoral Process', 6 Jun., p 16.

The Centre for Advanced Social Science (CASS) is of the opinion that INEC was not adequately prepared to conduct the polls and, as such, the integrity of the electoral process was compromised and some results discredited. A constitutional amendment that will ensure the independence, and thus efficiency of INEC was called for.

Roberts, F. O. and Obioha, Emeka, 2005, 'Electoral Violence and the Role of the Police in Nigeria', In Godwin Onu and Abubakar Momoh, eds., *Elections and Democratic Consolidation in Nigeria*, Lagos: A-Triad Associates, pp 394-412.

The paper discusses the optimal role of the police in managing electoral violence in Nigeria during civilian-to-civilian transitions.

Sho, Pam D. 2005, 'Too much Politics, Too Little Democracy in Nigeria, Interrogating the Correlation Between the 2003 Nigerian Elections and the Democratic Transition on Project' in Godwin Onu and Abubakar Momoh, eds., *Elections and Democratic Consolidation in Nigeria*, Lagos: A-Triad Associates, pp 232-247.

The paper states that there is a strong theoretical correlation between elections and democracy, however previous conduct of elections in Nigeria will obviously lead one to interrogate the validly of the correlation, and therefore the democratic character of these elections.

Soniyi, Tobi 2008, 'Presidential Poll: A Second Look at Appeal Court's Judgment', *The Punch* 24 Mar., pp 47.

The article throws more light on how the Appeal Court arrived at its verdict. It explains that Buhari and Atiku lost at the Appeal Court not because there are no irregularities and frauds during the election, and not because the generality of Nigerians voted for Yar 'Adua, or because the Judges compromised, but simply because the two petitions did not pass the tests of the law of procedure on election petition that is very cumbersome.

Sonowo, Biodun 1999, 'C'wealth Endorses Nigeria's Elections', *Daily Times*, 25 Mar, p.1

The article says that the commonwealth secretariat endorsed Nigeria's electoral process, saying that despite observed irregularities, the country was on course to democracy.

Suleiman, Tajudeen, 2008, 'Lessons from other Countries', *Tell*, Sept. pp 34. As INEC embarks on the delineation exercise, it is good to note that this is standard practice in many countries.

Transition Monitoring Group 2000, 'Final Report on the 1998-1999 Transition to Civil Rule Elections in Nigeria' Lagos: Transition Monitoring Group. 204p.

Provides reports on the 1998/1999 elections based on the observations of polling in various constituencies in all six zones of Nigeria.

Transition Monitoring Group 2007, 'April Polls What Observers Say', *Nigerian Tribune*, 26 Apr., p 15.

The transition monitoring group, with 50,000 Nigerian observers on ground, called for the polls to be cancelled, due to numerous lapses, irregularities and electoral malpractices, which characterised the election in many states.

Uhunmwhangho, Amen 2008, 'Electoral Fraud and other Malpractices in Nigeria: The Way Out', *The Constitution*, vol. 8, no. 1, pp 24-33.

The article reflects on the April 2007 elections and focuses on the various forms of electoral malpractices. It argues that the electoral malaise is a product of leadership failure.

The Guardian, 2008, 'Uwais Electoral Panel Queries INEC, SEIC's Independence', 12 Dec., p 1.

Amongst the recommendations made by the Uwais Electoral Panel, a proportional representation system was recommended so that universal adult suffrage would be made possible by ensuring that all votes are of equal value and that no valid vote cast is rendered useless, ineffective or wasted. The system will also facilitate representation of women and other disadvantaged groups.

Uzzi, Oluwole Osaze, 2006, 'The Electoral Act and 2007 Elections', in *Proceedings and Communiqué of INEC Forum on the Nigeria's 2007 General Election: The Challenges Ahead*, Abuja: INEC, pp. 156-165.

Takes a look at the Electoral Act 2006, which was to guide the conduct of the 2007 General Elections.

The Nation, 2008, 'Why we Upheld Yar' Adua's Election, by Appeal Court', Feb. 29, p 43.

The verdict of the presidential election petitions' tribunal on the 21 April 2007 election.

11

Postscript

Against the backdrop of the largely successful 2011 general elections in Nigeria, the 2015 Presidential and National Assembly elections held on 28 March and 11 April respectively were expected to deepen democracy in the country. Although the elections were held amidst extreme tension and fear of outbreak of violence, the eventual outcome negated those fears. The elections were adjudged to be free, fair and credible by both local and international observers, as well as a lot of Nigerians. Although there were initial logistical challenges, especially during the Presidential and National Assembly elections, the elections were generally peaceful all over the country.

In the Presidential election, Muhammadu Buhari of the All Progressives Congress (APC) defeated the incumbent, President Goodluck Jonathan of the People's Democratic Party (PDP), which had been in power for sixteen years. Buhari polled 15,424,921 votes, out of a total of 28,288,083 cast during the election while President Jonathan polled 12,853,162 votes. This was a significant development in Nigeria's electoral history, because it was the first time a ruling party would be defeated at the polls by an opposition party. What was even more significant was the fact that President Jonathan immediately accepted defeat, even before the final result was announced and congratulated his opponent, Muhammadu Buhari. This gesture of statesmanship was commended nationally and globally, as it helped to douse the political tension in the country, and probably helped to prevent post-election violence.

The Gubernatorial and State Assembly elections were also quite peaceful and well organized, although there were violent incidences in some of the keenly contested states in the southern parts of the country. There was however, a lower turn-out of voters compared to the Presidential election probably due to security concerns and apathy. According to the Independent National Electoral Commission (INEC), the body responsible for the conduct of the elections, a total of 6,050 candidates consisting of 760 gubernatorial candidates contested in 29 states; while 5,290 candidates contested for State Assembly seats in the 36 states of the Federation. The results indicated that the opposition APC won most of the Governorship positions contested.

On the whole, considering the inadequacies of the 1999, 2003 and 2007 general elections; the 2011 and 2015 elections, both adjudged credible by local and international observers, have provided a platform for the growth of Nigeria's democracy. Inspite of some lapses, the use of Smart Card Readers and Permanent Voters' Cards (PVC) by INEC to accredit voters and capture their biometric features (thereby making it difficult to rig), the orderly conduct of ordinary Nigerians, the integrity of the INEC Chairman and his team, and the largely impressive conduct of the security personnel were instrumental to ensuring a credible and acceptable general election. Indeed, it appears that some lessons have been learned this time around, and one only hopes that this will translate to good governance for the people of Nigeria.

www.ingramcontent.com/pod-product-compliance
Lightning Source LLC
Chambersburg PA
CBHW050653280326
41932CB00015B/2895